# CALIFORNIA GOLD

*SELECTED SOURCE MATERIALS*

*FOR COLLEGE RESEARCH PAPERS*

*Edited by*

EDWIN R. BINGHAM — 1920

UNIVERSITY OF OREGON

D. C. HEATH AND COMPANY *Boston*

# TABLE OF CONTENTS

# INTRODUCTION

## THE RESEARCH PAPER

THE process of developing new knowledge in most fields of study involves two separate steps: gathering accurate facts, and putting the facts together to see what they mean. The results of this procedure are often communicated to others through a written report which presents the information, tells where and how it was found so that the reader may verify it, and explains what conclusions may be drawn from it. Such a report is called a research paper. The form of the research paper and the steps used in collecting information for it have become standard for they have been developed over a long period of time. Writing a research paper gives the student experience in gathering evidence in a responsible manner, thinking about it logically, and presenting his ideas to others. The skills involved are useful in nearly every college course, as well as in many professions and businesses. Even more important, perhaps, the research paper gives the student a chance to do the kind of original thinking that develops new knowledge from recognized facts.

The material in this book has been assembled to give you training and practice in developing these skills. In it you will read reports of one of the most exciting phases of the Westward Movement — the California Gold Rush. After more than a century, tales about these days still capture the American imagination. Like other dramatic and colorful episodes in American history, the discovery of gold in California drew a varied assortment of individuals, a good number of whom, aware of the significance of their experience, kept a record of what they saw and heard. This booklet incorporates a small part of that rich record in the form of firsthand accounts thus putting the student where the researcher begins, in the presence of raw material which needs to be sorted out, interpreted, and reorganized in a meaningful way. Despite general similarities in experiences: with the elements, with informal law enforcement, with minorities, and with mining techniques, the reactions of the various observers often vary substantially, reflecting diverse backgrounds and attitudes as well as different situations. Sometimes the accounts confirm or supplement each other; sometimes they seem to be, or will in fact be, contradictory. Your first reading should provide a good picture of the subject as a whole, seen from a number of different angles. You should therefore begin working on your research paper by reading this booklet through to gain a general idea of what it contains.

The selections are reprinted just as they stand in early printed texts. Peculiarities of spelling, punctuation, and grammar are not corrected. The pagination of the original texts is supplied in the margin.

## The Topic

The success of a research paper depends to a large extent upon the skill with which the topic is selected and phrased. The most common weakness is choice of an excessively broad topic — one that promises much more than can be delivered in a short paper. "The California Gold Rush," for example, would be too large a topic. A thorough discussion of it based on this book would require more than ten thousand words — a considerable undertaking for most students and instructors. Length itself is no merit; a paper gains significance and interest in proportion to the depth of the analysis. The first research papers should therefore be written on relatively small topics to permit the maximum amount of analysis and interpretation. "Life in a Typical Mining Camp" would be more manageable and could be discussed significantly in two thousand words. For still shorter themes the topic should be narrowed still further: "Prices in the Mines," "The Miner's Dress," "Health Conditions in the Mines," for example. Discussing a small topic exhaustively provides the kind of training in analysis that you will find useful in all your future papers.

## The Outline

After you have surveyed your material and chosen your topic, you should make a trial outline. You should always remember that your first outline is a tentative one. Many students ruin their papers by clinging stubbornly to their original outlines. The final outline must be made inductively; that is, it must reflect what you discover to be important rather than what you considered to be important at the start. You should think about the organization of your paper in all stages of your reading, but you should not make the final outline until you have collected all your material and evaluated it carefully. Follow the outlining techniques recommended by your instructor.

## Note Cards

It would be possible to write short papers based on this book without the use of note cards. But to write the longer papers, and even some of the shorter ones, you will find it advantageous to make note cards. You will save time in this way because all the material on your particular subject, which is scattered throughout the book (or throughout the library in your future papers), will then lie before you in small units. You can bring together the cards on different parts of your subject and fit the material logically into your outline or rearrange it to conform to last-minute changes. You will do a better job on your paper because making note cards gives you a better opportunity to analyze your material carefully.

Every note card should be limited to a single topic. This is basic because one purpose of these notes is to enable you to study your material in several different arrangements. In addition, every card should contain three parts: a subject heading, composed by you, placed in the upper left-hand corner; the source, including the page number, in the upper right-hand corner or at the bottom; and the body of the note itself. Placing both the subject heading and the source at the top leaves the bottom of the card open for your own comments which you may wish to add.

The subject heading should be a catch word or phrase which identifies the contents of the card accurately. Such general headings as "Mining Methods" or "Justice in the Mining Camps" would be less helpful than more specific ones, such as "Panning Technique" or "Mining Camp Lynching." You will often have several cards with identical subject headings, but this should occur only when the contents of the cards deal with the same specific point.

Sources can be identified by abbreviating the author's name and the title if all sources are before you in one book, as they are in this instance, or if you have complete bibliographical cards for each source you used in the library. The page number (and the volume number in multi-volume works) must always be included.

The body of the note may be made up of your own summary, a direct quotation from the source, or both. The length of the summary may vary from a brief condensation to a rather complete paraphrase, depending upon the importance you place on the original passage. Whatever the length, the style of the summary must be entirely your own. It is inevitable that you will repeat many of the words of the original, but you must develop your own phrasing and sentence structure. You have not dealt honestly or profitably with your material if you present it in a style that resembles that of your source rather than you own. You must remember at all times that there is no such thing as a "near-quotation." You must present your information either in your own words or in an exact quotation. To fall between these alternatives defeats the value of research writing and leads to failure.

The following is an example of a note card for a paper dealing with mining camp justice. It is from information found in E. Gould Buffum, *Six Months in the Gold Mines* (1850).

---

Buffum, 20 Jan. 1849

Mining Camp Lynching

Several months after alleged incident, two French-men and Chilean charged with robbery and attempted murder. Charges substantiated in open-air trial although no overt act was alleged. Impromptu jury convicted them unanimously. Hostile crowd clamored for hanging. Buffum made vigorous, but unavailing protest. Victims swiftly and unceremoniously hanged and buried on spot.

Note to → yourself

Compare with other accounts of crimes and lynchings to arrive at some concept of the quality of mining camp justice.

---

Although you should use direct quotations sparingly in your first paper, you should learn to use them correctly. When you quote you must be scrupulously accurate. You should observe the following rules, both in the note cards and in the paper.

1. The source must be reproduced exactly, including punctuation marks and misspellings.

2. Short quotations, not exceeding three or four lines, should be enclosed in quotation marks and should be run into the text; longer quotations are preferably set off by indention (or, in a typewritten paper by single spacing and indention) without quotation marks.

3. Ellipsis marks (three spaced periods) must be used to indicate omissions within a quotation. If the omission comes at the end of a sentence or extends to more than a sentence, a fourth period is required for end punctuation.

4. Any material inserted by you must be enclosed in square brackets. It may be necessary to supply the antecedent of a pronoun or to insert an identifying name: "I [Buffum] mounted a stump, and in the name of God, humanity, and law, protested against such a course of proceeding; . . . " If the quoted part contains an error, you may insert the correction immediately following it or you may insert the word *sic* (Latin for "thus") to show that you are transcribing accurately. Archaic and British spellings need not be pointed out.

Direct quotations should be limited to passages of unusual effectiveness or importance.

## Writing the Paper

After you have completed all your note cards, you should study them carefully and make your final outline. You should not expect every card to fall neatly into place. Most cards will fit into a logical place in the outline, but a few stubborn ones will resist classification. You must be extremely cautious in dealing with these misfits. They may reveal a weakness in your organization or conclusion. They may point to a contradiction which needs to be explained. Under no circumstances should you discard information to avoid dealing with a conflict. You may never have a better opportunity to increase your knowledge than when you wrestle with the problem of organizing facts which seem contradictory. If you cannot account for an exception to your interpretation of the facts, you should say so and let the exception stand. Throw out only those cards which are clearly irrelevant or repetitious.

After you have organized your material you should review your notes and outline until you feel confident that you can discuss your subject with authority and zest. You must never forget that the research paper is an original, creative piece of writing. It is true that you obtained your facts from your reading, but the interpretation and the presentation are original with you.

You should write the first draft with as few interruptions as possible. Do not bother about footnotes and similar details until later. This procedure is recommended as an antidote to the dull, wooden style that results from merely filling in an outline. After you have completed the first draft you should check it with the outline for digressions and omissions. You should then make corrections, add the footnotes, and rewrite as often as necessary.

The footnotes, which usually appear at the bottom of the page or at the end of the paper, are indispensable in a research paper because you must tell the reader where you got the information that is not original with you. They must be included, not only because the elementary principle of honesty requires you to acknowledge your sources, but also because you must make it possible for your reader to follow up or verify any facts in which he becomes interested.

No matter which system of documentation you use, you should see to it that all your footnotes are clear, accurate, consistent, and brief. The system standardized by the Style Sheet of the Modern Language Association has been adopted by more than seventy journals and is finding favor in many English departments. The Style Sheet can be obtained for a slight charge from the Treasurer of the MLA, 100 Washington Square, New York 3, N. Y.

Your instructor will tell you whether your footnotes should cite the pagination of this book, or the pagination of the early texts, or both. One good scheme is to begin with some such footnote as this:

1 All the material used in this paper is reprinted in *California Gold,* edited by Edwin R. Bingham (Boston: Heath, 1959), hereafter abbreviated as CG.

The next footnote could then read:

2 Walter Colton, *Three Years in California* (New York: S. A. Rollo, 1850), p. 358 (CG, p. 1).

Or your first footnote might say:

1 All the material used in this paper is reprinted in *California Gold,* edited by Edwin R. Bingham (Boston: Heath, 1959); but my footnotes cite the original pagination, which the reprint supplies.

The next footnote would then say simply:

2 Walter Colton, *Three Years in California* (New York: S. A. Rollo, 1850), p. 358.

Research papers usually include a bibliography, an alphabetical list of books used in the preparation of the paper. Though a paper based on this book does not, strictly speaking, need a bibliography, you can gain valuable practice by compiling one for your paper, showing the various sources as they would be listed if you had consulted the original texts themselves. For the form, consult the same authority as for your footnotes.

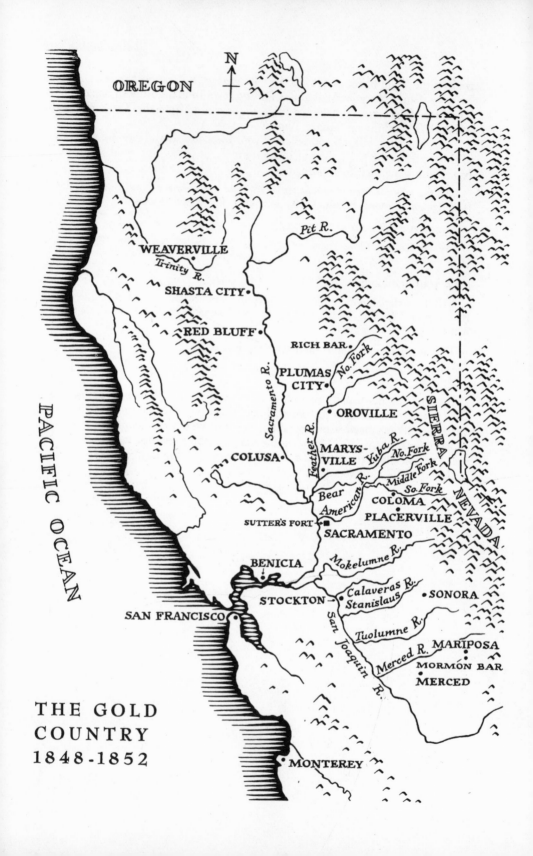

THE GOLD
COUNTRY
1848-1852

# Reverend Walter Colton, U. S. N.

From *Three Years in California.* New York (S. A. Rollo), 1850.

Reverend Walter Colton, born and reared in Vermont, was educated at Yale and ordained in the Congregational Church. After four years as professor of moral philosophy and belles-lettres at the Scientific and Military Academy in Middletown, Connecticut, he accepted the editorship of the *American Spectator and Washington City Chronicle* in the nation's capital. In 1831 he went to sea as a navy chaplain — a duty offered to him by President Jackson, who deemed it to be more suitable to Colton's then-failing health. He cruised first in Caribbean and then in Mediterranean waters and fashioned two travel books from the journeys. After a few years of various other sea and shore duties with the navy, he was ordered to California in 1845 and arrived there in July, 1846 just nine days after the Americans under John D. Sloat had taken possession of Monterey. He became the first ordained minister to reside in California and was soon appointed Alcalde of Monterey, a position which he occupied for three years. Colton, therefore, combined broad experience and literary talent in *Three Years in California* — the record of his stay in that area. The journal is broken into here on May 29, 1848 — the date on which news of the discovery reached Monterey.[1] Less than a year after publication of the journal, Walter Colton was dead.

[NEWS OF THE DISCOVERY STIRS MONTEREY]

242 *Monday, May* 29 [1848]. Our town was startled out of its quiet dreams to-day, by the announcement that gold had been discovered on the American Fork. The men wondered and talked, and the women too; but neither believed. The sibyls were less skeptical; they said the moon had, for several nights, appeared not more than a cable's length from the earth; that a white raven had been seen playing with an infant; and that an owl had rung the church bells. . . .

245 *Monday, June* 12. A straggler came in to-day from the American Fork, bringing a piece of yellow ore weighing an ounce. The young dashed the dirt from their eyes, and the old from their spectacles. One brought a spyglass, another an iron ladle; some wanted to melt it, others to hammer it, and a few were satisfied with smelling it. All were full of tests; and many, who could not be gratified in making their experiments, declared it a humbug. One lady sent me a huge gold ring, in the hope of reach-/ing the truth by comparison; while 246 a gentleman placed the specimen on the top of his gold-headed cane and held it up, challenging the sharpest eyes to detect a difference. But doubts still hovered on the minds of the great mass. They could not conceive that such a treasure could have lain there so long undiscovered. The idea seemed to convict them of stupidity. There is nothing of which a man is more tenacious than his claims to sagacity. He sticks to them like an old bachelor to the idea of his personal attractions, or a toper to the strength of his temperance ability, whenever he shall wish to call it into play. . .

*Tuesday, June* 20. My messenger sent to the mines, has returned with specimens of the gold; he dismounted in a sea of upturned faces. As he drew forth the yellow lumps from his pockets, and passed / them 247 around among the eager crowd, the doubts,

[1] The discovery itself had taken place in January of 1848, but news of it was slow in coming, due mostly to the efforts of the finders to keep it a secret. Word gradually leaked out, however, and it wasn't long before the reports began to spread across the continent and to other parts of the world.

1

which had lingered till now, fled. All admitted they were gold, except one old man, who still persisted they were some Yankee invention, got up to reconcile the people to the change of flag. The excitement produced was intense; and many were soon busy in their hasty preparations for a departure to the mines. The family who had kept house for me caught the moving infection. Husband and wife were both packing up; the blacksmith dropped his hammer, the carpenter his plane, the mason his trowel, the farmer his sickle, the baker his loaf, and the tapster his bottle. All were off for the mines, some on horses, some on carts, and some on crutches, and one went in a litter. An American woman, who had recently established a boarding-house here, pulled up stakes, and was off before her lodgers had even time to pay their bills. Debtors ran, of course. I have only a community of women left, and a gang of prisoners, with here and there a soldier, who will give his captain the slip at the first chance. I don't blame the fellow a whit; seven dollars a month, while others are making two or three hundred a day! that is too much for human nature to stand.

*Saturday, July* 15. The gold fever has reached every servant in Monterey; none are to be trusted in their engagement beyond a week, and as for compulsion, it is like attempting to drive fish into a net with the ocean before them. Gen. Mason, 248 Lieut. / Lanman, and myself, form a mess; we have a house, and all the table furniture and culinary apparatus re-quisite; but our servants have run, one after another, till we are almost in despair: even Sambo, who we thought would stick by from laziness, if no other cause, ran last night; and this morning, for the fortieth time, we had to take to the kitchen and cook our own breakfast. A general of the United States Army, the commander of a man-of-war, and the Alcalde of Monterey, in a smoking kitchen, grinding coffee, toasting herring, and pealing onions! . . .

252 *Thursday, Aug.* 16. Four citizens of Monterey are just in from the gold mines on Feather River, where they worked in company with three others. They employed about thirty wild Indians, who are attached to the rancho owned by one of the party. They worked precisely seven weeks and three days, and have divided seventy-six thousand eight hundred and forty-four dollars — nearly eleven thousand dollars to each. Make a dot there, and let me introduce a man, well known to me, who has worked on the Yuba river sixty-four days, and brought back, as the result of his individual labor, five thousand three hundred and fifty-six dollars. Make a dot there, and let me introduce another townsman, who has worked on the North Fork fifty-seven days, and brought back four thousand five hundred and thirty-four dollars. Make a dot there, and let me introduce a boy, fourteen years of age, who has worked on the Mokelumne fifty-four days, and brought back three thousand four hundred and sixty-seven dollars. Make another dot there, and let me introduce a woman, of Sonoranian birth, who / has worked in the dry 253 diggings forty-six days, and brought back two thousand one hundred and twenty-five dollars. Is not this enough to make a man throw down his leger and shoulder a pick? But the deposits which yielded these harvests were now opened for the first time; they were the accumulation of ages; only the foot-prints of the elk and wild savage had passed over them. Their slumber was broken for the first time by the sturdy arms of the American emigrant.

*Tuesday, Aug.* 28. The gold mines have upset all social and domestic arrangements in Monterey; the master has become his own servant, and the servant his own lord. The millionaire is obliged to groom his own horse, and roll his wheelbarrow; and the hidalgo — in whose veins flows the blood of all the Cortes — to clean his own boots! Here is lady L——, who has lived here seventeen years, the pride and ornament of the place, with a broomstick in her jewelled hand! . . . / And here am I, who have been 254 a man of some note in my day, loafing on the hospitality of the good citizens, and grateful for a meal, though in an Indian's wigwam. Why, is not this enough to make one wish the gold mines were in the earth's flaming centre, from which they sprung? Out on this yellow dust! it is worse than the cinders which buried Pompeii, for there, high and low shared the same fate! . . .

255   *Saturday, Sept.* 16. The gold mines are producing one good result; every creditor who has gone there is paying his debts. Claims not deemed worth a farthing are now cashed on presentation at nature's great bank. This has rendered the credit of every man here good for almost any amount. Orders for merchandise are honored which six months ago would have been thrown into the fire. There is none so poor, who has two stout arms and a pickaxe left, but he can empty any store in Monterey. Nor has the first instance yet occurred, in which the creditor has suffered. All distinctions indicative of means have vanished; the only capital required is muscle and an honest purpose. I met a man to-day from the mines in patched buckskins, rough as a badger from his hole, who had fifteen thousand dollars in yellow dust, swung at his back. Talk to him of brooches, gold-headed canes, and Carpenter's coats! why he can unpack a lump of gold that would throw all Chesnut-street into spasms. And there is more where this came from. *His* rights in the great domain are equal

256   to yours, and his / prospects of getting it out vastly better. With these advantages, he bends the knee to no man, but strides along in his buckskins, a lord of earth by a higher prescriptive privilege than what emanates from the partiality of kings. His patent is medallioned with rivers which roll over golden sands, and embossed with mountains which have lifted for ages their golden coronets to heaven. Clear out of the way with your crests, and crowns, and pedigree trees, and let this democrat pass. Every drop of blood in his veins tells that it flows from a great heart, which God has made and which man shall never enslave. Such are the genuine sons of California; such may they live and die.

[PREPARING FOR THE TRIP]

*Wednesday, Sept.* 20. A servant of James 257 McKinley, Esq., led to my door this morning a beautiful saddle-horse, with a message from his master, desiring me to accept the animal as a token of his regard. The gift was most opportune, as I was on the eve of a trip to the gold-mines. To guard against contingencies I purchased another, and, to prevent their being stolen, placed them both in the government corral, where a watch is posted night and day. My companions on the trip were to be Capt. Marcy, son of the late secretary of war, Mr. Botts, naval storekeeper, and Mr. Wilkinson, son of our ex-minister to Russia.

Having procured a suitable wagon, we freighted it lightly with provisions, articles of Indian traffic, tools for working in the mines, cooking utensils, and blankets to sleep in. To this we attached four mules, but little used to the harness, and of no great power. . . . The whole was put under the charge of a man who was half sailor and half teamster, and not much of / either. 258 Thus accoutred, the team was sent ahead, and we were to follow the next day.

[AT THE CAMPS]

*Friday, Sept.* 29. We met a company of Californians about mid-day, on their return from the mines, and a more forlorn looking group never / knocked at the gate 271 of a pauper asylum. They were most of them dismounted, with rags fastened round their blistered feet, and with clubs in their hands, with which they were trying to force on their skeleton animals. They inquired for bread and meat; we had but little of either, but shared it with them. They took from one of their packs a large bag of gold, and began to shell out a pound or two in payment. We told them they were welcome; still they seemed anxious to pay, and we were obliged to be positive in our refusal. This company, as I afterwards ascertained, had with them over a hundred thousand dollars in grain gold. One of them had the largest lump that had yet been found; it weighed over twenty pounds; and he seemed almost ready to part with it for a mess of pottage. What is gold where there is nothing to eat? — the gilded fly of the angler in a troutless stream.

273 *Saturday, Sept.* 30. The scenery, as we advanced, became more wild and picturesque. The hills lost their gentle slopes, and took the form of steep and rugged cones; the mountain ranges were broken by dark and rugged gorges; over crags that toppled high in air, the soaring pine threw its wild music on the wind; while merry streams dashed down the precipitous rocks, as if in haste to greet the green vale below. A short distance beyond us lay the richest gold mines that had yet been discovered; and nature, as if to guard her treasures, had thrown around them a steep mountain barrier. This frowning wall seemed as if riven in some great convulsion. The broad chasm, like a break in a huge Roman aqueduct, dropped to the level plain; while the bold bluffs of the severed barrier gazed at each other in savage grandeur. Beyond this gateway, a valley wandered for some distance, and then expanded into a plain, in the midst of which stood a beautiful grove of oak and pine. Crossing this, we wound over a rough, rocky elevation, and turned suddenly into a ravine, up which we discovered a line of tents glittering in the sun's rays. We were in the gold mines! I jumped from my horse, took a pick, and in five minutes found a piece of gold large enough to make a signet-ring. . . .

274 *Sunday, Oct.* 1. Another Sabbath, and our first in the mines. But here and there a digger has resumed his work. With most it is a day of rest, not so much perhaps from religious scruples, as conviction that the system requires and must have repose. He is a blind philosopher, as well as a stupid Christian, who cannot see, even in the physical benefits of the Sabbath, motives sufficient to sanctify its observance. He must be a callous soul, who, with the hope of heaven in his dreams, can wantonly profane its spirit.

*Monday, Oct.* 2. I went among the gold-diggers; found half a dozen at the bottom of the ravine, tearing up the bogs, and up to their knees in mud. Beneath these bogs lay a bed of clay, sprinkled in spots with gold. These deposits, and the earth mixed with them, were shovelled into bowls, taken to a pool near by, and washed out. The bowl, in working, is held / in both hands, 275 whirled violently back and forth through half a circle, and pitched this way and that sufficiently to throw off the earth and water, while the gold settles to the bottom. The process is extremely laborious, and taxes the entire muscles of the frame. In its effect it is more like swinging a scythe than any work I ever attempted.

Not having much relish for the bogs and mud, I procured a light crowbar and went to splitting the slate rocks which project into the ravine. I found between the layers, which were not perfectly closed, particles of gold, resembling in shape the small and delicate scales of a fish. These were easily scraped from the slate by a hunter's knife, and readily separated in the wash-bowl from all foreign substances. The layers in which they were found generally inclined from a vertical or horizontal position, and formed an acute angle with the bank of the ravine, in the direction of the current. In the reverse of this position, and where the inclination was with the current, they rarely contained any gold. The inference would seem to be, that these deposits are made by the currents when swelled by the winter rains, and poured in a rushing tide down these channels. It is only the most rapid stream that can carry this treasure, and even that must soon resign it to some eddy, or the rock that paves its footsteps.

There are about seventy persons at work in this ravine, all within a few yards of each other. They average about one ounce per diem each. They / who get less are dis- 276 contented, and they who get more are not satisfied. Every day brings in some fresh report of richer discoveries in some quarter not far remote, and the diggers are consequently kept in a state of feverish excitement. One woman, a Sonoranian, who was washing here, finding at the bottom of her bowl only the amount of half a dollar or so, hurled it back again into the water, and straightening herself up to her full height, strode off with the indignant air of one who feels himself insulted. Poor woman! how little thou knowest of those patient females, who in our large cities make a shirt or vest for ten cents! Were an ounce of diamonds to fall into one of our hands every day, we should hold out the other just as eager and impatient as if its fellow were empty. Such is human nature; and a miserable thing it is, too, especially when touched with the gold fever. . . .

278 *Wednesday, Oct. 4.* Our camping-ground is in a broad ravine through which a rivulet 279 wanders, and / which is dotted with the frequent tents of gold-diggers. The sounds of the crowbar and pick, as they shake or shiver the rock, are echoed from a thousand cliffs; while the hum of human voices rolls off on the breeze to mingle with the barking of wolves, who regard with no friendly eyes this intrusion into their solitude. They resemble their great progenetrix, trembling in stone, as the Vandals broke into Rome. But little care the gold-diggers about the wolves, it is enough for them to know that this ravine contains gold; and it must be dug out, though an earthquake may slumber beneath. If you want to find men prepared to storm the burning threshold of the infernal prison, go among gold-diggers.

The provisions with which we left San Jose are gone, and we have been obliged to supply ourselves here. We pay at the rate of four hundred dollars a barrel for flour; four dollars a pound for poor brown sugar, and four dollars a pound for indifferent coffee. And as for meat, there is none to be got except jerked beef, which is the flesh of the bullock cut into strings and hung up in the sun to dry, and which has about as much juice in it as a strip of bark dangling in the wind from a dead tree. Still, when moistened and toasted, it will do something towards sustaining life; so also will the sole of your shoe. And yet I have seen men set and grind it as if it were nutritious and sweetly flavored. Oh ye who lose your temper because your sirloin has rolled once too much on the spit, come to the mines of California and eat jerked-beef! . . .

*Wednesday, Oct. 11.* It is near sunset, 285 and the gold-diggers are returning from their labors, each one bearing on his head a brush-heap, with which he will kindle his evening fire. Their wild halloes, as they come in, fill the cliffs with their echoes. All are merry, whatever may have been the fortunes of the / day with them. Not one 286 among the whole can anticipate a more luxurious supper than a cake baked in the ashes, with a cup of coffee and a bit of jerked-beef, except in the case of a newcomer, who has brought with him a few pounds of buckwheat flour; he can have a pancake, that is if he has any thing with which to grease his pan, which is extremely doubtful. There is not a bottle of liquor in the ravine, and every one must, per force, turn in sober. Every streamlet preaches temperance, and the wind-stirred pine sings its soft eulogy on the charmed air. . . .

*Monday, Oct. 16.* I encountered this 289 morning, in the person of a Welchman, a pretty marked specimen of the gold-digger. He stood some six feet eight in his shoes, with giant limbs and frame. A leather strap fastened his coarse trowsers above his hips, and confined the flowing bunt of his flannel shirt. A broad-rimmed hat sheltered his browny features, while his unshorn beard and hair flowed in tangled confusion to his waist. To his back was lashed a blanket and bag of provisions; on one shoulder rested a huge crowbar, to which were hung a gold-washer and skillet; on the other rested a rifle, a spade, and pick, from which dangled a cup and pair of heavy shoes. He recognized me as the magistrate who had once arrested him for a breach of the peace. "Well, Senor Alcalde," said he, "I am glad to see you in these dig-/gings. You 290 had some trouble with me in Monterey; I was on a burster; you did your duty, and I respect you for it; and now let me settle the difference between us with a bit of gold: it shall be the first I strike under this bog." I told him there was no difference between us; that I knew at the time it was rum which had raised the rumpus. But before I had finished my disclaiming speech, his traps were on the ground, and his heavy pick was tearing up bog after bog from the marl in which it had struck its tangling roots. These removed, he struck a layer of clay: "Here she comes!" he ejaculated, and turned out a piece of gold that would weigh an ounce or more. "There," said he, "Senor Alcalde, accept that; and when you reach home, where I hope you will find all well, have a bracelet made of it for your good lady."

He continued to dig around the same place, but during the hour I remained with him found no other piece of gold — not a particle. This is no uncommon thing; I have seen a piece weighing six ounces taken from some little curve in a bank undulating in its bed, while not another of any size, after the most laborious search, could be found in its vicinity. This holds true of the larger pieces, but rarely of the scale gold. Where you find half an ounce of that, you may be pretty sure there is more near by. The same law which deposited that, has carried its results much further; and you will find a clue to them in the curves of the channel, 291 or the character and posi-/tion of the rocks which project into it. If the projection is smooth, or forms an obtuse angle with the current, there is no gold there, and you must look to the eddy directly below it. This eddy, or its deposit, can be examined only when the water has subsided. During the rainy season and when the snows are melting on the Sierra, no such investigations can be successfully prosecuted. Of all metals the most difficult to reach and secure under water is gold. It has a thousand modes of eluding your search, and escaping your scooping implements.

292   *Wednesday, Oct.* 18. We are camped in the centre of the gold mines, in the heart of the richest deposits which have been found, and where there are many hundred at work. I have taken some pains to ascer-

tain the average per man that is got out; it must be less than half an ounce per day. It might be more were there any stability among the diggers; but half their time is consumed in what they call prospecting; that is, looking up new deposits. An idle rumor, or mere surmise, will carry them off in this direction or that, when perhaps they gathered nothing for their weariness and toil. A locality where an ounce a day can be obtained by patient labor is constantly left for another, which rumor has enriched with more generous deposits. They who decry this instability in others, may hold out for a time, but yield at last to the same phrensied fickleness. I have never met with one who had the strength of purpose / to 293 resist these roving temptations. He will not swing a pick for an ounce a day, with the rumor of pounds ringing in his ears. He shoulders his implements to chase this phantom of hope.

*Thursday, Oct.* 19. All the gold-diggers through the entire encampment, were shaken out of their slumbers this morning by a report that a solid pocket of gold had been discovered in a bend of the Stanislaus. In half an hour a motley multitude, covered with crowbars, pickaxes, spades, rifles, and washbowls, went streaming over the hills in the direction of the new deposits. You would have thought some fortress was to be stormed, or some citadel sapped. I had seen too much of these rumored banks of gold to be moved from my propriety, and remained under my old camping-tree. Near this I pecked out from a small crevice of slate rock, a piece weighing about half an ounce. . . .

But evening is returning, and with it the 294 gold-diggers from their pursuit of the new deposit. Their jokes, as they clatter down the slopes of the ravine, are sufficient evidence that they have been on a wild-goose chase. Disappointment will make a single man sober, but when it falls on a multitude, is often converted into a source of railery and fun. There is something extremely consoling in having the company of others, when we have been duped through our vanity or exaggerated hopes. This comfort was deeply felt by the diggers this evening. All had lost a day, and with it the most enchanting visions of wealth. All had returned hungry as a wolf on a desert; or a recluse listening in his last penance to the sound of his cross-bones, shaken by the wind.

295    *Friday, Oct.* 20. I threw myself into my saddle at an early hour this morning, and started for a cañada, about ten miles distant. The foot-trail which I followed, lay over several sharp ridges to the quick waves of the Stanislaus, and then up a steep mountain spur. . . .

296    Ascending another ridge, the ravine, which had induced this adventure, lay in jagged wildness beneath. It was in uproarious life; an elk had been shot; and the miners were feasting on its fat ribs. The repast was hardly over, when the monté table, with its piles of gold, glimmered in the shade. It was the great camp of the Sonoranians, and hundreds were crowding around to reach the bank, and deposit their treasures on the turn of a card. They seemed to play for the excitement, and often doubled their stakes whether they won or lost. They apparently connect no moral obliquity with the game; one of them, who sleeps near my camping-tree, will kneel by the half hour on the sharp rock in his Ave Marias, while the keen night-wind cuts his scarce clad frame, then rise and stake his last dollar at monté. At the break of day he is on his knees again, and his prayer trembles up with the first trill of the waking birds. It was in this ravine that a few weeks since the largest lump of gold found in California was discovered. It weighs twenty-three pounds, is nearly pure, and cubic in its form. Its discovery shook the whole mines; the shout of the *eureka* swelled on the wind like the cheer of seamen when the pharos breaks through the stormy night. I waved my adieu to the miners, and fetching a bold circuit to the east, reached at night-fall my camping-tree.

*Monday, Oct.* 23. It was now near noon, 297 and / my day to cook the dinner; so I 298 hastened back to our camping-tree, and piling up the half-extinguished brands, soon raised a fire. Then taking a tin pan, which served alternately as a gold-washer and a bread-tray, I turned into it a few pounds of flour, a small solution of saleratus, and a few quarts of water, and then went to work it with my hands, mixing it up and adding flour till I got it to the right consistency; then shaping it into a loaf, raked open the embers, and rolled it in, covering it with the live coals. While this baking was going on, I placed in a stew-pan, after pounding it pretty well between two stones, a string of jerked-beef, with a small quantity of water, and lodged it on the fire. Then taking some coffee, which had been burnt the evening before, I tied it in the end of a napkin, and hammering it to pieces between two stones, turned it into a coffee-pot filled with water, and placed that, too, on the fire. In half an hour or so my bread was baked, my jerk-beef stewed, and my coffee boiled. I settled the latter by turning on it a pint of cold water. The bread was well done; a little burnt on one side, and somewhat puffed up, like the expectations of the gold-digger in the morning, or the vanity of a stump-orator just after a cheer. My companions returned, and seating ourselves on the ground, each with a tin cup of coffee, a junk of bread, and a piece of the stewed jerky, our dinner was soon dispatched, and with a relish which the epicure never yet felt or fancied. The water here is slightly impregnated with iron and / sulphur; the 299 one acting as a tonic, the other as an aperient. And then this fine mountain air, some eight hundred feet above the level of the sea, all conduce to health and buoyancy of spirits. Among the hundred gold-diggers around, not one hypochondriac throws on rock or rill the shadow of a long countenance. Even they who hardly get out gold enough to pay their way, laugh at their bad luck, and hope for better success tomorrow. They have yet plenty of tickets in the lottery, and some of them may turn out prizes. At any rate, they are not going to despond while these glens contain an undisturbed bar, or these hills lift their cones of white rock in the sun. . . .

306   *Wednesday, Nov. 1.* There are several persons among the gold-diggers here who rarely use any implement but their wooden bowls. Into these they scrape the dirt left by others, which they stir and whirl till the gold gradually works its way to the bottom. The earth, as these heavier particles descend, is thrown off by the hands, and the gold remains. This process is what they call dry washing; it is resorted to where there is no water in the vicinity, and will answer pretty well where the gold is found in coarse grains; but the final particles, of course, escape. The Sonoranians obviate this difficulty to some extent by calling their lungs into requisition. They rub the earth into their bowls, through their hands, detaching and throwing away all the pebbles, and then blow off the sand and dust, leaving the gold at the bottom. But on some of the streams, particularly the Yuba, the gold is too fine even for this process. It is amusing to see a group of Sonoranians, seated around a deposit, blowing the earth out of their bowls. But for the dust they raise, you would think they were cooling hasty-pudding. Their cheeks swell out, like the chops of a squirrel, carrying half the beech-nuts on a tree to his hole. A more provident fellow he than his two-legged superior! He lays in his stores against the 307 inclemency of / winter; while the Sonoranian squanders his at the gambling-table. There is more practical wisdom in an ant-hill than is often found in a city. But I am digressing again — a propensity which I shall never get over.

*Thursday, Nov. 2.* Quite a sensation was produced among the gold-diggers this morning by the arrival of a wagon from Stockton, freighted with provisions and a barrel of liquor. The former had been getting scarce, and the latter had long since entirely given out. The prices of the first importation were — flour, two dollars a pound; sugar and

coffee, four dollars; and the liquor, which was nothing more or less than New England rum, was twenty dollars the quart. But few had bottles: every species of retainer was resorted to; some took their quart cups, some their coffee-pots, and others their sauce-pans; while one fellow, who had neither, offered ten dollars to let him suck with a straw from the bung. All were soon in every variety of excitement, from prattling exhilaration, to roaring inebriety. Some shouted, some danced, and some wrestled; a son of Erin poured out his soul on the beauties of the Emerald isle; a German sung the songs of his father-land; a Yankee apostrophized the mines, which swelled in the hills around; an Englishman challenged all the bears in the mountain glens to mortal combat; and a Spaniard, posted aloft on a beetling crag, addressed the universe. The multitudinous voices which rang / from every chasm and cove 308 of the ravine, rivalled the roar that went up around the tower of Babel. But night has come; the camp-fires burn dim; and the revellers are at rest, save here and there one who strides about in his delirium, commanding silence among the wolves who bark from the hills. What exciting, elevating, and expanding powers there are in a barrel of New England rum! . . .

*Sunday, Nov. 5.* I rose this morning with 311 the intention of proposing to the diggers a religious service. But mid-day came, and only here and there one broke from slumbers doubly deep from the overpowering fatigues of the week. In a shaded recess of the hills three of us found a little sanctuary: . . .

*Tuesday, Nov. 7.* The price of provisions 313 here is no criterion of their market value on the seaboard, or even at the embarcadaros nearest the mines. The cost of a hundred pounds of flour at Stockton, only sixty miles distant, is twenty dollars; but here it is two hundred dollars. This vast disparity is owing to the difficulty of transportation and the absence of competition. But few can be persuaded to leave the expectations of the pick for the certainties of the pack — the promises of the cradle for the fulfilments of the freighted wagon. All live on drafts upon the future, and though disappointed a hundred times, still believe the results of to-morrow will more than redeem the broken pledges of to-day. Though all else may end in failure, hope is not bankrupt here.

The soil in the mines is evidently volcanic; it resembles in places the ashes which cover Pompeii. You can walk through it when dry, though every footstep stirs a little cloud; but when saturated with the winter rain you slump to the middle. No horse can force his way forward; every struggle but sinks him the deeper, and the miner himself retires to his cabin, as thoroughly cut off from the peopled districts of the coast, as a sailor wrecked on some rock at sea. Years must elapse before human enterprise can bridge a path to these mines, or render communication practicable in the rainy season; nor at any period can heavy machinery be transported here without an immense 314 outlay of capital. The quartz rock / has yet some time to roll back the sunlight before it crumbles under the steam-stamper.

*Wednesday, Nov. 8.* Some fifty thousand persons are drifting up and down these slopes of the great Sierra, of every hue, language, and clime, tumultuous and confused as a flock of wild geese taking wing at the crack of a gun, or autumnal leaves strown on the atmospheric tides by the breath of the whirlwind. All are in quest of gold; and, with eyes dilated to the circle of the moon, rush this way and that, as some new discovery, or fictitious tale of success may suggest. Some are with tents, and some without; some have provisions, and some are on their last ration; some are carrying crowbars; some pickaxes and spades; some wash-bowls and cradles; some hammers and drills, and powder enough to blow up the rock of Gibralter — if they can but get under it, as the monkeys do, when they make their transit, through a sort of Thames tunnel, from the golden but barren sands of Africa to the green hills of Europe. Wise fellows they, notwithstanding the

length of their tails — they won't stay on the Congo side of the strait, to gather gold, when, by crossing, they can gather grapes. Wisdom is justified of her children.

But I was speaking of the gold-hunters here on the slopes of the Sierra. Such a mixed and motley crowd — such a restless, roving, rummaging, ragged multitude, never before roared in the rookeries of man. As for mutual aid and sympathy — Samson's / foxes had as much of it, turned tail to, with 315 firebrands tied between. Each great camping-ground is denoted by the ruins of shovels and shanties, the bleaching bones of the dead, disinhumed by the wolf, and the skeleton of the culprit, still swinging in the wind, from the limb of a tree, overshadowed by the raven. . . .

[REPORT ON CONDITIONS AT THE MINES]

*Saturday, Dec. 2.* I found Monterey, on 339 my return from the mines, under the same quiet air in which her green hills had soared since I first beheld their waving shade. Many had predicted my precipitate return, from the hardships and baffled attempt of the tour; but I persevered, taking rough and tumble from the first, and have returned with improved health. I met with but very few cases of sickness in the mines, and these obviously resulting from excessive imprudence. What but maladies could be expected, where the miner stands by the hour in a cold mountain stream, with a broiling sun overhead, and then, perhaps, drinking every day a pint of New England rum? Why, the rum itself would shatter any constitution not lightning-proof. I wish those who send this fire-curse here were wrapped in its flames till the wave of repentance should baptize them into a better life.

*Monday, Dec. 25.* The multitudes who 341 are in the mines, suffer in health and constitution from the extreme changes of temperature which follow day and night. In some of the ravines in which we camped, these variations vibrated through thirty and forty degrees. In mid-day we were driven into the shade to keep cool, and in the night into two or three blankets to keep warm. The heat is ascribable in part to the nature of the soil, its naked sandy features, its power of radiation, and the absence of circulation in the glens. But the cold comes with the visits of the night wind from the frosty slopes of the Sierra Nevada.

These extreme variations follow the 342 miner through / the whole region in which his tempting scenes of labor lie, and require a degree of prudence seldom met with in that wild woodland life. The consequence is, a group of maladies under which the strongest constitution at length breaks down. But I am convinced from personal experience, that with proper precaution and suitable food, many, and most of these evils may be obviated. The southern mines are in elevations which exempt them from the maladies incident to the low lands which fringe the streams farther north. There are no stagnant waters, no decomposition of vegetable matter, no miasma drifting about in the fog, to shake and burn you with alternate chill and fever. I never enjoyed better health and spirits; and never encountered in a great moving mass, notwithstanding their irregularities, so few instances of disease traceable to local causes. I have seen more groaners and grunters in one metropolitan household, than in any swarming ravine in the southern mines.

365 *Thursday, April 26.* The gold region, which contains deposits of sufficient richness to reward the labor of working them, is strongly defined by nature. It lies along the foot hills of the Sierra Nevada — a mountain range running nearly parallel with the coast — and extends on these hills about five hundred miles north and south, by thirty or forty east and west. From the slopes of the Sierra, a large number of streams issue, which cut their channels through these hills, and roll with greater or less volume to the Sacramento and San Joaquin rivers . . .

The streams which break into these rivers 366 from / the Sierra Nevada, are from ten to thirty miles distant from each other. They commence with Feather river on the north, and end with the river Reys on the south. They all have numerous tributaries; are rapid and wild on the mountain slopes, and become more tranquil and tame as they debouch upon the plain. Still their serpentine waters, flashing up among the trees which shadow their channels give a picturesque feature to the landscape, and relieve it of that monotony which would otherwise fatigue the eye. But very few of these rivers have sufficient depth and regularity to render them navigable. Their sudden bends, falls, and shallows would puzzle even an Indian canoe, and strand any boat of sufficient draft to warrant the agency of steam.

The alluvial deposits of gold are confined mainly to the banks and bars of these mountain streams, and the channels of the gorges, which intersect them, and through which streams are forced when swollen by the winter rains. In the hills and table-lands, which occupy the intervals between these currents and gorges, no alluvial deposits have been found. Here and there a few detached pieces have been discovered, forming an exception to some general law by which the uplands have been deprived of their surface treasures. The conclusion at which I have arrived, after days and weeks of patient research, and a thousand inquiries made of others, is, that the alluvial deposits of gold in California are mainly confined to the banks and bars of her streams, / and the ravines which intersect 367 them. The only material exception to this general law is found in those intervening deposits, from which the streams have been diverted by some local cause, or some convulsion of nature. Aside from these, no surface gold to any extent has been found on the table-lands or plains. Even the banks of the Sacramento and San Joaquin, stretching a distance of five hundred miles through their valleys, have not yielded an ounce. The mountain streams, long before they discharge themselves into these rivers, deposit their precious treasures. They contribute their waters, but not their gold. Like cunning misers they have stowed this away, and no enchantments can make them whisper of its whereabouts. If you would find it, you must hunt for it as for hid treasures.

*Monday, May 14.* Much has been said of the amounts of gold taken from the mines by Sonoranians, Chilians, and Peruvians, and carried out of the country. As a general fact, this apprehension and alarm is without any sound basis. Not one pound of gold in ten, gathered by these foreigners, is shipped off to their credit: it is spent in the country for provisions, clothing, and in the hazards of the gaming-table. It falls into the hands of those who command the avenues of commerce, and ultimately reaches our own mints. I have been in a camp of five hundred Sonoranians, who had not gold enough to buy a month's provisions—all had gone, through their
368 im-/provident habits, to the capacious pockets of the Americans. To drive them out of California, or interdict their operations, is to abstract that amount of labor from the mines, and curtail proportionably the proceeds. If gold, slumbering in the river banks and mountains of California, be more valuable to us than when stamped into eagles and incorporated into our national currency, then drive out the Sonoranians: but if you would have it *here* and not *there*, let those diggers alone. When gold shall begin to fail, or require capital and machinery, you will want these hardy men to quarry the rocks and feed your stampers; and when you shall plunge into the Cinnebar mountains, you will want them to sink your shafts and kindle fires under your great quicksilver retorts. They will become the hewers of wood and drawers of water to American capital and enterprise. But if you want to perform this drudgery yourself, drive out the Sonoranians, and upset that cherished system of political economy founded in a spirit of wisdom and national justice.
374 *Wednesday, June 20.* The causes which exclude slavery from California lie within a nut-shell. All here are diggers, and free

white diggers wont dig with slaves. They know they must dig themselves: they have come out here for that purpose, and they wont degrade their calling by associating it with slave-labor: self-preservation is the first law of nature. They have nothing to do with slavery in the abstract, or as it exists in other communities; not one in ten cares a button for its abolition, nor the Wilmot proviso either: all they look at is their own position; they must themselves swing the pick, and they wont swing it by the side of negro slaves. That is their feeling, their determination, and the upshot of the whole business. An army of half a million, backed by the resources of the United States, could not shake their purpose. Of all men with whom I have ever met, the most firm, resolute, and indomitable, are the emigrants into California. They feel that they have got into a new world, where they have a right to shape and settle things in their own way. No mandate, unless it / comes like a thunder-bolt straight out of 375 heaven, is regarded. They may offer to come into the Union, but they consider it an act of condescension, like that of Queen Victoria in her nuptials with Prince Albert. . . .

WHO SHOULD STAY AND WHO COME

The indiscretion with which so many 393 thousands are rushing to California will be a source of regret to them, and of sorrow to their friends. Not one in twenty will bring back a fortune, and not more than one in ten secure the means of defraying the expenses of his return. I speak now of those whose plans and efforts are confined to the mines, and who rely on the proceeds of their manual labor; when they have defrayed the expenses incident to their position, liqui-/dated all demands for food, 394 clothing, and implements for the year, their yellow heap will dwindle to a point. This might serve as the nucleus of operations which are to extend through a series of years; but as the result of the enterprise, involving privation and hardship, is a failure, no man should come to California under the impression that he can in a few months pick a fortune out of its mines. He may here and there light on a more productive deposit, but the chances are a hundred to one that his gains will be slenderly and laboriously acquired. He is made giddy with the reports of sudden wealth; these are the rare *prizes*, while the silence of the grave hangs over the multitudinous *blanks*.

A young man endowed with a vigorous constitution, and who possesses sterling habits of sobriety and application, and who has no dependencies at home, can do well in California. But he should come with the resolute purpose of remaining here eight or ten years, and with a spirit that can throw its unrelaxed energies into any enterprise which the progress of the country may develop. He must identify himself for the time being with all the great interests which absorb attention, and quicken labor. If he has not the enterprise and force of purpose which this requires, he should remain at home. . . .

### THE PROFESSIONS AND PURSUITS

396   All the secular professions and more privileged or prescribed pursuits in California are crowded to overflowing. Physicians are without patients; lawyers without clients; surveyors without lands; hydrographers without harbors; actors without audiences; painters without pupils; financiers without funds; minters without metals; printers without presses; hunters without hounds, and fiddlers without fools. And all these must take to the plough, the pickaxe, and spade. Even California, with all her treasured hills and streams, fell under that primal malediction which threw its death-shade on the infant world. It is as true here as among the granite rocks of New England — in the sweat of thy face shalt thou eat bread. Let none think to escape this labor-destiny here; it environs the globe, and binds every nation and tribe in its inexorable folds.

The merchant, whose shrewdness avails him everywhere else, will often be wrecked here. The markets of a single month have all the phases of its fickle moon. The slender crescent waxes into the circle; and the full orb passes under a total eclipse. The man that figured on its front is gone, and with him the hopes of the millionaire. . . .

### WRONGS OF CALIFORNIA

The neglect and wrongs of California 397 will yet find a tongue. From the day the United States flag was raised in this country, she has been the victim of the most unrelenting oppression. Her farmers were robbed of their stock to meet the exigences of war; and her emigrants forced into the field to maintain the conquest. Through the exactions of the customhouse the comforts and necessaries of life were oppressively taxed. No article of food or raiment could escape this forced contribution; it reached the plough of the farmer, the anvil of the smith; the blanket that protected your person, the salt that seasoned your food, the shingle that roofed your cabin, and the nail that bound your coffin. Even the light of heaven paid its contribution in its windowed tariff. And who were the persons on whom these extortions fell? Citizens whom the government had promised to relieve of taxation, and emigrants who had exhaust-/ed their last means in reach- 398 ing their new abode! There was treachery and tyranny combined in the treatment which they received. A less provocation sunk the dutied tea in the harbor of Boston, and severed the indignant colonies from the British crown.

Nor does this gross injustice stop here: this oppressive tax was enforced at a time when there was but little specie in the country; the whole circulating medium was absorbed in its unrighteous demands. Nor was the case materially relieved by the discovery of gold; this precious ore was extorted at ten dollars the ounce, and forfeited at that arbitrary valuation if not redeemed within a given time. There was no specie by which it could be redeemed, and it went to the clutches of the government at ten dollars, when its real value at our mints is eighteen dollars. If this be not robbery, will some one define what that word means? It was worse than robbery — it was swindling under the color of law. All this has been carried on against a community without a representation in our national legislature, and without any civil benefits in return. Not even a light-house to relieve its onerous injustice. Hundreds of thousands, not to say millions thus extorted, are now locked up in the sub-treasury chest at San Francisco. Every doubloon, dollar, and dime that reaches the country is forced under that inexorable key. In this absorption of the circulating medium, commercial loans can be effected only on ruinous rates of interest, and the civil government itself is bankrupt. . . .

[SURFACE GOLD AND DEEP MINING]

403    The surface gold in California will in a few years be measurably exhausted; the occasional discovery of new deposits cannot long postpone such a result; nor will it be delayed for any great number of years, by any more scientific and thorough method of securing the treasure. California will prove no exception in these respects to other sections of the globe where surface gold has been found. The great question is,

will her mountains be exhausted with her streams and valleys? Will her rock gold give out with her alluvial deposits? The gold-bearing quartz is the sheet-anchor at which the whole argosy rides; if this parts, your golden craft goes to fragments. . . .

. . . Though the gold may not ooze from 404 the quartz as water drips from a rock, yet it is *there,* and often beads from the surface like a tear that has lost its way among the dimples of a lady's cheek. In other instances it shows itself only in fine veins; and in others still, is wholly concealed from the naked eye, and even eludes the optical instrument; but when reduced to powder with the quartz, flies to the embrace of quicksilver, and takes a virgin shape, massive and rich. The specimens of quartz which have been subjected to experiment, have yielded from one to three dollars the pound. These specimens were gathered at different points, in the foot range of the Sierra Nevada, and are deemed only a fair average of the yield that may be derived from the quartz.

The gold rocks of Georgia and Virginia yield, on an average, less than half a cent to the pound, and yet the profits are sufficient to justify deep mining. What then must be the profits of working a rock which lies near the surface, and which yields over a dollar to the pound! . . .

# E. Gould Buffum

From *Six Months in the Gold Mines from A Journal of Three Years in Upper and Lower California, 1847–1849*. Philadelphia (Lea and Blanchard), 1850.

Edward Gould Buffum, elder son of Arnold Buffum a well-known New England abolitionist and philanthropist, was born in Rhode Island about 1820. He chose journalism for a career and was affiliated with the New York *Herald* at the time of the war with Mexico. In 1846 Buffum joined the New York Volunteers as a lieutenant and was sent to San Francisco, arriving in March, 1847. After news of the discovery of gold Lt. Buffum was ordered to Los Angeles, where he and other members of the regiment spent three dreary, impatient months waiting for the deactivation of their unit. Free at last, Buffum rushed to the gold mines, arriving in October, and was one of the few to record the early scenes of the rush. Later Buffum became editor-in-chief of the *Alta California*, a pioneer California newspaper. He also entered politics briefly as a member of the legislature from San Francisco, but declined the speakership of the House. After a time he returned to the New York *Herald* and was sent to Paris in 1859 as special correspondent, serving in that capacity until his death in October, 1867.

[THE TRIP TO THE MINES]

25 ARMED with a pickaxe, shovel, hoe, and rifle, and accoutred in a red flannel shirt, corduroy pants, and heavy boots, and accompanied by two friends, I found myself, on the afternoon of the 25th of October, 1848, wending my way to the only wharf in San Francisco, to take passage for the golden hills of the Sierra Nevada. The scenes that for days had met my eyes, and even as I was stepping on board the launch, might have damped the ardour of a more adventurous man. Whole launch-loads of miserable victims of fever and ague were daily arriving from the mining region — sallow, weak, emaciated and dispirited — but I had nerved myself for the combat, and doubt not that I would have taken passage when I did and as I did, had the arch-enemy of mankind himself stood helmsman on the little craft that was to bear me to El Dorado. We had engaged and paid our passage, and such 26 was our eagerness to get a / conveyance of some kind, that we had not even looked at the frail bark in which we were to entrust our now more than ever before valuable bodies.

The "Ann" was a little launch of about ten tons burden, a mere ship's boat, entirely open, and filled with barrels and merchandise of every kind, and eight human beings, who, besides ourselves, had taken passage in her. I looked at her, — there was not room upon her deckless hull to stow a brandy bottle securely. We tried to reason the captain into an idea of the danger of proceeding with so much freight, but the only reply he gave us was, that "he received four dollars a hundred for it." There was no alternative, so in we jumped, and about dusk the boat was under way, and scudding with a fair wind across the bay of San Francisco. . . .

The beautiful plain on which is now 32 located the thriving and populous city of Sacramento, was, when I first landed there, untenanted. There was not a house upon it, the only place of business being an old store-ship laid up upon its bank. Where now, after a lapse of only a year, a flourishing city with a population of twelve thousand stands, I pitched my tent on the edge of a broad prairie.

To complete the party with which we intended going to the mines, we were obliged to wait at the Embarcadero for /

14

33 three of our disbanded soldiers, who had left the Pueblo de los Angeles about the time we did, and were coming by land through the Tulare valley, as we required their horses to pack the provisions we had brought with us.

We pitched our tent, cooked our provisions, and anxiously waited the arrival of the men, a prey to the greatest excitement, —continually hearing as we did, the most extravagant stories from the mining region. The intense heat of the summer solstice had given way to autumn's cooling breezes, and parties were daily arriving at and leaving the Embarcadero; the former with their pockets well lined with gold-dust, and the latter with high hopes and beating hearts. . . .

On the 7th of November our party 35 arrived, — their horses, of which they brought five, jaded with the travel in the mountains; and it was not until the 16th that we were able to make a start. Being, of course, entirely ignorant of the best locality to which to proceed, and being all young, strong, and enthusiastic, we determined to strike out a new path, and go on an exploring expedition in the mountains, in the hope that fortune would throw in our way the biggest of all lumps, and that we might possibly find the fountain head of El Dorado, where, gushing in a rich and golden lava from the heart of the great Sierra, a stream of molten gold should appear before our enraptured eyes. . . .

[After several false starts and some aimless wandering Buffum and his party reached a ranch on Bear River.]

43 . . . Johnson is an American, who many years since obtained a large grant of fertile land on Bear River, and has been living here for years within fifteen miles of a stream whose banks and bed were filled with incalculable riches.

We procured some provisions here, and started for the Yuba, and without any mishaps reached the camping ground, about three miles from the river, early in the afternoon. We camped, and Higgins and myself started on a hunting expedition, for the purpose of getting some game for supper. We made our way into the hills, and were travelling slowly, trailing our rifles, when we stopped suddenly, dumbfounded, before two of the most curious and uncouth-looking objects that ever crossed my sight. They were two Indian women, engaged in gathering acorns. They were entirely naked, with the exception of a *coyote* skin extending from the waists to the knees. Their heads were shaved, and the tops of them covered with a black tarry paint, and a huge pair of military whiskers were daubed on 44 their cheeks with / the same article. They had with them two conical-shaped wicker baskets, in which they were placing the

acorns, which were scattered ankle deep around them. Higgins, with more gallantry than myself, essayed a conversation with them, but made a signal failure, as after listening to a few sentences in Spanish and English, they seized their acorn baskets and ran. The glimpse we had taken of these mountain beauties, and our failure to enter into any conversation with them, determined us to pay a visit to their headquarters, which we knew were near by. Watching their footsteps in their rapid flight, we saw them, after descending a hill, turn up a ravine, and disappear. We followed in the direction which they had taken, and soon reached the Indian *rancheria*. It was located on both sides of a deep ravine, across which was thrown a large log as a bridge, and consisted of about twenty circular wigwams, built of brush, plastered with mud, and capable of containing three or four persons. As we entered, we observed our flying beauties, seated on the ground, pounding acorns on a large rock indented with holes similar to those which so puzzled me at "Camp Beautiful." We were suddenly surrounded upon our entrance by thirty or forty male Indians, entirely naked, who had their bows and quivers slung over their shoulders, and who stared most suspiciously at us and our rifles. Finding one of them who spoke Spanish, I entered into a conversation with him — told him we had only come to pay a visit to the *rancheria*, and, as a token of peace offering, gave him about two pounds of musty bread and some tobacco which I happened to have in my game-bag. This pleased him highly, and from that moment till we left, *Pule-u-le*, as he informed me his name was, appeared my most intimate and sworn friend. I apologized to him for the unfortunate fright which we had caused a portion of his household, and assured him that no / harm was intended, as I entertained the greatest respect for the ladies of his tribe, whom I considered far superior in point of ornament, taste, and natural beauty to those of any other race of Indians in the country. Pule-u-le exhibited to me the interior of several of the wigwams, which were nicely thatched with sprigs of pine and cypress, while a matting of the same material covered the bottom. During our presence our two female attractions had retired into one of the wigwams, into which Pule-u-le piloted us, where I found some four or five squaws similarly bepitched and clothed, and who appeared exceedingly frightened at our entrance. But Pule-u-le explained that we were friends, and mentioned the high estimation in which I held them, which so pleased them that one of the runaways left the wigwam and soon brought me in a large piece of bread made of acorns, which to my taste was of a much more excellent flavour than musty hard bread.

Pule-u-le showed us the bows and arrows, and never have I seen more beautiful specimens of workmanship. The bows were some three feet long, but very elastic and some of them beautifully carved, and strung with the intestines of birds. The arrows were about eighteen inches in length, accurately feathered, and headed with a perfectly clear and transparent green crystal, of a kind which I had never before seen, notched on the sides, and sharp as a needle at the point.

The arrows, of which each Indian had at least twenty, were carried in a quiver made of *coyote* skin.

I asked Pule-u-le if he had ever known of the existence of gold prior to the entrance of white men into the mines. His reply was that, where he was born, about forty miles higher up the river, he had, when a boy, picked it from the rocks in large pieces, and amused himself by throwing / them into the river as he would pebbles. A portion of the tribe go daily to the Yuba River, and wash out a sufficient amount of gold to purchase a few pounds of flour, or some sweetmeats, and return to the *rancheria* at night to share it with their neighbours; who in their turn go the next day, while the others are chasing hare and deer over the hills. There were no signs around them of the slightest attempt to cultivate the soil. Their only furniture consisted of woven baskets and earthen jars, and Pule-u-le told me that in the spring he thought they should all leave and go over the "big mountain," to get from the sight of the white man.

Highly pleased with our visit, and receiving a very earnest invitation to "call again," we left the *rancheria* and proceeded towards the camp. . . .

[THE MINES]

Next morning early, in better spirits than we had enjoyed for a week previously, we started for Yuba River. About a mile from the camping-place we struck into the mountains, the same range at whose base we had been before travelling, and which are a portion of the Sierra Nevada. The hills here were steep and rugged, but covered with a magnificent growth of oak and red-wood. As we reached the summit of a lofty hill, the Yuba River broke upon our view, winding like a silver thread beneath us, its banks dotted with white tents, and fringed with trees and shrubbery.

We had at last reached the "mines," although a very different portion of them than that for which we started. We turned out our tired horses, and immediately set forth on an exploring expedition. As my clothing was all dirty and wet, I concluded to indulge in the luxury of a new shirt, and going down to the river found a shrewd Yankee in a tent surrounded by a party of naked Indians, and exposing for sale jerked beef at a dollar a pound, flour at a dollar and a half do., and for a coarse striped 50 shirt which / I picked up with the intention of purchasing, he coolly asked me the moderate price of sixteen dollars! I looked at my dirty shirt, then at the clean new one I held in my hand, and finally at my little gold bag, not yet replenished by digging, and concluded to postpone my purchase until I had struck my pick and crowbar into the bowels of the earth, and extracted therefrom at least a sufficiency to purchase a shirt. . . . Upon reaching the bar, a curious scene presented itself. About one hundred men, in miner's costume, were at work, performing the various portions of the labour necessary in digging the earth and working a rocking machine. The apparatus then used upon the Yuba River, and which has always been the favourite assistant of the gold-digger, was the common rocker or cradle, constructed in the simplest manner. It consists of nothing more than a wooden box or hollowed log, two sides and one end of which are closed, while the other end is left open. At the end which is closed and called the "mouth" of the machine, a sieve, usually made of a plate of sheet iron, or a piece of raw hide, perforated with holes about half an inch in diameter, is rested upon the sides. A num- 51 ber of "bars" / or "rifflers," which are little pieces of board from one to two inches in height, are nailed to the bottom, and extend laterally across it. Of these, there are three or four in the machine, and one at the "tail," as it is called, i.e. the end where the dirt is washed out. This, with a pair of rockers like those of a child's cradle, and a handle to rock it with, complete the description of the machine, which being placed with the rockers upon two logs, and the "mouth" elevated at a slight angle above the tail, is ready for operation. Modified and improved as this may be, and as in fact it already has been, so long as manual labour is employed for washing gold, the "cradle" is the best agent to use for that purpose. The manner of procuring and washing the golden earth was this. The loose stones and surface earth being removed from any portion of the bar, a hole from four to six feet square was opened, and the dirt extracted therefrom was thrown upon a raw hide placed at the side of the machine. One man shovelled the dirt into the sieve, another dipped up water and threw it on, and a third rocked the "cradle." The earth, thrown upon the sieve, is washed through with the water, while the stones and gravel are retained and thrown off. The continued motion of the machine, and the constant stream of water pouring through it, washes the earth over the various bars of rifflers to the "tail," where it runs out, while the gold, being of greater specific gravity, sinks to the bottom, and is prevented from escaping by the rifflers. When a certain amount of earth has been thus washed (usually about sixty pans full are called "a washing"), the gold, mixed with a heavy black sand, which is always found mingled with gold in California, is taken out and washed in a tin pan, until nearly all the sand is washed away. It is then put into a cup or pan, and when the day's labour is over is dried before the fire, / and the sand remaining 52 carefully blown out. This is a simple explanation of the process of gold-washing in the placers of California. At present, however, instead of dipping and pouring on water by hand, it is usually led on by a hose or forced by a pump, thereby giving a better and more constant stream, and saving the labour of one man. The excavation is continued until the solid rock is struck, or the water rushing in renders it impossible to obtain any more earth, when a new place is opened. We found the gold on the Yuba in exceedingly fine particles, and it has always been considered of a very superior quality. We inquired of the washers as to their success, and they, seeing we were "green horns," and thinking we might possibly interfere with them, gave us either evasive answers, or in some cases told us direct lies. We understood from them that they were making about twenty dollars per day, while I afterwards learned, from the most positive testimony of two men who were at work there at the time, that one hundred dollars a man was not below the average estimate of a day's labour. . . .

The labour on Yuba River appeared very severe, the excavations being sometimes 53 made to a depth of twelve / feet before the soil containing the gold, which was a gravelly clay, was reached. We had not brought our tools with us, intending, if our expedition in the mountains had succeeded, that one of our party should return for our remaining stock of provisions and tools. We had no facilities for constructing a machine, and no money to buy one (two hundred dollars being the price for which a mere hollowed pine log was offered us), and besides, all the bars upon which men were then engaged in labour were "claimed," a claim at that time being considered good when the claimant had cleared off the top soil from any portion of the bar. We returned to our camp, and talked over our prospects, in a quandary what to do. Little did we then dream that, in less than six months, the Yuba River, then only explored some three miles above where we were, would be successfully wrought for forty miles above us, and that thousands would find their fortunes upon it.

We concluded to return to the *Embarcadero*, and take a new start. Accordingly, next morning we packed up and set off, leaving at work upon the river about two hundred men. Having retraced our steps, we arrived at Sutter's Fort in safety on the evening of November 30th, just in time to find the member of our party whom we had left behind, packing all our remaining provisions and tools into a cart, ready to start for the "dry diggings" on the following morning. . . .

60   The "dry diggings" of Weaver's Creek[1]

[1] Buffum was mistaken in the use of the name Weaver's Creek. It was rather, Weber's Creek.

being a fair specimen of dry diggings in all parts of the mining region, a description of them will give the reader a general idea of the various diggings of the same kind in California. They are called "dry" in contradistinction to the "wet" diggings, or those lying directly on the banks of streams, and where all the gold is procured by washing. As I before said, the stream coursed between lofty tree-clad hills, broken on both sides of the river into little ravines or gorges. In these ravines most of the gold was found. The loose stones and top earth being thrown off, the gravelly clay that followed it was usually laid aside for washing, and the digging continued until the bottom rock of the ravine was reached, commonly at a depth of from one to six feet. The surface of this rock was carefully cleared off, and usually found to contain little crevices and holes, the latter in miner's parlance called "pockets," and in which / the gold was 61 found concealed, sparkling like the treasures in the cave of Monte Cristo. A careful examination of the rock being made, and every little crevice and pocket being searched with a sharp pointed-knife, gold in greater or less quantities invariably made its appearance. I shall never forget the delight with which I first struck and worked out a crevice. It was the second day after our installation in our little log hut; the first having been employed in what is called "prospecting," or searching for the most favourable place at which to commence operations. I had slung pick, shovel, and bar upon my shoulder, and trudged merrily away to a ravine about a mile from our house. Pick, shovel, and bar did their duty, and I soon had a large rock in view. Getting down into the excavation I had made, and seating myself upon the rock, I commenced a careful search for a crevice, and at last found one extending longitudinally along the rock. It appeared to be filled with a hard, bluish clay and gravel, which I took out with my knife, and there at the bottom, strewn along the whole length of the rock, was bright, yellow gold, in little pieces about the size and shape of a grain of barley. Eureka! Oh how my heart beat! I sat still and looked at it some minutes before I touched it, greedily drinking in the pleasure of gazing upon gold that was in my very grasp, and feeling a sort of independent bravado in allowing it to remain there. When my eyes were sufficiently feasted, I scooped it out with the point of my knife and an iron spoon, and placing it in my pan, ran home with it very much delighted. I weighed it, and found that my first day's labour in the mines had made me thirty-one dollars richer than I was in the morning.

The gold, which, by some great volcanic eruption, has been scattered upon the soil over an extensive territory, by the continual rains of the winter season has 62 been sunk / into the hills, until it has reached either a hard clay which it cannot penetrate, or a rock on which it rests. The gold in the hills, by the continual rains, has been washing lower and lower, until it has reached the ravines. It has washed down the ravines until it has there reached the rock, and thence, it has washed along the bed of the ravines until it has found some little crevice in which it rests, where the water can carry it no farther. Here it gathers, and thus are formed the "pockets" and "nests" of gold, one of which presents such a glowing golden sight to the eye of the miner, and such a field for his imagination to revel in. How often, when I have struck one of these, have I fondly wished that it might reach to the centre of the earth, and be filled as it was at its mouth with pure, bright, yellow gold.

Our party's first day's labour produced one hundred and fifty dollars, I having been the most successful of all. But we were satisfied, although our experiences had not fulfilled the golden stories we had heard previous to our reaching the *placers*. Finding the average amount of gold dug on Weaver's Creek at that time to be about an ounce per day to a man, we were content so long as we could keep pace with our neighbours. There is a spirit of emulation among miners which prevents them from being ever satisfied with success whilst others around them are more successful. We continued our labours for a week, and found, at the end of that time, our whole party had dug out more than a thousand dollars; and after paying for our house, and settling between ourselves our little private expenses, we were again on a clear track, unencumbered by debt, and in the heart of a region where treasures of unknown wealth were lying hidden in the earth on which we daily trod. . . .

But I have digressed in my narrative, and 69 must now return to Culoma. We purchased from one of the stores two hundred pounds of flour, for which we paid three hundred dollars, one hundred pounds of pork for two hundred dollars, and sugar and coffee at a dollar a pound, amounting to another hundred dollars, making in all six hundred dollars expended for about two months' provisions. We crossed the South Fork, and mounting a lofty hill over-looking the river, encamped for the night on its summit. The next day we descended the hill, and passing through a long and watered valley, struck the "divide" or ridge, which overhangs the river at a point three miles above the "Spanish Bar," at dusk. We again encamped, anxious for a long and invigorating sleep to prepare us for a descent in the morning. . . .

The banks of the Middle Fork, on which 70 we encamped, were rugged and rocky. Awful and mysterious mountains of huge granite boulders towered aloft with solemn grandeur, seeming piled up upon each other as though some destroying angel had stood on the summit of the lofty hills and cast promiscuously these rocks headlong down the steep.

What a wild scene was before us! A river 71 rapidly coursing through a pile of rocks, and on each side of it hills that seemed to reach the clouds. The mountains that over-look this river are about two miles in height, and are probably as difficult of travel as any in the world.

It puzzled us greatly to find a camping-place, although we had no tent to pitch, and only wanted room to spread our blankets on a rock. I searched the river up and down for fifty yards in this laudable endeavor, and finally succeeded in finding a little triangular crevice, formed by two boulders resting against each other, into which I crept, and slept that night, with the pleasant anticipation that the rocks above might possibly give way, in which case my gold-digging dreams would meet with a woful denouement by my being crushed to atoms. No such fate overtook me, however, and the next morning I arose fresh and hearty, to commence my first day's labour on the golden banks of the Middle Fork.

We had packed on the back of one of our mules a sufficient number of boards from Culoma to construct a machine, and the morning after our arrival placed two of our party at work for this purpose, while the rest of us were to dig; and, taking our pans, crowbars, and picks, we commenced operations. Our first attempt was to search around the base of a lofty boulder, which weighed probably some twenty tons, in hopes of finding a crevice in the rock on which it rested, in which a deposit of gold might have been made; nor were we unsuccessful. Around the base of the rock was a filling up of gravel and clay, which we removed with much labour, when our eyes were gladdened with the sight of gold strewn all over its surface, and intermixed with a blackish sand. This we gathered up and washed in our pans, and ere night four of us had dug and washed twenty-six ounces of gold, being about four hundred 72 and / sixteen dollars. The process of pan-washing is the simplest mode of separating the golden particles from the earth with which it is amalgamated. A common-sized tin pan is filled with the soil containing the gold. This is taken to the nearest water and sunk until the water overspreads the surface of the pan. The earth is then thoroughly mixed with water and the stones taken out with the hand. A half rotary motion is given to the pan with both hands; and, as

it is filled, it is lifted from the water, and the loose light dirt which rises to the surface washed out, until the bottom of the pan is nearly reached. The gold being heavier than the earth, sinks by its own weight to the bottom, and is there found at the close of the washing, mixed with a heavy black sand. This is placed in a cup or another pan till the day's labour is finished, when the whole is dried before the fire and the sand carefully blown away. The gold which we found the first day was principally procured by washing, although two pieces, one weighing thirteen and the other seventeen dollars, were taken from a little pocket on the rock. We returned to camp exceedingly elated with our first attempt; and gathering some green branches of trees built a fire, cooked some venison, crawled into our holes and went to sleep.

The next day, our machine being ready, we looked for a place to work it, and soon found a little beach, which extended back some five or six yards before it reached the rocks. The upper soil was a light black sand, on the surface of which we could see the particles of gold shining, and could in fact gather them up with our fingers. In digging below this, we struck a red, stony gravel that appeared perfectly alive with gold, shining and pure. We threw off the top earth and commenced our washings with the gravel, which proved so rich, that, excited by curiosity, we weighed the gold extracted from the first washing of fifty / pansful of earth, and found seventy-five 73 dollars, or nearly five ounces of gold to be the result. We made six washings during the day, and placed in our common purse that night a little over two pounds, — about four hundred dollars worth of gold dust.

Our camp was merry that night. Seated on the surface of a huge rock, we cooked and ate our venison, drank our coffee, and revelled in the idea that we had stolen away from the peopled world, and were living in an obscure corner, unseen by its inhabitants, with no living being within many miles of us, and in a spot where gold was almost as plentiful as the pebble stones that covered it.

After working three days with the machine, the earth we had been washing began to give out, and it became necessary for us to look for a new place: accordingly on the fourth morning, we commenced "prospecting." Three of us started down, and three up the river. I sauntered on ahead of the party on the lower expedition until, about three hundred yards from camp, I found a pile of rocks that I thought afforded a reasonable "prospect." I started down to the river bank, and seated myself at the foot of a vast rock to look around me. I observed above me, and running in a direct course down the rocky bank, a large crevice, which I carefully searched as high up as I could reach, but found only a very small quantity of gold. Being disappointed in this, I determined to trace the crevice to its outlet, confident that there a deposit of gold must have been made. I traced the crevice down nearly to the edge of the water, where it terminated in a large hole or pocket, on the face of a rock which was filled with closely packed gravel. With a knife and spoon I dug this out, and till when near the bottom of the pocket, I found the earth which I brought up in my spoon contained gold, and the last spoonful 74 I took from the pocket was nearly / pure gold in little lumpy pieces. I gathered up all the loose gold, when I reached the stony bottom of the pocket, which appeared to be of pure gold, but upon probing it, I found it to be only a thin covering which by its own weight and the pressure above it, had spread and attached itself to the rock. Crossing the river, I continued my search, and, after digging some time, struck upon a hard, reddish clay, a few feet from the surface. After two hours' work, I succeeded in finding a "pocket" out of which I extracted three lumps of pure gold, and one small piece mixed with oxydized quartz. Elated with my good luck, I returned to camp, and weighing the gold, found the

first lot amounted to twelve and a half ounces, or two hundred dollars, and the four lumps last found, to weigh sixteen and three quarter ounces. The largest pieces weighed no less than seven ounces troy. My success this day was, of course, entirely the result of accident; but another of the party had also found a pocket containing about two hundred and seventy dollars, and a place which promised a rich harvest for our machine.

The gold thus found in pockets and crevices upon the river banks, is washed from the hills above them. In searching for the course of the metal, I have found small quantities by digging on the hill-tops, and am fully persuaded that the gold is washed by the rains, until seeking, as it always does, a permanent bottom, it rests in any pocket or crevice that can prevent it from being washed further, or falls into a stream running at the base of the hills, to find a resting-place in its bed, or be again deposited on its banks. If this theory be true, the beds of the rivers whose banks contain gold must be very rich in the precious metal, and recent labours in damming and turning the courses of certain portions of them, have so proved. The richest deposits of gold upon the rivers are found on what / are called 75 the "bars." These bars are places where there is an extension of the bank into the river, and round which the stream winds, leaving, of course, a greater amount of surface than there is upon the bank generally. They are covered with large rocks deeply imbedded in the soil, which upon most of them is a red gravel, extending to the solid formation of rock beneath.

There are two theories upon which the superior richness of the bars can be accounted for. The first is, that the river in its annual overflows has made the deposits of gold here, and that being more level and broad than the river's banks, they retain a larger quantity of the gold thus deposited. The other, and the only one that accounts for the formation of the bars themselves, is, that where they now are, the river formerly ran; and that they were once the river's bed, but that from some natural cause, the channel has been changed and a new one made; and thus, are left dry, these large portions of the river's bed which annually receive fresh deposits of gold from it in its overflow. . . .

77   The banks of the Middle Fork have proved richer than those of any other tributary of the Sacramento River. The fork is the central one of three streams, which rise in the Sierra Nevada, and course their way to the American Fork, a large branch of the Sacramento, into which they empty. The first exploration of the Middle Fork was made in the latter part of June, 1848, by a party of Mormons who had been at work upon the South Fork, and had left them for the hills in search of richer deposits than were found there. The first diggings were made at the Spanish Bar, which is about twelve miles in a direct line from Sutter's Mill, and has yielded at least a million of dollars. The Middle Fork has now been explored to its very source in the Sierra, but has not been found so rich above as it was below. Since my first trip there, I have travelled for thirty miles on both its banks, and never yet washed a pan of its earth without finding gold in it. When the immense tide of emigration began to pour 78 in from the United States, the Mid-/dle Fork was the grand headquarters of the enthusiastic gold-hunters, and its banks have been torn to their very bottoms, and incalculable treasures taken from them. Within the past summer and fall, at least ten thousand people have been at work upon this river, and at the fair average of one ounce, or even ten dollars per day to a man, more than ten millions of dollars worth of gold dust have been extracted on this river alone. Its bank having ceased to furnish a very large amount of gold, the river itself has in many places been diverted from its wonted course, a channel dug for it through a bar, and its bed wrought, — in many cases yielding an immense quantity of the precious metal, and in others, comparatively nothing. This is now about the

only profitable labour that can be performed here, as the banks of the stream have been completely riddled; but when companies with capital and scientific mining apparatus shall commence operations here, a rich harvest will follow.

About ten miles beyond the Middle Fork, and coursing in the same direction, is another stream, the North Fork, whose banks have proved nearly equal in richness to those of the Middle Fork. Within the past spring and summer some fifteen points on this river have been dammed, the channel turned, and the bed of the river dug. In one case, a party of five dammed the river near what is now called "Smith's Bar." The time employed in damming off a space of some thirty feet was about two weeks, after which from one to two thousand dollars a day were taken out by the party, for the space of ten days, — the whole amount of gold extracted being fifteen thousand dollars. Another party above them made another dam, and in one week took out five thousand dollars. In other cases, where unfavourable points in the river were selected, little or no gold was found; and a fair average of the amount taken / out, in 79 parts of the river which were dammed, I think I can safely state at fifty dollars per day to a man.

Here is an immense field for a combination of capital and labour. As yet no scientific apparatus has been introduced, and severe manual labour alone has produced such golden results. When steam and money are united for the purpose, I doubt not that the whole waters of the North and Middle Forks will be turned from their channels, and immense canals dug through the rugged mountains to bear them off. There are placers upon the Middle Fork, where, within a space of twenty square feet, are lying undisturbed pounds of gold. This may appear startling; but facts and experience have led me to an analogical mode of reasoning, which has proved it to my own mind conclusively. A Frenchman and his boy, who were working on the Middle Fork in November, 1848, found a place in the river where they could scrape from the bottom the sands which had gathered in the crevices and pockets of the rocks. These were washed in a machine, and in four days' time the father and son had taken from the river's bed three thousand dollars, and this with nothing but a hoe and spade. Two men on Kelsey's Bar, on the Middle Fork, adopted the same process, and in two days washed from the earth, thus procured, fifty pounds of gold, amounting to nearly ten thousand dollars. The great difficulty in the way of labouring in this manner is, that there are very few places where the water is sufficiently shallow to permit it, and the river bed is so rocky, and the current so strong, that it is only in places where it becomes a pool of still water that the soil can be taken from its bottom.

The width of the Middle Fork is in most places about thirty feet, and that of the North a little less. The current of both rivers is very strong, being at the rate of five or six miles an hour. The beds of these 80 rivers are com-/posed of huge rocks, tumbled together as they are upon the banks; and it is in the crevices and pockets of these rocks that the gold has secreted itself. Where the stream is narrow and the current strong, the probability is that there is but little gold; but where it expands, and the water becomes more quiet, the gold has settled peacefully, there to remain till the hand of some irreverent Yankee shall remove it from its hiding-place.

During the months of September, October, and November, and sometimes a part of December, the rivers are at their lowest ebb, when the water is from three to eight feet deep in the Middle and North Forks. In the latter part of December, or the early part of January, when the yearly rains commence, the rivers are continually rising and falling, as the rains cease or commence again. About the first of March, the snows which have fallen during the winter begin to melt on the mountains, and flow in little streams down the mountain sides. Every warm day raises the rivers perceptibly,

sometimes to the extent of four feet in a single day, so that in the heat of summer they are fifteen feet higher than in the fall. The only practicable time for damming is in the fall, or early in the spring.

When I dropped the thread of this narrative, I left myself about to start up the hill on my return with the remainder of the party to Weaver's Creek. We found the journey up more toilsome than it had been before, as the soil was reduced to a pasty consistency, into which we sank ankle deep at every step, and the rocks were rendered so slimy and slippery by the rain, that it was with great difficulty we could maintain our foothold when climbing over them. After a tedious three hours' / struggle, how- 81 ever, we succeeded in reaching the top, where we encamped again, and the next day travelled to the summit of the hill which overlooks Culoma. There we again encamped, and the following morning entered the settlement. The country between the mill and the Middle Fork is made up of a succession of hills, covered with oak trees, and interspersed with beautifully watered valleys. In these valleys the soil is a rich black loam, while the hills are barren, and of a red, gravelly soil. As yet no attempts at agriculture have been made in this region, but I am satisfied that the valleys would produce the common field crops in great profusion.

We reached the mill about nine o'clock in the morning, a little too late to get a breakfast at one of the stores, where sometimes the proprietor was sufficiently generous to accommodate a traveller with a meal for the moderate price of five dollars. The only resource was to lay a cloth on the storekeeper's counter, and make a breakfast on crackers, cheese, and sardines. In order not to make a rush upon the trade, we divided ourselves into three parties, each going to a different store. Mac and myself went together, and made a breakfast from the following items; — one box of sardines, one pound of seabiscuit, one pound of butter, a half-pound of cheese, and two bottles of ale. We ate and drank with great gusto, and, when we had concluded our repast called for the bill. It was such a curiosity in the annals of retail grocery business, that I preserved it, and here are the items. It may remind some of Falstaff's famous bill for bread and sack.

| | |
|---|---|
| One box of sardines | $16.00 |
| One pound of hard bread | 2.00 |
| One pound of butter | 6.00 |
| A half-pound of cheese | 3.00 |
| Two bottles of ale | 16.00 |
| Total | $43.00 |

82    A pretty expensive breakfast, thought we! If I ever get out of these hills, and sit and sip my coffee and eat an omelet, at a mere nominal expense, in a marble palace, with a hundred waiters at my back, I shall send back a glance of memory at the breakfast I ate at Culoma sawmill.

We laid over at the mill during the day, and travelled a mile or two up and down the South Fork "prospecting." It appeared remarkable that here, where the gold was first discovered, and while hundreds and thousands were crowding to the mines, not a single man was at work upon the South Fork. But very little digging has ever been done at the mill, although I doubt not there will yet be found vast deposits of gold on the banks of the South Fork. We tried several places, and invariably found gold, but in such small quantities that we thought it would not be profitable to work there; and the day after, as the rain had ceased, we went into Weaver's Creek, with a huge load of blankets on our backs, sweating under a broiling sun.

We found our companions there, anxiously waiting for our return, and eager to listen to the glowing report we made them of our early success, but disappointed almost as much as we were at the unfortunate ending of the affair. We determined to settle down quietly for the rest of the winter in our log house, and take our chance among the dry diggings. It had by this time commenced snowing; and from the first until the fifteenth of January it continued falling heavily, so that by the middle of January it was about four feet deep on a level. All labour was of course suspended, and we lay by in our log house, and amused ourselves by playing cards, reading, washing our clothing, and speculating on the future results of gold-digging. By the middle of January the snow ceased, and the rain again commenced; and in a few days, the snow / having been entirely washed 83 off the surface, we anticipated being soon able to recommence operations.

A scene occurred about this time that exhibits in a striking light, the summary manner in which "justice" is dispensed in a community where there are no legal tribunals. We received a report on the afternoon of January 20th, that five men had been arrested at the dry diggings, and were under trial for a robbery. The circumstances were these: — A Mexican gambler, named Lopez, having in his possession a large amount of money, retired to his room at night, and was surprised about midnight by five men rushing into his apartment, one of whom applied a pistol to his head, while the others barred the door and proceeded to rifle his trunk. An alarm being given, some of the citizens rushed in, and arrested the whole party. Next day they were tried by a jury chosen from among the citizens, and sentenced to receive thirty-nine lashes each, on the following morning. Never having witnessed a punishment inflicted by Lynch-law, I went over to the dry diggings on a clear Sunday morning, and on my arrival found a large crowd collected around an oak tree, to which was lashed a man with a bared back, while another was applying a raw cowhide to his already gored flesh. A guard of a dozen men, with loaded rifles pointed at the prisoners, stood ready to fire in case of an attempt being made to escape. After the whole had been flogged, some fresh charges were preferred against three of the men — two Frenchmen, named Garcia and Bissi, and a Chileno, named Manuel. These were charged with a robbery and attempt to murder, on the Stanislaus River, during the previous fall. The unhappy men were removed to a neighbouring house, and being so weak from their punishment as to be unable to stand, were laid stretched upon the floor. As it was not possible for them to attend, they were tried 84 / in the open air, in their absence, by a crowd of some two hundred men, who had organized themselves into a jury, and appointed a *pro tempore* judge. The charges against them were well substantiated, but amounted to nothing more than an attempt at robbery and murder; no overt act being even alleged. They were known to be bad men, however, and a general sentiment seemed to prevail in the crowd that they ought to be got rid of. At the close of the trial, which lasted some thirty minutes, the Judge put to vote the question whether they had been proved guilty. A universal affirmative was the response; and then the question, "What punishment shall be inflicted?" was asked. A brutal-looking fellow in the crowd, cried out, "Hang them." The proposition was seconded, and met with almost universal approbation. I mounted a stump, and in the name of God, humanity, and law, protested against such a course of proceeding; but the crowd, by this time excited by frequent and deep potations of liquor from a neighbouring groggery, would listen to nothing contrary to their brutal desires, and even threatened to hang me if I did not immediately desist from any further remarks. Somewhat fearful that such might be my fate, and seeing the utter uselessness of further argument with them, I ceased, and prepared to witness the horrible tragedy. Thirty minutes only were allowed the unhappy victims to prepare themselves to enter on the scenes of eternity. Three ropes were procured, and attached to the limb of a tree. The prisoners were marched out, placed upon a wagon, and the ropes put round their necks. No time was given them for explanation. They vainly tried to speak, but none of them understanding English, they were obliged to employ their native tongues, which but few of those assembled understood. Vainly they called for an interpreter, for their cries 85 were drowned by the yells of a / now

infuriated mob. A black handkerchief was bound around the eyes of each; their arms were pinioned, and at a given signal, without priest or prayer-book, the wagon was drawn from under them, and they were launched into eternity. Their graves were dug ready to receive them, and when life was entirely extinct, they were cut down and buried in their blankets. This was the first execution I ever witnessed. — God grant that it may be the last! . . .

Our life at Weaver's Creek became 89 exceedingly monotonous. There were about three hundred people then at work at this point, and whenever a new ravine was opened, everybody swarmed to it, and in a few days it was "dug out." Moreover, dry digging is exceedingly uncertain. Where it is necessary to search among the crevices of rocks to find the gold deposits, one may at times dig and delve through the whole day without striking a single deposit of gold. In this respect they are entirely different and far inferior in point of certainty to the wet diggings upon the banks of rivers. In the latter, where the gold is nearly equally distributed among the earth, a certain amount of labour will produce a certain reward; while in the former, success may not attend the operations of the gold-digger. There is a remarkable peculiarity in the gold of all dry diggings, which is, that the formation of gold in every ravine is different, so much so that one acquainted with the character / of the gold in any certain 90 region can easily tell by a glance at a piece of gold from what ravine it was extracted. This can only be accounted for on the theory, that in a narrow and deep ravine, where the water runs swiftly during the rainy season, the gold courses further over the rocks, and is more thoroughly washed, while in a shallow and wide ravine, where but little water runs, it settles upon the first rock on which it strikes, and retains its distinctive marks.

Tired of the old ravines, I started one morning into the hills, with the determination of finding a new place, where I could labour without being disturbed by the clang of picks and shovels around me. Striking in an easterly direction, I crossed a number of hills and gorges, until I found a little ravine about thirty feet in length embosomed amid low undulating hills. It attracted my attention, I know not why, and clearing off a place about a yard in length, I struck the soil which contained the gold. The earth on the top was a light black gravel, filled with pebbly stones, which apparently contained no gold. Below this was another gravel of a reddish colour, and in which the fine particles of gold were so mingled that they shone and sparkled through the whole of it. A little pool of water, which the rains had formed just below me, afforded a favourable place to test the earth, and scooping up a panful, I took it down and washed it, and it turned out about two dollars. I continued digging and washing until I reached a slate rock, in the crevices of which I found many little nests or clusters of gold, some of them containing eight or ten dollars. These latter were intermixed with a heavy red clay from which the gold was almost inseparable. The gold was of the finest quality, both in size and richness, and I flattered myself that I had here at last found a quiet place, where I could labour alone and undisturbed, and appropriate to myself the entire riches of 91 the / whole ravine. When I reached and had explored the surface of the slate rock, I tried the experiment of breaking the rock itself into small pieces and washing it. This proved as rich as the red gravel, turning out two dollars to a pan-ful. The results of that day's labour were one hundred and ninety dollars worth of gold dust, and I returned to the house with a most profound secrecy resting on my countenance, and took good care not to expose to my companions the good luck I had experienced. But either my eyes betrayed me, or some prying individual had watched me, for the next morning, when busily at work in my ravine, I found myself suddenly surrounded by twenty good stout fellows, all equipped with their implements of labour. I could say or do nothing. Pre-emption rights are

things unknown here, and the result of the matter was, that in three days the little ravine, which I had so fondly hoped would be my own property, was turned completely upside down. About ten thousand dollars worth of gold dust was extracted from it, from which I realized a little over a thousand. Merely the body of the ravine, however, was dug, and after it was entirely deserted, many a day I went to it, solitary and alone, and took from one to three ounces out of its banks. In the early discovery of the mines, and the first working of the "dry diggings," it was supposed that the gold existed only in the beds of the ravines. But since a more philosophical idea of the cause of gold deposits has been entertained, it is found that, in many cases, depending upon the character of the soil, the banks upon each side prove richer in gold than the ravines themselves. The gold having descended from the hillsides, should it before reaching the ravine strike a rocky gravel or hard clay, will remain there instead of descending farther; and thus it happens universally, that when gold is found upon the sides or banks of a ravine, the soil is of one of these / descriptions. 92 Accident has proved this oftener than scientific reasoning. When we first reached Weaver's Creek, we found, in the very heart of the settlement, a ravine which seemed to have been completely "dug out," so much so that, by labouring in it, it would not yield five dollars a day to a man. Report said that nearly one hundred thousand dollars had been taken from it about the time of its discovery, and it was supposed there was little or none remaining. One day, however, about the first of February, an ignorant Irishman sank a hole about six feet deep on the bank, twelve feet from the bed of the ravine. He struck a hard solid white clay, through which gold could scarcely penetrate, and by washing it, took out the first day nearly one hundred dollars worth of gold. This, of course, attracted crowds to the old ravine, and before a week had elapsed, nearly fifteen thousand dollars had been taken from the place which was supposed to be entirely worthless. Among the prizes was one piece weighing twenty-eight ounces, and valued at four hundred and forty-eight dollars; and I have no doubt that to this day the banks of many of the ravines are as rich in the pure metal as were their beds on the first discovery. . . .

96    Among the peculiarities consequent upon the extraction of gold, may be mentioned the fact, that in Weaver's Creek, during the whole winter of 1848, the price paid in silver or gold coin for gold dust was from six to eight dollars per ounce. I, myself, bought some hundred ounces of a Mexican for six dollars and a half. The only object in selling gold for coin was to procure specie for gambling purposes, — and gambling was the life of two-thirds of the residents there at that period. At the same time, communication with San Francisco and Sacramento City having been closed by the rains, provisions were enormously high. A few items will give an idea of gold-mine prices. Flour was selling at one dollar per pound, dried beef at two dollars, sugar at a dollar, coffee seventy-five cents, molasses four dollars per gallon, pork two dollars per pound, miserable New England rum at fifty cents per glass or eight dollars per bottle, and tobacco at two dollars per pound. At these prices, the trader and transporter realized a greater profit from the miner's labour than the miner himself; but provisions must be had, and no price, however great, could deter the labourer from purchasing the necessaries of life.

About the first of March, the long and severe winter broke up, and, tired of our winter quarters, our party made a division of the remaining provisions and cooking utensils, broke up housekeeping, and most of us started for the Middle Fork. Our travel was not diversified by anything new or strange, and, upon striking the river, we proceeded up it about eighteen miles above 97 the "Spanish Bar" to a / bar opposite the "Big Bar," where we pitched our camp, constructed a machine, and commenced operations.

The soil on this bar was exceedingly sandy, and the surface was covered with huge imbedded rocks, which required an immense amount of severe manual labour to remove. Below this was a red gravel, which was united with gold, the washing of which turned out about four ounces per day to each man. I was again dreaming of fortune and success, when my hopes were blasted by an attack of a terrible scourge that wrought destruction through the northern mines during the winter of 1848. I allude to the land scurvy. The exposed and unaccustomed life of two-thirds of the miners, and their entire subsistence upon salt meat, without any mixture of vegetable matter, had produced this disease, which was experienced more or less by at least one-half of the miners within my knowledge. Its symptoms and progress may not be uninteresting. It was first noticed in the "Dry Diggings," where, about the middle of February, many persons were rendered unable to walk by swellings of the lower limbs, and severe pains in them. It was at first supposed to be rheumatism, and was treated as such. But it withstood the most powerful applications used in that complaint, and was finally decided to be scurvy. So long as the circumstances which caused it continued, the disease made rapid progress. Many, who could obtain no vegetables, or vegetable acids, lingered out a miserable existence and died — while others, fortunate enough to reach the settlements where potatoes and acids could be procured, recovered. I noticed its first attack upon myself by swelling and bleeding of the gums, which was followed by a swelling of both legs below the knee, which rendered me unable to walk; and for three weeks I was laid up in my tent, obliged to feed upon the very articles / that had caused the 98 disease, and growing daily weaker, without any reasonable prospect of relief. There were, at that time, about eight hundred persons at work on the river, and hoping to get some medicine, I despatched one of my companions one morning, with instructions to procure me, if possible, a dose of salts, and to pay for it any price that should be asked. He returned at night with the consoling news that he had failed, having found only two persons who had brought the article with them, and they refused to sell it at any price.

I was almost in despair: with only a blanket between myself and the damp, cold earth, and a thin canvass to protect me from the burning sun by day, and the heavy dews by night, I lay day after day enduring the most intense suffering from pain in my limbs, which were now becoming more swollen, and were turning completely black. Above me rose those formidable hills which I must ascend ere I could obtain relief. I believe I should have died, had not accident discovered the best remedy that could have been produced. In the second week of my illness, one of our party, in descending the hill on which he had been deer-hunting, found near its base, and strewn along the foot-track, a quantity of beans which sprouted from the ground and were in leaf. Some one, in descending the hill with a bag of them on his back, had probably dropped them. My companion gathered a quantity and brought them into camp. I had them boiled, and lived entirely on them for several days, at the same time using a decoction of the bark of the Spruce tree. These seemed to operate magically, and in a week after commencing the use of them, I found myself able to walk, — and as soon as my strength was partially restored, I ascended the hill, and with two companions walked into Culoma, and by living princi-
99 pally upon a vegetable diet, which I pro- / cured by paying three dollars per pound for potatoes, in a very short time I recovered. . . .
100  About this time, reports were daily arriving at the settlements of outrages committed by Indians upon whites in the vicinity of the North and Middle Forks. A report which afterwards proved to be strictly correct, came to the mill, that a party of Indians had descended to the camp of five white men on the North Fork, while the latter were engaged in labour, had broken the locks of their rifles which were in their

tents, and then fallen upon and cruelly beaten and murdered them. A large party, headed by John Greenwood, a son of the celebrated mountaineer, was immediately mustered at the mill, and started in pursuit of the Indians, and tracked them to a large Indian *rancheria* on Weaver's Creek. This they attacked, and after killing about twenty of them, took thirty prisoners, and marched to the mill. Here they underwent a trial, and six of them, having been proved to have been connected with the party who killed the white men, were sentenced to be shot. They were taken out in the afternoon after their arrival, followed by a strong guard, and, as was anticipated, a little distance ahead being allowed them, they ran. They had no sooner started than the unerring aim of twenty mountaineers' rifles was upon them, and the next moment five of the six lay weltering in their blood. Soon after this several expeditions were fitted out, who scoured the country in quest of Indians, until now a / redskin is scarcely 101 ever seen in the inhabited portion of the northern mining region. Their *rancherias* are deserted, the graves of their ancestors are left to be desecrated by the white man's foot-print, and they have gone, — some of them to seek a home beyond the rugged crest of the Sierra Nevada, while others have emigrated to the valley of the Tulares, and the whole race is fast becoming extinct. . . .

[SACRAMENTO AND SAN FRANCISCO]

The city of Sacramento had assumed a 110 very different aspect at the time I reached it on my return from the northern mines, from that which it exhibited when I previously left it. Where the old store-ship used to be, on the banks of the Sacramento, tall-masted ships were moored, and the extensive plain on which I pitched my tent was dotted with houses. Around the fort itself, which is nearly two miles from the bank of the river, houses had begun to spring up. Building-lots which, four months previously, had sold at from fifty to two hundred dollars, were now held by their

11 owners at from one to three thou-/sand. I looked on with astonishment at the remarkable progress, and then little thought that the ensuing six months would develop a growth, both in size and prices, which would entirely outstrip what I then witnessed.

Getting on board a launch, I spent a weary five days in sailing down the Sacramento, and arrived at San Francisco in the early part of May. What a change had occurred in six months! San Francisco, when I saw it before, was almost entirely deserted, everybody having gone to the mines. Now it was being daily recruited by the arrival of travellers across the plains, by vessels around Cape Horn, by Sandwich Islanders, Chinese, French, English, and Mexicans. The age of speculation had commenced. The building-lots which, when I landed in San Francisco, were granted by the alcaldes for the sum of fifteen dollars, and in the autumn before were worth but five hundred, had now risen in value to from three to five thousand. Hundreds and thousands of men with capital were arriving, who readily seized upon the opportunities for speculating. Houses were going up on the vacant lots, and the town beginning to assume an air of business. Goods of all kinds had fallen in price, owing to the arrival of fleets of loaded ships from all parts of the world, and in some cases from wilful neglect on the part of consignees. Large hotels had been erected, and life began to be rendered comfortable. Gambling in all its forms was carried on to an enormous extent, and money, as before, was almost as plentiful as the sea-sands. . . .

[RECAPITULATION AND ADVICE]

131  It is proper, before closing this work, and it will probably be expected, that I should make a sort of recapitulation, and give some advice in regard to prospects and plans of proceeding in the gold mines of California. To advise is always a difficult task, and in this instance it is peculiarly so; but I will endeavour to give a fair statement of facts,

and the best advice I can. The number of persons at present labouring in the various portions of the mining region is about one hundred thousand. Of these, at least one-third are Mexicans, Chilenos, Pacific Islanders, and Chinese, and the remainder Americans, English, French, and Germans; and I should divide their locations as follows: on the North, Middle, and South Forks, say twenty thousand; on the Stanislaus, Mokelumne, Tuolumne, Merced, Mariposa, and other tributaries of the San Joaquin, forty thousand; on Yuba and Feather Rivers, twenty thousand; and, scattered over the various dry diggings, twenty thousand more. During the past summer and autumn, I should estimate the average quantity of gold dug daily at eight dollars to a man; for although it is by no means uncommon for an individual to "strike a lucky / place," and some days take out 132 from a hundred to a thousand dollars, others spend whole days in search and labour, without finding more than two or three dollars a day. From my own experience in the mines I am, however, satisfied, that, during six months in the year, a stout man, with health, energy, and perseverance, can average sixteen dollars a day in almost any portion of the placers; and that, for twenty years, from three to ten dollars a day can be made by individual labour. Still, I would advise all who are in good positions at home to remain there. The labour and hardships consequent upon the life of a gold-digger are of the most severe and arduous nature. Prying and breaking up huge rocks, shovelling dirt, washing it with wet feet all day, and sleeping on the damp ground at night, with nothing above but a thin covering of canvass, or a leaky log roof, are not by any means agreeable to one who has been accustomed to the civilized life of cities. Richelieu says, that "the pen is mightier than the sword." Many a fine, spruce young clerk coming to California with golden dreams of wealth before him has proved, to his sorrow, that the crowbar is heavier than the pen. I hesitate not to say, that the labour of gold-digging is unequalled by any other in the world with severity. It combines within itself the various arts of canal-digging, ditching, laying stone walls, ploughing, and hoeing potatoes, — and adding to this a life in the wilds of the mountains, living upon poor provisions, continually exposed either to the burning rays of the sun, or the heavy dews of night, and the occupation becomes anything but a pleasant one. But to a man endowed with a constitution to endure hardship, with hands that have been accustomed to labour, and with a heart which suffers not itself to be sorrowed with disappointment, there was never a better opportunity in the world to make a fortune, than there is at present in Cali-/

133 fornia. To mechanics, especially, there are great inducements; for if they do not choose to labour in the mines, with the wages which I have previously stated as being paid to them in San Francisco and the other towns of Northern California, they may, in one year, save more money than in five in any other portion of the United States.

To those who do come, I would give a few words of advice, which may be of service. Bring with you very little clothing and provisions, as they will only prove a burden. These can be purchased in San Francisco almost at New York prices. Never come without money, as gold is not to be found in the streets of San Francisco. You may be delayed several days before going to the mines, and board at from sixteen to fifty dollars a week will soon make a large hole in a small sum of money. Arrived at San Francisco, beware of the vices prevalent there. Drinking and gaming are the principal, and in fact the only amusements of the town, and many a poor fellow, landing there with high hopes, has been fleeced and turned adrift upon society with a broken heart. Purchase no provisions in San Francisco. The expenses of transportation are so great, (freight up the river being from two to four cents per pound, and by teams to the various mining points from fifteen to fifty,) that your provisions will cost more in money and time than they would if purchased in the mines. Flour is

now selling in the gold regions at about fifty cents per pound; this seems like a great price, but you will find it cheaper than to carry it with you, and will soon find that it is much easier to pay fifty cents for a pound of flour when you are making sixteen dollars a day, than it is to pay three cents when you are making but one. For the same reason that you should carry no provisions, carry but little clothing. A mere change is sufficient, and clothes / can 13 always be purchased at reasonable rates in all parts of the mines.

The best season for proceeding to the mines is about the end of the month in August. The waters which have been swollen by the melting of the snows in the summer, have then subsided, and the heat of the summer months has then given way to the cooling breezes of autumn. From that time till the middle of December, the weather is most delightful, and the opportunities for profitable labour are far better than at any other time. About the middle of December, the rainy season commences; the rivers immediately commence rising, and labour is prevented both by this and the inclemency of the weather. The life of the miner during the winter months is exceedingly unpleasant, and I would advise no one to proceed to the gold region after the month of November. The rainy season usually closes about the middle of February, but the roads are exceedingly muddy until the first of March, and from that time till July, labour can be performed to advantage in the various dry-diggings, and upon some of the rivers. By this time the hot and sickly season commences, and the waters upon the rivers are at their greatest height. The thermometer ranges from 90° to 120° in the shade at noonday, and the heavy dews of night fall upon the labourer, who has been all day at work beneath a broiling sun. This of course produces disease, and in that wild region, where the comforts and attendance that should ever surround a sick man's bed, are unknown, disease is usually followed by death. The most prevalent diseases during this time are fever and ague, and bilious fevers of the most virulent nature. But I am satisfied that, setting aside the prevalence of diseases common to all new countries, a large portion of the sickness of the summer months is caused by the exposure consequent upon the present 35 mode of / life of the miner. When the same comforts are introduced, when good houses are built, and wholesome provisions can be procured, the mining regions of California will compare favourably with Illinois, Indiana, or any of the new states in point of healthiness.

It has been a frequent inquiry in the United States, "In what kind of soil is gold found?" The answer is, that it is found in no one particular kind of soil, but in every variety from the common loose black earth to the hardest clay. I have found, in the dry diggings of Weaver's Creek, pieces of gold, some of them weighing nearly a quarter of an ounce, lying in the upper black soil within two inches of the surface. It is sometimes found embedded in a hard white clay, at other times in a red, and at others in a blue clay. As a general thing, I have found that where the gold is coarse, it usually descends until it reaches one of the above-mentioned clays, while the finer particles rest upon the gravelly stratum nearer the surface, and thus fine gold is most frequently found mingled with red gravel.

In regard to bringing machines to California for the purpose of washing gold, I must caution the miners to be careful and judicious in their selection. Some of the more recent inventions are valuable, especially the "Quicksilver Gold Separator," which is constructed to operate with quicksilver in such manner as to save the fine particles of gold which in the ordinary cradles or rockers are lost. The only object of a machine of any kind is to break up and keep in motion a larger quantity of earth than a pan would hold, and at the same time prevent the gold from being lost. I saw, last spring, hundreds of huge, bulky machines, which had been brought round Cape Horn, and which would require, each one of them, a large ox-team to convey them to the mining region, lying piled upon the / beach of San Francisco, destined never to 136 fulfil the object for which they were intended, and ere this probably used for firewood, or in constructing habitations for their owners to dwell in. There are, however, some small hand machines manufactured in New York, which are really of great use to the gold-digger.

A great mistake has been made by people who have emigrated to California, or who have desired to emigrate, in considering it merely as a temporary home, a sort of huge goose, out of which a few feathers were to be plucked, and then forsaken. It is for this reason that the life of the miner is at present tenfold more arduous than it otherwise would be, and never was there a more egregious error in regard to the character of the country. Gold is not the only product of the soil in California. Her fertile valleys and rich prairies are capable, when cultivated, of producing an untold store of agricultural wealth. Her lofty pines and spreading oak trees afford an abundant supply of material for the erection of comfortable dwellings. Her thousand streams, pouring down every hillside and winding through her plains, furnish an inexhaustible supply of water-power, and her forests, mountains, and lakes abound with game of every description. In the immense valleys of the Sacramento and San Joaquin, are millions of acres of land entirely unreclaimed, upon which any man may settle and make a fortune in a few years by the cultivation of the soil. Some hundred and fifty miles above Sacramento City, on the Sacramento River, are large tracts of valuable, well-watered land, much of which is unreclaimed, other portions being for sale at mere nominal prices. On one of these tracts, at "Lawson's Rancho," wheat was last year raised at an average of forty-five bushels to the acre, and is now selling delivered on the rancho at six dollars a bushel! Cattle bring from forty to a hundred dollars a / head, potatoes twenty-five cents 137 per pound, milk two dollars per gallon, butter from one to two dollars per pound, and every product of a farm is at corresponding prices. With the continued growth of California, the demand for all these articles, most of which are now brought from the Sandwich Islands, Chili, and Oregon, must necessarily increase, and I am satisfied that the cultivation of the soil will yet be a more profitable labour than extracting the gold from it.

California is a habitable country, and should be looked upon no longer as a mere temporary residence. A state government has been organized, the sheltering hand of law stretched over its borders, and life there can be made as comfortable as life in any other portion of the world. Let then the gold-digger come, and from the never-failing hills gather a rich supply of treasure. Let the farmer come, and from the abundant soil produce the necessaries of life, and enrich himself from them. Let the mechanic and labourer come, and build up the towns of this new country, and let the ladies of our land come, and with their smiles bring peace and happiness into the wilderness.

> "The world was sad! — the garden
>   was a wild! —
> And man, the hermit sighed, till
>   woman smiled!"

In this connexion, it may be well to state, that although California presents one of the finest fields in the world for mechanical and industrial pursuits, it is as yet an unpromising region for what are called "the learned professions;" and I would advise no more "of the ilk" to wend this way. The country is already overrun with young lawyers and doctors, who are too feeble physically to succeed as gold-diggers, and seek in vain for fees. Nearly all the law business done here is in the hands of a few prominent individuals, who are handsomely paid for what they do, but could readily transact ten times the amount of busi-/ness that is ever placed in their hands. Public opinion is more stringent here than in the older states, and contracts are faithfully fulfilled, whether written or verbal, without evasion, under the technicalities or subtleties of the law. The medical profession is somewhat more in demand, but it is so crowded that few succeed, and most persons who come here to practise medicine, are compelled to resort to some other means of obtaining a livelihood. Hydropathy is the popular treatment, and a good bath is thought to be far more conducive to health than bleeding or calomel.

# Bayard Taylor

*From* Eldorado or Adventures in the Path of Empire, Comprising a Voyage to California via Panama; Life in San Francisco and Monterey; Pictures of the Gold Region; and Experiences of Mexican Travel. *New York* (G. P. Putnam's Sons), 1894.

Bayard Taylor (1825–1878), poet, journalist, novelist, and short-story writer, was the son of a Pennsylvania Quaker family. *Eldorado,* first published in 1850, came early in his career and grew out of letters and notes written in California, where he was sent by the New York *Tribune* to observe and record scenes and incidents of the gold rush. Despite his youth, Taylor's comments are rather sophisticated and his style is polished. Following the California assignment, Taylor traveled widely in Africa, India, and in the Near and Far East. His report on these adventures appeared shortly thereafter in a series of travel books published in the 1850's. He went on to become a highly productive writer but fell short of any real distinction. A translation of Faust (2 vols., 1870–1871) helped him to secure a nonresident professorship of German at Cornell in 1870. Taylor held this post for seven years and then was made minister to Germany in 1878. He died the same year.

FIRST IMPRESSIONS OF SAN FRANCISCO
[AUGUST, 1849]

54 THE OHIO's boat put us ashore at the northern point of the anchorage, at the foot of a steep bank, from which a high pier had been built into the bay. A large vessel lay at the end, discharging her cargo. We scrambled up through piles of luggage, and among the crowd collected to witness our arrival, picked out two Mexicans to carry our trunks to a hotel. The barren side of the hill before us was covered with tents and canvas houses, and nearly in front a large two-story building displayed the sign: "Fremont Family Hotel."

55 As yet, we were only in the suburbs of the town. Crossing the shoulder of the hill, the view extended around the curve of the bay, and hundreds of tents and houses appeared, scattered all over the heights, and along the shore for more than a mile. A furious wind was blowing down through a gap in the hills, filling the streets with clouds of dust. On every side stood buildings of all kinds, begun or half-finished, and the greater part of them mere canvas sheds, open in front, and covered with all kinds of signs, in all languages. Great quantities of goods were piled up in the open air, for want of a place to store them. The streets were full of people, hurrying to and fro, and of as diverse and bizarre a character as the houses: Yankees of every possible variety, native Californians in *sarapes* and sombreros, Chilians, Sonorians, Kanakas from Hawaii, Chinese with long tails, Malays armed with their everlasting creeses, and others in whose embrowned and bearded visages it was impossible to recognize any especial nationality. We came at last into the plaza, now dignified by the name of Portsmouth Square. It lies on the slant side of the hill, and from a high pole in front of a long one-story adobe building used as the Custom House, the American flag was flying. On the lower side stood the Parker House — an ordinary frame house of about sixty feet front — and towards its entrance we directed our course.

Our luggage was deposited on one of the rear porticos, and we discharged the porters, after paying them two dollars each — a sum so immense in comparison to the service rendered that there was no longer any doubt of our having actually landed in California. There were no lodgings to be

33

had at the Parker House — not even a place to unroll our blankets; but one of the proprietors accompanied us across the plaza to 56 the City Hotel, where we ob-/tained a room with two beds at $25 per week, meals being in addition $20 per week. . . .

Many of the passengers began speculation at the moment of landing. The most ingenious and successful operation was made by a gentleman of New York, who took out fifteen hundred copies of The Tribune and other papers, which he disposed of in two hours, at one dollar a-piece! Hearing of this I bethought me of about a dozen papers which I had used to fill up crevices in packing my valise. There was a newspaper merchant at the corner of the City Hotel, and to him I proposed the sale of them, asking him to name a price. "I shall want to make a good profit on the retail price," said he, "and can't give more than ten dollars for the lot." I was satisfied with the wholesale price, which was a gain of just four thousand per cent!

57 I was forced to believe many things, which in my communications to The Tribune I was almost afraid to write, with any hope of their obtaining credence. It may be interesting to give here a few instances of the enormous and unnatural value put upon property at the time of my arrival. The Parker House rented for $110,000 yearly, at least $60,000 of which was paid by the gamblers, who held nearly all the 58 second story. Adjoining it on / the right was a canvas-tent fifteen by twenty-five feet, called "Eldorado," and occupied likewise by gamblers, which brought $40,000. On the opposite corner of the plaza, a building called the "Miner's Bank," used by Wright and Co., brokers, about half the size of a fire-engine house in New York, was held at a rent of $75,000. A mercantile house paid $40,000 rent for a one-story building of twenty feet front; the United States Hotel, $36,000; the Post Office, $7,000, and so on to the end of the chapter. A friend of mine, who wished to find a place for a law-office, was shown a cellar in the earth, about twelve feet square and

six deep, which he could have at $250 a month. One of the common soldiers at the battle of San Pasquale was reputed to be among the millionaires of the place, with an income of $50,000 *monthly*. A citizen of San Francisco died insolvent to the amount of $41,000 the previous Autumn. His administrators were delayed in settling his affairs, and his real estate advanced so rapidly in value meantime, that after his debts were paid his heirs had a yearly income of $40,000. These facts were indubitably attested; every one believed them, yet hearing them talked of daily, as matters of course, one at first could not help feeling as if he had been eating of "the insane root."

The prices paid for labor were in proportion to everything else. The carman of Mellus, Howard and Co. had a salary of $6,000 a year, and many others made from $15 to $20 daily. Servants were paid from $100 to $200 a month, but the wages of the rougher kinds of labor had fallen to about $8. Yet, notwithstanding the number of gold-seekers who were returning enfeebled and disheartened from the mines, it was difficult to obtain as many workmen as the forced growth of the city demanded. A gentleman who arrived in April told me he then found but thirty or / forty houses, 59 the population was then so scant that not more than twenty-five persons would be seen in the streets at any one time. Now, [August, 1849] there were probably five hundred houses, tents and sheds, with a population, fixed and floating, of six thousand. People who had been absent six weeks came back and could scarcely recognize the place. Streets were regularly laid out, and already there were three piers, at which small vessels could discharge. It was calculated that the town increased daily by from fifteen to thirty houses; its skirts were rapidly approaching the summits of the three hills on which it is located.

A curious result of the extraordinary abundance of gold and the facility with which fortunes were acquired, struck me at the first glance. All business was transacted on so extensive a scale that the ordinary habits of solicitation and compliance on the one hand and stubborn cheapening on the other, seemed to be entirely forgotten. You enter a shop to buy something; the owner eyes you with perfect indifference, waiting for you to state your want; if you object to the price, you are at liberty to leave, for you need not expect to get it cheaper; he evidently cares little whether you buy it or not. One who has been some time in the country will lay down the money, without wasting words. The only exception I found to this rule was that of a sharp-faced Down-Easter just opening his stock, who was much distressed when his clerk charged me seventy-five cents for a coil of rope, instead of one dollar. This disregard for all the petty arts of money-making was really a refreshing feature of society. Another equally agreeable trait was the punctuality with which debts were paid, and the general confidence which men were obliged to place, perforce, in each other's honesty. Perhaps this latter fact was owing, in part, to the impossibility of protecting wealth, 60 and / consequent dependence on an honorable regard for the rights of others.

. . . Business was over about the usual hour, and then the harvest-time of the gamblers commenced. Every "hell" in the place, and I did not pretend to number them, was crowded, and immense sums were staked at the monte and faro tables. A boy of fifteen, in one place, won about $500, which he coolly pocketed and carried off. One of the gang we brought in the Panama won $1,500 in the course of the evening, and another lost $2,400. A fortunate miner made himself conspicuous by betting large piles of ounces on a single throw. His last stake of 100 oz. was lost, and I saw him the following morning dashing through the streets, trying to break his own neck or that of the magnificent *garañon* he bestrode.

Walking through the town the next day, I was quite amazed to find a dozen persons busily employed in the street before the United States Hotel digging up the earth with knives and crumbling it in their hands.

They were actual gold-hunters, who obtained in this way about $5 a day. After blowing the fine dirt carefully in their hands, a few specks of gold were left, which they placed in a piece of white paper. A number of children were engaged in the same business, picking out the fine grains by / applying to them the head of a pin, 61 moistened in their mouths. I was told of a small boy having taken home $14 as the result of one day's labor. On climbing the hill to the Post Office I observed in places, where the wind had swept away the sand, several glittering dots of the real metal, but, like the Irishman who kicked the dollar out of his way, concluded to wait till I should reach the heap. The presence of gold in the streets was probably occasioned by the leakings from the miners' bags and the sweepings of stores; though it may also be, to a slight extent, native in the earth, particles having been found in the clay thrown up from a deep well.

The arrival of a steamer with a mail ran the usual excitement and activity of the town up to its highest possible notch. The little Post Office, half-way up the hill, was almost hidden from sight by the crowds that clustered around it. Mr. Moore, the new Postmaster, who was my fellow-traveler from New York, barred every door and window from the moment of his entrance, and with his sons and a few clerks, worked steadily for two days and two nights, till the distribution of twenty thousand letters was completed. . . .

. . . We made hasty tours through all 62 the shops on Clay, Kearney, Washington and Montgomery streets, on the hunt of the proper equipments. Articles of clothing were cheaper than they had been or were afterwards; tolerable blankets could be had for $6 a pair; coarse flannel shirts, $3; Chilian spurs, with rowels two inches long, $5, and Mexican sarapes, of coarse texture but gay color, $10. We could find no saddle-bags in the town, and were necessitated to pack one of the mules. Among our camping materials were a large hatchet and plenty of rope for making lariats; in addition to which each of us carried a wicker flask slung over one shoulder. We laid aside our civilized attire, stuck long sheath-knives into our belts, put pistols into our pockets and holsters, and buckled on the immense spurs which jingled as they struck the ground at every step. Our "animals" were already in waiting; an *alazan,* the Californian term for a sorrel horse, a beautiful brown mule, two of a cream color and a dwarfish little fellow whose long forelock and shaggy mane gave him altogether an elfish character of cunning and mischief. . . .

CAMP-LIFE, AND A RIDE TO THE DIGGINGS

79   After discussing our further plans, it was decided to visit the Mokelumne Diggings, which were the most accessible from Stockton. Accordingly, . . . our mules were driven in from the plain and saddled for the journey. The sun was shining hotly as we rode over the plain to Stockton, and the tent-streets of the miraculous town glowed like the avenues of a brick-kiln. The thermometer stood at 98°, and the parched, sandy soil burnt through our very boot-soles. We therefore determined to wait till evening before starting for another stage to the Mokelumne. . . .

Mr. Raney, who had just established a line of conveyance to the Mokelumne, kindly offered to accompany us as far as his ranche on the Calaveras River, twenty-four miles distant. . . .

81   Leaving the ranche soon after sunrise, we entered the hills. . . .

After traveling about fourteen miles, we were joined by three miners, and our mules, taking a sudden liking for their horses, jogged on at a more brisk rate. The instincts of the mulish heart form an interesting study to the traveler in the mountains. I would, were the comparison not too ungallant, liken it to a woman's for it is quite as uncertain in its sympathies, bestowing its affections where least expected, and when bestowed, quite as constant, so long as the object is not taken away. Sometimes a horse, sometimes an ass, captivates the fancy of a whole drove of mules; but often an animal nowise akin. Lieut. Beale told me that his whole train of mules once took a stampede on the plains of the Cimarone, and ran half a mile, when they halted in apparent satisfaction. The cause of their freak was found to be a buffalo calf which had strayed from the herd. They were frisking around it / in the greatest delight, 82 rubbing their noses against it, throwing up their heels and making themselves ridiculous by abortive attempts to neigh and bray, while the poor calf, unconscious of its attractive qualities, stood trembling in their midst. It is customary to have a horse in the *atajos,* or mule-trains, of the traders in Northern Mexico, as a sort of magnet to keep together the separate atoms of the train, for, whatever the temptation, they will never stray far from him.

We turned from the main road, which led to the Upper Bar and took a faint trail leading over the hills to the Lower Bar. . . . Crossing several steep spurs, we reached the top of the divide overlooking the Mokelumne Valley, and here one of the most charming mountain landscapes in the world opened to our view. Under our very feet, as it seemed, flowed the river, and a little corner of level bottom, wedged between the bases of the hills, was dotted with the tents of the gold-hunters, whom we could see burrowing along the water. . . .

Coming down the almost perpendicular side of the hill, my saddle began to slip over the mule's straight shoulders, and dismounting, I waded the rest of the way knee-deep in dust. Near the bottom we came upon the Sonorian Town, as it was called, from the number of Mexican miners encamped there. The place / which was a regularly 83 laid-out town of sapling houses, without walls and roofed with loose oak boughs, had sprung up in the wilderness in three weeks: there were probably three hundred persons living in or near it. Under the open canopies of oak we heard, as we passed along, the jingle of coin at the monte tables, and saw crowds gathered to watch the progress of the game. . . .

### THE DIGGINGS ON MOKELUMNE RIVER

84  Our first move was for the river bottom, where a number of Americans, Sonorians, Kanakas and French were at work in the hot sun. The bar, as it was called, was nothing more nor less than a level space at the junction of the river with a dry arroyo or "gulch", which winds for about eight miles among the hills. It was hard and rocky, with no loose sand except such as had lodged between the large masses of stone, which must of course be thrown aside to get at the gold. The whole space, containing about four acres, appeared to have been turned over with great labor, and all the holes slanting down between the broken strata of slate, to have been explored to the bottom. No spot could appear more unpromising to the inexperienced gold-hunter. Yet the Sonorians, washing out the loose dust and dirt which they scraped up among the rocks, obtained from $10 to two ounces daily. The first party we saw had just succeeded in cutting a new channel for the shrunken waters of the Mokelumne, and were commencing operations on about twenty yards of the river-bed, which they had laid bare. They were ten in number, and their only implements were shovels, a rude cradle for the top layer of earth, and flat wooden bowls for washing 85 out the sands. Bap-/tiste took one of the bowls which was full of sand, and in five minutes showed up a dozen grains of bright gold. The company had made in the forenoon about three pounds; we watched them at their work till the evening, when three pounds more were produced, making an average of seven ounces for each man. The gold was of the purest quality and most beautiful color. When I first saw the men, carrying heavy stones in the sun, standing nearly waist-deep in water, and grubbing with their hands in the gravel and clay,

there seemed to me little virtue in resisting the temptation to gold digging; but when the shining particles were poured out lavishly from a tin basin, I confess there was a sudden itching in my fingers to seize the heaviest crowbar and the biggest shovel.

A company of thirty, somewhat further down the river, had made a much larger dam, after a month's labor, and a hundred yards of the bed were clear. They commenced washing in the afternoon and obtained a very encouraging result. The next morning, however, they quarreled, as most companies do, and finally applied to Mr. James and Dr. Gillette, two of the principal operators, to settle the difficulty by having the whole bed washed out at their own expense and taking half the gold. As all the heavy work was done, the contractors expected to make a considerable sum by the operation. Many of the Americans employed Sonorians and Indians to work for them, giving them half the gold and finding them in provisions. Notwithstanding the enormous prices of every article of food, these people could be kept for about a dollar daily — consequently those who hired them profited handsomely.

After we had taken the sharp edge off our curiosity, we returned to our quarters. Dr. Gillette, Mr. James, Captain Tracy and several other of the miners entertained us with a hospitality / as gratifying as it was 86 unexpected. In the evening we sat down to a supper prepared by Baptiste and his partner, Mr. Fisher, which completed my astonishment at the resources of that wonderful land. There, in the rough depth of the hills, where three weeks before there was scarcely a tent, and where we expected to live on jerked beef and bread, we saw on the table green corn, green peas and beans, fresh oysters, roast turkey, fine Goshen butter and excellent coffee. I will not pretend to say what they cost, but I began to think that the fable of Aladdin was nothing very remarkable, after all. The genie will come, and had come to many whom I saw in California; but the rubbing of the lamp — aye, there's the rub. There is nothing in the world so hard on the hands.

I slept soundly that night on the dining-table, and went down early to the river, where I found the party of ten bailing out the water which had leaked into the river-bed during the night. They were standing in the sun, and had two hours' hard work before they could begin to wash. Again the prospect looked uninviting, but when I went there again towards noon, one of them was scraping up the sand from the bed with his knife, and throwing it into a basin, the bottom of which glittered with gold. Every knifeful brought out a quantity of grains and scales, some of which were as large as the finger-nail. At last a two-ounce lump fell plump into the pan, and the diggers, now in the best possible humor, went on with their work with great alacrity. Their forenoon's digging amounted to nearly six pounds. It is only by such operations as these, through associated labor, that great profits are to be made in those districts which have been visited by the first eager horde of gold hunters. The deposits most easily reached are soon exhausted by the 87 crowd, and the / labor required to carry on further work successfully deters single individuals from attempting it. Those who, retaining their health, return home disappointed, say they have been humbugged about the gold, when in fact, they have humbugged themselves about the *work.* If any one expects to dig treasures out of the earth, in California, without severe labor, he is woefully mistaken. Of all classes of men, those who pave streets and quarry limestone are best adapted for gold diggers.

Wherever there is gold, there are gamblers. Our little village boasted of at least a dozen monte tables, all of which were frequented at night by the Americans and Mexicans. The Sonorians left a large portion of their gold at the gaming tables, though it was calculated they had taken $5,000,000 out of the country during the summer. The excitement against them prevailed also on the Mokelumne, and they were once driven away; they afterwards quietly returned, and in most cases worked in companies, for the benefit and under the protection of some American. They labor steadily and faithfully, and are considered honest, if well watched. The first colony of gold-hunters attempted to drive out all foreigners, without distinction, as well as native Californians. . . .

Dr. Gillette, to whom we were indebted for many kind attentions, related to me the manner of his finding the rich gulch which attracted so many to the Mokelumne Diggings. The word *gulch,* which is in general use throughout the diggings, may not be familiar to many ears, though its sound somehow expresses its meaning, without further definition. It denotes a mountain ravine differing from ravines elsewhere as the mountains of California / differ from 88 all others — more steep, abrupt and inaccessible. The sound of *gulch* is like that of a sudden plunge into a deep hole which is just the character of the thing itself. It bears the same relation to a ravine that a "cañon" does to a pass or gorge. About two months previous to our arrival, Dr. Gillette came down from the Upper Bar with a companion, to "prospect" for gold among the ravines in the neighborhood. There were no persons there at the time, except some Indians belonging to the tribe of José Jesus. One day at noon, while resting in the shade of a tree, Dr. G. took a pick and began carelessly turning up the ground. Almost on the surface, he struck and threw out a lump of gold of about two pounds weight. Inspired by this unexpected result, they both went to work, laboring all that day and the next, and even using part of the night to quarry out the heavy pieces of rock. At the end of the second day they went to the village on the Upper Bar and weighed their profits, which amounted to fourteen pounds! They started again the third morning under pretence of hunting, but were suspected and followed by the other diggers, who came upon them just as they commenced work. The news rapidly spread, and there was soon a large number of men on the spot, some of whom obtained several pounds per day, at the start. The gulch had been well dug up for the large lumps, but there was still great wealth in the earth and sand, and several operators only waited for the wet season to work it in a systematic manner.

The next day Col. Lyons, Dr. Gillette and myself set out on a visit to the scene of these rich discoveries. Climbing up the rocky bottom of the gulch, as by a staircase, for four miles, we found nearly every part of it dug up and turned over by the picks of the miners. Deep holes, sunk between the solid strata / or into the precipitous sides of the mountains, showed where veins of the metal had been struck and followed as long as they yielded lumps large enough to pay for the labor. The loose earth, which they had excavated, was full of fine gold, and only needed washing out. A number of Sonorians were engaged in dry washing this refuse sand — a work which requires no little skill, and would soon kill any other men than these lank and skinny Arabs of the West. Their mode of work is as follows: — Gathering the loose dry sand in bowls, they raise it to their heads and slowly pour it upon a blanket spread at their feet. Repeating this several times, and throwing out the worthless pieces of rock, they reduce the dust to about half its bulk; then, balancing the bowl on one hand, by a quick, dexterous motion of the other they cause it to revolve, at the same time throwing its contents into the air and catching them as they fall. In this manner everything is finally winnowed away except the heavier grains of sand mixed with gold, which is carefully separated by the breath. It is a laborious occupation, and one which, fortunately, the American diggers have not attempted. This breathing the fine dust from day to day, under a more torrid sun, would soon impair the strongest lungs.

We found many persons at work in the higher part of the gulch, searching for veins and pockets of gold, in the holes which had already produced their first harvest. Some of these gleaners, following the lodes abandoned by others as exhausted, into the sides of the mountain, were well repaid for their perseverance. Others, again, had been working for days without finding anything. Those who understood the business obtained from one to four ounces daily. Their only tools were the crowbar, pick and knife, and many of them, following the veins under strata of rock which lay deep below the surface, were obliged to work while lying flat / on their backs, in cramped and narrow holes, sometimes kept moist by springs. They were shielded, however, from the burning heats and preserved their health better than those who worked on the bars of the river.

There are thousands of similar gulches among the mountains, nearly all of which undoubtedly contain gold. Those who are familiar with geology, or by carefully noting the character of the soil and strata where gold is already found, have learned its indications, rarely fail in the selection of new spots for digging. It is the crowd of those who, deceived in their extravagant hopes, disheartened by the severe labor necessary to be undergone, and bereft of that active and observing spirit which could not fail to win success at last, that cry out with such bitterness against the golden stories which first attracted them to the country. I met with hundreds of such persons, many of whom have returned home disgusted forever with California. They compared the diggings to a lottery, in which people grew rich only by accident or luck. There is no such thing as accident in Nature, and in proportion as men understand her, the more sure a clue they have to her buried treasures. There is more gold in California than ever was said or imagined: ages will not exhaust the supply. From what I first saw on the Mokelumne, I was convinced that the fabled Cibao of Columbus, splendid as it seemed to his eager imagination, is more than realized there. . . .

From all I saw and heard, while at the Mokelumne Diggings, I judged there was as much order and security as could be attained without a civil organization. The inhabitants had elected one of their own number Alcalde, before whom all culprits were tried by a jury selected for the purpose. Several thefts had occurred, and the offending parties been severely punished after a fair trial. Some had been whipped and cropped, or maimed in some other way, and one or two of them hung. Two or three who had stolen largely had been shot down by the injured party, the general feeling among the miners justifying such a course when no other seemed available. We met near Livermore's Ranch, on the way to Stockton, a man whose head had been shaved and his ears cut off, after receiving one hundred lashes, for stealing ninety-eight pounds of gold. It may conflict with popular ideas of morality, but, nevertheless, this extreme course appeared to have produced good results. In fact, in a country without not only bolts and bars, but any effective system of law and government, this Spartan severity of discipline seemed the only security against the most frightful disorder. The result was that, except some 93 petty / acts of larceny, thefts were rare. Horses and mules were sometimes taken, but the risk was so great that such plunder could not be carried on to any extent. The camp or tent was held inviolate, and like the patriarchal times of old, its cover protected all it enclosed. Among all well-disposed persons there was a tacit disposition to make the canvas or pavilion of rough oak-boughs as sacred as once were the portals of a church.

### A GALLOP TO STOCKTON, WITH SOME WORDS ON LAW AND SOCIETY

97 All the roads from Stockton to the mines 98 were filled with *atajos* / of mules, laden with freight. They were mostly owned by Americans, many of them by former trappers and mountaineers, but the packers and drivers were Mexicans, and the *aparéjos* and *alforjas* of the mules were of the same fashion as those which, for three hundred years past, have been seen on the hills of Grenada and the Andalusian plains. With good mule-trains and experienced packers,

the business yielded as much as the richest diggings. The placers and gulches of Mokelumne as well as Murphy's Diggings and those on Carson's Creek, are within fifty-five miles of Stockton; the richest diggings on the Stanislaus about sixty, and on the Tuolumne seventy. The price paid for carrying to all the nearer diggings averaged 30 cents per lb. during the summer. A mule-load varies from one to two hundred lbs., but the experienced carrier could generally reckon beforehand the expenses and profits of his trip. The intense heat of the season and the dust of the plains tended also to wear out a team, and the carriers were often obliged to rest and recruit themselves. One of them, who did a good business between Stockton and the Lower Bar of the Mokelumne, told me that his profits were about $3,000 monthly.

The history of law and society in Cali- 99 fornia, from the period of the golden discoveries, would furnish many instructive lessons to / the philosopher and the states- 100 man. The first consequence of the unprecedented rush of emigration from all parts of the world into a country almost unknown, and but half reclaimed from its original barbarism was to render all law virtually null, and bring the established authorities to depend entirely on the humor of the population for the observance of their orders. The countries which were nearest the golden coast — Mexico, Peru, Chili, China and the Sandwich Islands — sent forth their thousands of ignorant adventurers, who speedily outnumbered the American population. Another fact, which none the less threatened serious consequences, was the readiness with which the worthless and depraved class of our own country came to the Pacific Coast. From the beginning, a state of things little short of anarchy might have been reasonably awaited.

Instead of this, a disposition to maintain order and secure the rights of all, was shown throughout the mining districts. In the absence of all law or available protection, the people met and adopted rules for their mutual security — rules adapted to their situation where they had neither guards nor prisons, and where the slightest license given to crime or trespass of any kind must inevitably have led to terrible disorders. Small thefts were punished by banishment from the placers, while for those of large amount or for more serious crimes, there was the single alternative of hanging. These regulations, with slight change, had been continued up to the time of my visit to the country. In proportion as the emigration from our own States increased, and the digging community assumed a more orderly and intelligent aspect, their severity had been relaxed, though punishment was still strictly administered for all offences. There had been, as nearly as I could learn, not more than twelve or fifteen executions in all, about 101 half of which / were inflicted for the crime of murder. This awful responsibility had not been assumed lightly, but after a fair trial and a full and clear conviction, to which was added, I believe in every instance, the confession of the criminal.

In all the large digging districts, which had been worked for some time, there were established regulations, which were faithfully observed. Alcaldes were elected, who decided on all disputes of right or complaints of trespass, and who had power to summon juries for criminal trials. When a new placer or gulch was discovered, the first thing done was to elect officers and extend the area of order. The result was, that in a district five hundred miles long, and inhabited by 100,000 people, who had neither government, regular laws, rules, military or civil protection, nor even locks or bolts, and a great part of whom possessed wealth enough to tempt the vicious and depraved, there was as much security to life and property as in any part of the Union, and as small a proportion of crime. The capacity of a people for self-government was never so triumphantly illustrated. Never, perhaps, was there a community formed of more unpropitious elements; yet from all this seeming chaos grew a harmony beyond what the most sanguine apostle of Progress could have expected.

The rights of the diggers were no less definitely marked and strictly observed. Among the hundreds I saw on the Mokelumne and among the gulches, I did not see a single dispute nor hear a word of complaint. A company of men might mark out a race of any length and turn the current of the river to get at the bed, possessing the exclusive right to that part of it, so long as their undertaking lasted. A man might dig a hole in the dry ravines, and so long as he left a shovel, pick or crowbar to show that he still intended working it, he was safe from trespass. His / tools 102 might remain there for months without being disturbed. I have seen many such places, miles away from any camp or tent, which the digger had left in perfect confidence that he should find all right on his return. There were of course exceptions to these rules — the diggings would be a Utopia if it were not so — but they were not frequent. The Alcaldes sometimes made awkward decisions, from inexperience, but they were none the less implicitly obeyed. I heard of one instance in which a case of trespass was settled to the satisfaction of both parties and the Sheriff ordered to pay the costs of Court — about $40. The astonished functionary remonstrated, but the power of the Alcalde was supreme, and he was obliged to suffer.

The treatment of the Sonorians by the American diggers was one of the exciting subjects of the summer. These people came into the country in armed bands, to the number of ten thousand in all, and took possession of the best points on the Tuolumne, Stanislaus and Mokelumne Rivers. At the Sonorian camp on the Stanislaus there were, during the summer, several thousands of them, and the amount of ground they dug up and turned over is almost incredible. For a long time they were suffered to work peaceably, but the opposition finally became so strong that they were ordered to leave. They made no resistance, but quietly backed out and took refuge in other diggings. In one or two places, I was told, the Americans, finding there was no chance of having a fight, coolly invited them back again! At the time of my visit, however, they were leaving the country in large numbers, and there were probably not more than five thousand in all scattered along the various rivers. Several parties of them, in revenge for the treatment they experienced, committed outrages on their way home, stripping small parties 103 of the emigrants by / the Gila route of all they possessed. It is not likely that the country will be troubled with them in future.

### SAN FRANCISCO BY DAY AND NIGHT

112   A better idea of San Francisco, in the beginning of September, 1849, cannot be given than by the description of a single day. Supposing the visitor to have been long enough in the place to sleep on a hard plank and in spite of the attacks of innumerable fleas, he will be awakened at daylight by the noises of building, with which the hills are all alive. The air is temperate, and the invariable morning fog is just beginning to gather. By sunrise, which gleams hazily over the Coast Mountains across the Bay, the whole populace is up and at work. The wooden buildings unlock their doors, the canvas houses and tents throw back their front curtains; the lights on the water are warped out from ship to ship; carts and porters are busy along the beach; and only the gaming-tables, thronged all night by the votaries of chance, are idle and deserted. The temperature is so fresh as to inspire an active habit of body, and even without the stimulus of trade and speculation there would be few sluggards at this season.

As early as half-past six the bells begin to sound to breakfast, and for an hour thenceforth, their incessant clang and the braying of immense gongs drown all the 113 hammers that are busy on a / hundred roofs. The hotels, restaurants and refectories of all kinds are already as numerous as gam-ing-tables, and equally various in kind. The tables d'hôte of the first class, (which charge $2 and upwards the meal,) are abundantly supplied. There are others, with more simple and solid fare, frequented by the large class who have their fortunes yet to make. At the United States and California restaurants, on the plaza, you may get an excellent beefsteak, scantily garnished with potatoes, and a cup of good coffee or chocolate, for $1. Fresh beef, bread, potatoes, and all provisions which will bear importation, are plenty; but milk, fruit and vegetables are classed as luxuries, and fresh butter is rarely heard of. On Montgomery street, and the vacant space fronting the water, venders of coffee, cakes and sweetmeats have erected their stands, in order to tempt the appetite of sailors just arrived in port, or miners coming down from the mountains.

By nine o'clock the town is in the full flow of business. The streets running down to the water, and Montgomery street which fronts the Bay, are crowded with people, all in hurried motion. The variety of characters and costumes is remarkable. Our own countrymen seem to lose their local peculiarities in such a crowd, and it is by chance epithets rather than by manner, that the New Yorker is distinguished from the Kentuckian, the Carolinian from the Down-Easter, the Virginian from the Texan. The German and Frenchman are more easily recognized. Peruvians and Chilians go by in their brown ponchos, and the sober Chinese, cool and impassive in the midst of excitement, look out of the oblique corners of their long eyes at the bustle, but are never tempted to venture from their own line of business. The eastern side of the plaza, in front of the Parker House and a canvas hell called the Eldorado, are the general rendezvous of business and amusement / — combining 114 'change, park, club-room and promenade all in one. There, everybody not constantly employed in one spot may be seen at some time of the day. The character of the groups scattered along the plaza is oftentimes very interesting. In one place are three or four speculators bargaining for lots, buying and selling "fifty varas square" in towns, some of which are canvas and some only paper; in another, a group of miners, brown as leather, and rugged in features as in dress; in a third, perhaps, three or four naval officers speculating on the next cruise, or a knot of genteel gamblers, talking over the last night's operations.

The day advances. The mist which after sunrise hung low and heavy for an hour or two, has risen above the hills, and there will be two hours of pleasant sunshine before the wind sets in from the sea. The crowd in the streets is now wholly alive. Men dart hither and thither, as if possessed with a never-resting spirit. You speak to an acquaintance — a merchant, perhaps. He utters a few hurried words of greeting, while his eyes send keen glances on all sides of you; suddenly he catches sight of somebody in the crowd; he is off, and in the next five minutes has bought up half a cargo, sold a town lot at treble the sum he gave, and taken a share in some new and imposing speculation. It is impossible to witness this excess and dissipation of business, without feeling something of its influence. The very air is pregnant with the magnetism of bold, spirited, unwearied action, and he who but ventures into the outer circle of the whirlpool, is spinning, ere he has time for thought, in its dizzy vortex.

115 . . . About twelve o'clock, a wind begins to blow from the north-west, sweeping with most violence through a gap between the hills, opening towards the Golden Gate. The bells and gongs begin to sound for dinner, and these two causes tend to lessen the crowd in the streets for an hour or two. Two o'clock is the usual dinner-time for business men, but some of the old and successful merchants have adopted the fashionable hour of five. Where shall we dine to-day? the restaurants display their signs invitingly on all sides; we have choice of the United States, Tortoni's, the Alhambra, and many other equally classic resorts, but Delmonico's, like its distin-

guished original in New York, has the highest prices and the greatest variety of dishes. We go down Kearney street to a two-story wooden house on the corner of Jackson. The lower story is a market; the walls are garnished with quarters of beef and / mutton; a huge pile of Sandwich 116 Island squashes fills one corner, and several cabbage-heads, valued at $2 each, show themselves in the window. We enter a little door at the end of the building, ascend a dark, narrow flight of steps and find ourselves in a long, low room, with ceiling and walls of white muslin and a floor covered with oil-cloth.

There are about twenty tables disposed in two rows, all of them so well filled that we have some difficulty in finding places. Taking up the written bill of fare, we find such items as the following:

SOUPS

Mock Turtle . . . . . . . . . . . . $0.75
St. Julien . . . . . . . . . . . . . . 1.00

FISH

Boiled Salmon Trout,
  Anchovy sauce . . . . . . . . . . 1.75

BOILED

Leg Mutton, caper sauce . . . . . . 1.00
Corned Beef, Cabbage . . . . . . . . 1.00
Ham and Tongues . . . . . . . . . . 0.75

ENTREES

Fillet of Beef, mushroom sauce . . . $1.75
Veal Cutlets, breaded . . . . . . . . 1.00
Mutton Chop . . . . . . . . . . . . 1.00
Lobster Salad . . . . . . . . . . . . 2.00
Sirloin of Venison . . . . . . . . . . 1.50
Baked Maccaroni . . . . . . . . . . 0.75
Beef Tongue, sauce piquante . . . . 1.00

So that, with but a moderate appetite, the dinner will cost us $5, if we are at all epicurean in our tastes. There are cries of "steward!" from all parts of the room — the word "waiter" is not considered sufficiently respectful, seeing that the waiter may have been a lawyer or merchant's clerk a few months before. The dishes look very small as they are placed on the table, but they are skilfully cooked and very palatable to men that have ridden in from the diggings. The appetite one acquires in California is something remarkable. For two months after my arrival, my sensations were like those of a famished wolf.

In the matter of dining, the tastes of all nations can be gratified here. There are French restaurants on the plaza and on Dupont street; an extensive German establishment on Pacific street; the *Fonda Peruana*; the Italian Confectionary; and 117 three Chinese / houses, denoted by their long three-cornered flags of yellow silk. The latter are much frequented by Americans, on account of their excellent cookery, and the fact that meals are $1 each, without regard to quantity. Kong-Sung's house is near the water; Whang-Tong's in Sacramento Street, and Tong-Ling's in Jackson street. There the grave Celestials serve up their chow-chow and curry, besides many genuine English dishes; their tea and coffee cannot be surpassed.

The afternoon is less noisy and active than the forenoon. Merchants keep within-doors, and the gambling-rooms are crowded with persons who step in to escape the wind and dust. The sky takes a cold gray cast, and the hills over the bay are barely visible in the dense, dusty air. Now and then a watcher, who has been stationed on the hill above Fort Montgomery, comes down and reports an inward-bound vessel, which occasions a little excitement among the boatmen and the merchants who are awaiting consignments. Toward sunset, the plaza is nearly deserted; the wind is merciless in its force, and a heavy overcoat is not found unpleasantly warm. As it grows dark, there is a lull, though occasional gusts blow down the hill and carry the dust of the city out among the shipping.

The appearance of San Francisco at night, from the water, is unlike anything I ever beheld. The houses are mostly of canvas, which is made transparent by the lamps within, and transforms them, in the darkness, to dwellings of solid light. Seated on the slopes of its three hills, the tents pitched among the chapparal to the very summits, it gleams like an amphitheatre of fire. Here and there shine out brilliant points, from the decoy-lamps of the gaming-houses; and through the indistinct murmur of the streets comes by fits the sound of music from their hot and crowded pre-/cincts. The picture has in it something 118 unreal and fantastic, it impresses one like the cities of the magic lantern, which a motion of the hand can build or annihilate.

The only objects left for us to visit are the gaming-tables, whose day has just fairly dawned. We need not wander far in search of one. Denison's Exchange, the Parker House and Eldorado stand side by side; across the way are the Verandah and Aguila de Oro; higher up the plaza the St. Charles and Bella Union; while dozens of second-rate establishments are scattered through the less frequented streets. The greatest crowd is about the Eldorado; we find it difficult to effect an entrance. There are about eight tables in the room, all of which are thronged; copper-hued Kanakas, Mexicans rolled in their sarapes and Peruvians thrust through their ponchos, stand shoulder to shoulder with the brown and bearded American miners. The stakes are generally small, though when the bettor gets into "a streak of luck," as it is called, they are allowed to double until all is lost or the bank breaks. Along the edge of the room is a spacious bar, supplied with all kinds of bad liquors, and in a sort of gallery, suspended under the ceiling, a female violinist tasks her talent and strength of muscle to minister to the excitement of play.

The Verandah, opposite, is smaller, but boasts an equal attraction in a musician who has a set of Pandean pipes fastened at his chin, a drum on his back, which he beats with sticks at his elbows, and cymbals in his hands. The piles of coin on the monte tables clink merrily to his playing, and the throng of spectators, jammed together in a sweltering mass, walk up to the bar between the tunes and drink out of sympathy with his dry and breathless throat. At the Aguila de Oro there is a full band of Ethiopian serenaders, and at the other hells, violins, 119 guitars or wheezy accordeons, as / the case may be. The atmosphere of these places is rank with tobacco-smoke, and filled with a feverish, stifling heat, which communicates an unhealthy glow to the faces of the players.

We shall not be deterred from entering by the heat and smoke or the motley characters into whose company we shall be thrown. There are rare chances here for seeing human nature in one of its most dark and exciting phases. Note the variety of expression in the faces gathered around this table! They are playing monte, the favorite game in California, since the chances are considered more equal and the opportunity of false play very slight. The dealer throws out his cards with a cool, nonchalant air; indeed, the gradual increase of the hollow square of dollars at his left hand is not calculated to disturb his equanimity. The two Mexicans in front, muffled in their dirty sarapes, put down their half-dollars and dollars and see them lost, without changing a muscle. Gambling is a born habit with them, and they would lose thousands with the same indifference. Very different is the demeanor of the Americans who are playing; their good or ill luck is betrayed at once by involuntary exclamations and changes of countenance, unless the stake should be very large and absorbing, when their anxiety, though silent, may be read with no less certainty. They have no power to resist the fascination of the game. Now counting their winnings by thousands, now dependent on the kindness of a friend for a few dollars to commence anew, they pass hour after hour in those hot, unwholesome dens. There is no appearance of arms, but let one of the players, impatient with his losses and maddened by the poisonous fluids he has drank, threaten

one of the profession, and there will be no scarcity of knives and revolvers. . . .

### POST-OFFICE EXPERIENCE

A day or two after my arrival, the 208 Steamer Unicorn came into the harbor, being the third which had arrived without bringing a mail. These repeated failures were too much for even a patient people to bear; an indignation meeting in Portsmouth Square was called, but a shower, heralding the rainy season, came on in time to prevent it. Finally, on the last day of October, on the eve of the departure of another steamer down the coast, the Panama came in, bringing the mails for July, August and September all at once! Thirty-seven mail-bags were hauled up to the little Post-Office that night, and the eight clerks were astounded by the / receipt of forty-five 209 thousand letters, besides uncounted bushels of newspapers. I was at the time domiciled in Mr. Moore's garret and enjoying the hospitalities of his plank-table; I therefore offered my services as clerk-extraordinary, and was at once vested with full powers and initiated into all the mysteries of counting, classifying and distributing letters.

The Post-Office was a small frame building, of one story, and not more than forty feet in length. The entire front, which was graced with a narrow portico, was appropriated to the windows for delivery, while the rear was divided into three small compartments — a newspaper room, a private office, and kitchen. There were two windows for the general delivery, one for French and Spanish letters, and a narrow entry at one end of the building, on which faced the private boxes, to the number of five hundred, leased to merchants and others at the rate of $1.50 per month. In this small space all the operations of the Office were carried on. The rent of the building was $7,000 a year, and the salaries of the clerks from $100 to $300 monthly, which, as no special provision has been made by Government to meet the expense, effectually confined Mr. Moore to these narrow limits. For his strict and conscientious adherence to the law, he received the violent censure of a party of the San Franciscans, who would have had him make free use of the Government funds.

The Panama's mail-bags reached the Office about nine o'clock. The doors were instantly closed, the windows darkened, and every preparation made for a long siege. The attack from without commenced about the same time. There were knocks on the doors, taps on the windows, and beseeching calls at all corners of the house. The interior was well lighted; the bags were emptied on the floor, and ten pairs of hands engaged 210 in the assortment and / distribution of their contents. The work went on rapidly and noiselessly as the night passed away, but with the first streak of daylight the attack commenced again. Every avenue of entrance was barricaded; the crowd was told through the keyhole that the Office would be opened that day to no one: but it all availed nothing. Mr. Moore's Irish servant could not go for a bucket of water without being surrounded and in danger of being held captive. . . .

We labored steadily all day, and had the satisfaction of seeing the huge pile of letters considerably diminished. Towards evening the impatience of the crowd increased to a most annoying pitch. They knocked; they tried shouts and then whispers and then shouts again; they implored and threatened by turns; and not seldom offered large bribes for the delivery of their letters. "Curse such a Post-Office and such a Post-Master!" said one; "I'll write to the Department by the next steamer. *We'll* see whether things go on in this way much longer." Then comes a messenger slyly to the back-door: "Mr.—— sends his compliments, and says you would oblige him very much by letting me have his letters; he won't say anything about it to anybody." A clergyman, or perhaps a naval officer, follows, relying on a white cravat or gilt buttons for the favor which no one else can obtain. Mr. Moore politely but firmly refuses; and

so we work on, unmoved by the noises of the besiegers. The excitement and anxiety of the public can scarcely be told in words. Where the source that governs business, satisfies affection and supplies intelligence had been shut off from a whole community for three months, the rush from all sides to supply the void, was irresistible.

In the afternoon, a partial delivery was made to the owners of / private boxes. It 211 was effected in a skillful way, though with some danger to the clerk who undertook the opening of the door. On account of the crush and destruction of windows on former occasions, he ordered them to form into line and enter in regular order. They at first refused, but on his counter-refusal to unlock the door complied with some difficulty. The moment the key was turned, the rush into the little entry was terrific; the glass faces of the boxes were stove in, and the wooden partition seemed about to give way. In the space of an hour the clerk took in postage to the amount of $600; the principal firms frequently paid from $50 to $100 for their correspondence.

We toiled on till after midnight of the second night, when the work was so far advanced that we could spare an hour or two for rest, and still complete the distribution in time for the opening of the windows, at noon the next day. So we crept up to our blankets in the garret, worn out by forty-four hours of steady labor. . . .

ELECTION SCENES AND MINING CHARACTERS

The Election Day[1] dawned wet and 252 cheerlessly. From the folds of our canvas door, we looked out on the soaked and trickling hills and the sodden, dripping tents. Few people were stirring about the place, and they wore such a forlorn look that all idea of getting up a special enthusiasm was at once abandoned. There was no motion made in the matter until towards noon, as most of the miners lay dozing in

[1] The Election of November 13, 1849, at which time the Constitution was voted on and state officers were elected.

their tents. The Alcalde acted as Judge, which was the first step; next there were two Inspectors to be appointed. I was requested to act as one, but, although I had been long enough in the country to have held the office, I declined to accept until after application had been made to some of the inhabitants. The acquiescence of two of the resident traders relieved me of the responsibility. The election was held in the largest tent in the place, the Inspectors being seated behind the counter, in close proximity to the glasses and bottles, the calls for which were quite as frequent as the votes. I occupied a seat next the Alcalde, on a rough couch covered with an India-rubber blanket, where I passed the day in looking on the election and studying the singular characters present.

As there were two or three candidates for State offices in the place, the drumming up of voters gave one a refreshing reminiscence of home. The choosing of candidates from lists, nearly all of whom were entirely unknown, was very amusing. Names, in many instances, were made to stand for principles; accordingly, a Mr. Fair got many votes. One of the candidates, who had been on the river a few days previous, wearing a 253 high-crowned silk hat, / with narrow brim, lost about twenty votes on that account. Some went no further than to vote for those they actually knew. One who took the opposite extreme, justified himself in this wise: — "When I left home," said he, "I was determined to *go it blind*. I went it blind in coming to California, and I'm not going to stop now. I voted for the Constitution, and I've never seen the Constitution. I voted for all the candidates, and I don't know a damned one of them. I'm going it blind all through, I am." The Californians and resident Mexicans who were entitled to vote, were in high spirits, on exercising the privilege for the first time in their lives. It made no difference what the ticket was; the fact of their having voted very much increased their self-importance, for the day at least.

The votes polled amounted to one hundred and five, all of which were "For the Constitution." The number of miners on the Bar, who were entitled to vote, was probably double this number, but those who were at work among the gulches remained in their tents, on account of the rain. A company on the other side of the river was completely cut off from the polls by the rise of the flood, which made it impossible for them to cross. . . . / . . . The 254 candidates, whose interest it was to search out all delinquents, finally exhausted the roll, and the polls were closed. The returns were made out in due form, signed and dispatched by a messenger to the Double Spring, to await the carrier from the Upper Bar, who was to convey them to Stockton.

During the few days I spent on the Mokelumne, I had an opportunity of becoming acquainted with many curious characteristics and incidents of mining life. It would have been an interesting study for a philosopher, to note the different effects which sudden enrichment produced upon different persons, especially those whose lives had previously been passed in the midst of poverty and privation. The most profound scholar in human nature might here have learned something which all his previous wisdom and experience could never teach. It was not precisely the development of new qualities in the man, but the exhibition of changes and contrasts of character, unexpected and almost unaccountable. The world-old moral of gold was completely falsified. Those who were unused to labor, whose daily ounce or two seemed a poor recompense for weary muscles and flagging spirits, might carefully hoard their gains; but they whose hardy fibre grappled with the tough earth as naturally as if it knew no fitter play, and made the coarse gravel and rocky strata yield up their precious grains, were as profuse as princes and as open-hearted as philanthropists. Weather-beaten tars, wiry, delving Irishmen, and stalwart foresters from the wilds of Missouri, became a race of sybarites and epicureans. Secure in possessing the "Open Sesamé" to the exhaustless treasury under their feet, they gave free rein to every whim or impulse which could possibly be gratified.

255   It was no unusual thing to see a company of these men, who had never before had a thought of luxury beyond a good beefsteak and a glass of whiskey, drinking their champagne at ten dollars a bottle, and eating their tongue and sardines, or warming in the smoky camp-kettle their tin canisters of turtle-soup and lobster-salad. It was frequently remarked that the Oregonians, though accustomed all their lives to the most simple, solid and temperate fare, went beyond every other class of miners in their fondness for champagne and all kinds of cordials and choice liquors. These were the only luxuries they indulged in, for they were, to a man, cautious and economical in the use of gold.

256   There was one character on the river, whom I had met on my first visit in August and still found there on my return. He possessed sufficient individuality of appearance and habits to have made him a hero of fiction; Cooper would have delighted to have stumbled upon him. His real name I never learned, but he was known to all the miners by the cognomen of "Buckshot" — an appellation which seemed to suit his hard, squab figure very well. He might have been forty years of age or perhaps fifty; his face was but slightly wrinkled, and he wore a heavy black beard which grew nearly to his eyes and entirely concealed his mouth. When he removed his worn and dusty felt hat, which was but seldom, his large, square forehead, bald crown and serious gray eyes gave him an appearance of reflective intellect; — a promise hardly verified by his conversation. He was of a stout and sturdy frame, and always wore clothes of a coarse texture, with a flannel shirt and belt containing a knife. I guessed from a slight peculiarity of his accent that he was a German by birth, though I believe he was not considered so by the miners.

The habits of "Buckshot" were still more eccentric than his appearance. He lived entirely alone, in a small tent, and seemed rather to shun than court the society of others. His tastes were exceedingly luxurious; he always had the best of everything in the market, regardless of its cost. The finest hams, at a dollar / and a half the 257 pound; preserved oysters, corn and peas, at six dollars a canister; onions and potatoes, whenever such articles made their appearance; Chinese sweetmeats and dried fruits, were all on his table, and his dinner was regularly moistened by a bottle of champagne. He did his own cooking, an operation which cost little trouble, on account of the scarcity of fresh provisions. When particularly lucky in digging, he would take his ease for a day or two, until the dust was exhausted, when he would again shoulder his pick and crowbar and commence burrowing in some lonely corner of the rich gulch. He had been in the country since the first discovery of the placers, and was reported to have dug, in all, between thirty and forty thousand dollars, — all of which he had spent for his subsistence. I heard him once say that he never dug less than an ounce in one day, and sometimes as much as two pounds. The rough life of the mountains seemed entirely congenial to his tastes, and he could not have been induced to change it for any other, though less laborious and equally epicurean.

Among the number of miners scattered through the different gulches, I met daily with men of education and intelligence, from all parts of the United States. It was never safe to presume on a person's character, from his dress or appearance. A rough, dirty, sunburnt fellow, with unshorn beard, quarrying away for life at the bottom of some rocky hole, might be a graduate of one of the first colleges in the country, and a man of genuine refinement and taste. I found plenty of men who were not outwardly distinguishable from the inveterate trapper or mountaineer, but who, a year before, had been patientless physicians, briefless lawyers and half-starved editors. It was this infusion of intelligence which gave the gold hunting communities notwithstanding their barbaric exterior and / 258 mode of life, an order and individual security which at first sight seemed little less than marvellous.

Since my first visit, the use of quicksilver had been introduced on the river, and the success which attended its application to gold-washing will bring it henceforth into general use. An improved rocker, having three or four lateral gutters in its bottom which were filled with quicksilver, took up the gold so perfectly that not the slightest trace of it could be discovered in the refuse earth. The black sand, which was formerly rejected, was washed in a bowl containing a little quicksilver in the bottom, and the amalgam formed by the gold yielded four dollars to every pound of sand. Mr. James, who had washed out a great deal of this sand, evaporated the quicksilver in a retort, and produced a cake of fine gold worth nearly five hundred dollars. The machines sold at one thousand dollars apiece, the owners having wisely taken the precaution to have them patented.

There is no doubt that, by means of quicksilver, much of the soil which has heretofore been passed by as worthless, will give a rich return. . . . A heap of refuse earth, left by the common rocker after ten thousand dollars had been washed, yielded still another thousand to the new machine. Quicksilver was enormously high, four dollars a pound having been paid in Stockton. When the mines of Santa Clara shall be in operation, the price will be so much reduced that its use will become universal and the annual golden harvest be thereby greatly increased. It will be many years before all the placers or gold deposits are touched, no matter how large the emigration to California may be. The region in which all 259 the mining operations / are now carried on, extending from the base of the proper Sierra Nevada to the plains of Sacramento and San Joaquin, is upwards of five hundred miles in length by fifty in breadth. Towards the head of the Sacramento River gold is also found in the granite formation, and there is every reason to believe that it

exists in the valleys and cañons of the great snowy ridge.

### THE RAINY SEASON

I left the Mokelumne River the after- 260 noon following Election Day, and retraced my path to Jackson's Creek, which I reached at dark. . . .

. . . The little community established on 261 the knoll numbered about sixty persons. They were all settled there for the winter, though the gold dug did not average more than half an ounce to each man, daily.

Next morning, I crossed the hills to Sutter's Creek, where I found the settlement increased by several new arrivals. From this place my path branched off to the north, crossing several mountain ridges to Amador's Creek, which, like the streams I had already passed, was lined with tents and winter cabins. I questioned several miners about their profits, but could get no satisfactory answer. Singularly enough, it is almost impossible to learn / from the 262 miners themselves, unless one happens to be a near acquaintance, the amount of their gains. If unlucky, they dislike to confess it; if the contrary, they have good reason for keeping it secret. When most complaining, they may be most successful. . . .

Leaving Amador's Creek, a walk of seven miles took me to Dry Creek, where I found a population of from two to three hundred, established for the winter. The village was laid out with some regularity, and had taverns, stores, butchers' shops and monte tables. The digging was going on briskly, and averaged a good return. The best I could hear of, was $114 in two days, contrasted with which were the stories of several who had got nothing but the fever and ague for their pains. The amount of sickness on these small rivers during the season had been very great, and but a small part of it, in my opinion, was to be ascribed to excesses of any kind. All new countries, it is well known, breed fever and ague, and this was especially the case in the gold region, where, before the rains came on,

263 the miner was exposed / to intense heat during the day and was frequently cold under double blankets at night. The water of many of the rivers occasions diarrhea to those who drink it, and scarcely one out of a hundred emigrants escapes an attack of this complaint.

At all these winter settlements, however small, an alcalde is chosen and regulations established, as near as possible in accordance with the existing laws of the country. Although the authority exercised by the alcalde is sometimes nearly absolute, the miners invariably respect and uphold it.

Thus, at whatever cost, order and security are preserved; and when the State organization shall have been completed the mining communities, for an extent of five hundred miles, will, by a quiet and easy process, pass into regularly constituted towns, and enjoy as good government and protection as any other part of the State. Nothing in California seemed more miraculous to me than this spontaneous evolution of social order from the worst elements of anarchy. It was a lesson worth even more than the gold.

[Taylor left the Mokelumne River area on the day following the election. He visited various other camps on the way back to Sacramento where the following account begins.]

### NIGHT IN SACRAMENTO CITY

272 Sacramento City was one place by day and another by night, and of the two, its night-side was the most peculiar. As the day went down dull and cloudy, a thin fog gathered in the humid atmosphere, through which the canvas houses, lighted from within, shone with a broad, obscure gleam, that confused the eye and made the streets most familiar by daylight look strangely different. They bore no resemblance to the same places, seen at mid-day, under a break of clear sunshine, and pervaded with the stir of business life. The town, regular as it was, became a bewildering labyrinth of half-light and deep darkness, and the perils of traversing it were greatly increased by the mire and frequent pools left by the rain.

To one, venturing out after dark for the first time, these perils were by no means imaginary. Each man wore boots reaching to the knees — or higher, if he could get them — with the pantaloons tucked inside, but there were pit-falls, into which had he fallen, even these would have availed little. In the more frequented streets, where drinking and gambling had full swing, there was a partial light, streaming out through doors and crimson window-curtains, to guide his steps. Sometimes a platform of
273 plank re-/ceived his feet; sometimes he skipped from one loose barrel-stave to

another, laid with the convex-side upward; and sometimes, deceived by a scanty piece of scantling, he walked off its further end into a puddle of liquid mud. Now, floundering in the stiff mire of the mid-street, he plunged down into a gulley and was "brought up" by a pool of water; now, venturing near the houses a scaffold-pole or stray beam dealt him an unexpected blow. If he wandered into the outskirts of the town, where the tent-city of the emigrants was built, his case was still worse. The briery thickets of the original forest had not been cleared away, and the stumps, trunks, and branches of felled trees were distributed over the soil with delightful uncertainty. If he escaped these, the lariats of picketed mules spread their toils for his feet, threatening entanglement and a kick from one of the vicious animals; tentropes and pins took him across the shins, and the horned heads of cattle, left where they were slaughtered, lay ready to gore him at every step. A walk of any distance, environed by such dangers, especially when the air was damp and chill, and there was a possibility of rain at any moment, presented no attractions to the weary denizens of the place.

A great part of them, indeed, took to their blankets soon after dark. They were generally worn out with the many excitements of the day, and glad to find a position of repose. Reading was out of the question to the most of them when candles were $4 per lb. and scarce at that; but in any case, the preternatural activity and employment of mind induced by the business habits of the place would have made impossible anything like quiet thought. I saw many persons who had brought the works of favorite authors with them, for recreation at odd hours, but of all the works thus brought, I never saw one read. Men pre-

274 ferred — or rather it grew, / involuntarily, into a custom — to lie at ease instead, and turn over in the brain all their shifts and manoeuvres of speculation, to see whether any chance had been left untouched. Some, grouped around a little pocket-stove, beguile an hour or two over their cans of steaming punch or other warming concoction, and build schemes out of the smoke of their rank Guayaquil *puros* — for the odor of a genuine Havana is unknown. But, by nine o'clock at farthest, nearly all the working population of Sacramento City are stretched out on mattrass, plank or cold earth, according to the state of their fortunes, and dreaming of splendid runs of luck or listening to the sough of the wind in the trees.

There is, however, a large floating community of overland emigrants, miners and sporting characters, who prolong the wakefulness of the streets far into the night. The door of many a gambling-hell on the levee, and in J and K streets, stands invitingly open; the wail of torture from innumerable musical instruments peals from all quarters through the fog and darkness. Full bands, each playing different tunes discordantly, are stationed in front of the principal establishments, and as these happen to be near together, the mingling of the sounds in one horrid, ear-splitting, brazen chaos, would drive frantic a man of delicate nerve. All one's old acquaintances in the amateur-music line, seem to have followed him. The gentleman who played the flute in the next room to yours, at home, has been hired at an ounce a night to perform in the drinking-tent across the way; the very French horn

whose lamentations used to awake you dismally from the first sweet snooze, now greets you at some corner; and all the squeaking violins, grumbling violincellos and rowdy trumpets which have severally plagued you in other times, are congregated here, in loving proximity. The very strength, loudness and confusion of / the noises, 275 which, heard at a little distance, have the effect of one great scattering performance, marvellously takes the fancy of the rough mountain men.

Some of the establishments have small companies of Ethiopian melodists, who nightly call upon "Susanna!" and entreat to be carried back to Old Virginny. These songs are universally popular, and the crowd of listeners is often so great as to embarrass the player at the monte tables and injure the business of the gamblers. I confess to a strong liking for the Ethiopian airs, and used to spend half an hour every night in listening to them and watching the curious expressions of satisfaction and delight in the faces of the overland emigrants, who always attended in a body. The spirit of the music was always encouraging; even its most doleful passages had a grotesque touch of cheerfulness — a mingling of sincere pathos and whimsical consolation, which somehow took hold of all moods in which it might be heard, raising them to the same notch of careless good-humor. The Ethiopian melodies well deserve to be called, as they are in fact, the national airs of America. Their quaint, mock-sentimental cadences, so well suited to the broad absurdity of the words — their reckless gaiety and irreverent familiarity with serious subjects — and their spirit of antagonism and perseverance — are true expressions of the more popular sides of the national character. They follow the American race in all its emigrations, colonizations and conquests, as certainly as the Fourth of July and Thanksgiving Day. The penniless and half despairing emigrant is stimulated to try again by the sound of "It'll never do to give it up so!" and feels a pang of home-sickness at the burthen of the "Old Virginia Shore."

At the time of which I am writing, Sacramento City boasted the only theatre in California. Its performances, three times 276 a / week, were attended by crowds of the miners, and the owners realized a very handsome profit. The canvas building used for this purpose fronted on the levee, within a door or two of the City Hotel; it would have been taken for an ordinary drinking-house but for the sign: "EAGLE THEATRE," which was nailed to the top of the canvas frame. Passing through the bar-room we arrive at the entrance; the prices of admission are: Box, $3; Pit, $2. The spectators are dressed in heavy overcoats and felt hats, with boots reaching to the knees. The box-tier is a single rough gallery at one end, capable of containing about a hundred persons; the pit will probably hold three hundred more, so that the receipts of a full house amount to $900. The sides and roof of the theatre are canvas, which, when wet, effectually prevents ventilation, and renders the atmosphere hot and stifling. The drop-curtain, which is down at present, exhibits a glaring landscape, with dark-brown trees in the foreground, and lilac-colored mountains against a yellow sky.

The overture commences; the orchestra is composed of only five members, under the direction of an Italian, and performs with tolerable correctness. The piece for the night is "The Spectre of the Forest," in which the celebrated actress, Mrs. Ray, "of the Royal Theatre, New Zealand," will appear. The bell rings; the curtain rolls up; and we look upon a forest scene, in the midst of which appears Hildebrand, the robber, in a sky-blue mantle. The foliage of the forest is of a dark-red color, which makes a great impression on the spectators and prepares them for the bloody scenes that are to follow. The other characters are a brave knight in a purple dress, with his servant in scarlet, they are about to storm the robber's hold and carry off a captive maiden. Several acts are filled with the 277 usual amount of fighting and ter-/rible speeches; but the interest of the play is carried to an awful height by the appearance of two spectres, clad in mutilated tent-covers, and holding spermaceti candles in their hands. At this juncture Mrs. Ray rushes in and throws herself into an attitude in the middle of the stage: why she does it, no one can tell. This movement, which she repeats several times in the course of the first three acts, has no connection with the tragedy; it is evidently introduced for the purpose of showing the audience that there is, actually, a female performer. The miners, to whom the sight of a woman is not a frequent occurrence, are delighted with these passages and applaud vehemently.

In the closing scenes, where Hildebrand entreats the heroine to become his bride, Mrs. Ray shone in all her glory. "No!" said she, "I'd rather take a basilisk and wrap its cold fangs around me, than be clasped in the embraces of an 'artless robber." . . . For her "'art-rending" personations, Mrs. Ray received $200 a week, and the wages of the other actors were in the same proportion. A musical gentleman was paid $96 for singing "The Sea! the Sea!" in a deep bass voice. The usual sum paid musicians was $16 a night. A Swiss organ-girl, by playing in the various hells, accumulated $4000 in the course of five or six months.

Before I left the place, the number of 279 emigrants settled there for the winter amounted to two or three thousand. They were all located on the vacant lots, which had been surveyed by the original owners of the town and were by them sold to others. The emigrants, who supposed that the land belonged of right to the United States, boldly declared their intention of retaining possession of it. Each man voted himself a lot, defying the threats and remonstrances of the rightful owners. The town was greatly agitated for a time by these disputes; meetings were held by both parties, and the spirit of hostility ran to a high pitch. At the time of my leaving the country, the matter was still unsettled, but the flood which occurred soon after, by sweeping both squatters and speculators off the ground, balanced accounts for awhile and left the field clear for a new start.

In the gambling-hells, under the excitement of liquor and play, a fight was no unusual occurrence. More than once, while walking in the streets at a late hour, I heard the report of a pistol; once, indeed, I came near witnessing a horrid affray, in which one of the parties was so much injured that he lay for many days blind, and at the point of death. I was within a few steps of the door, and heard the firing in time to retreat. The punishment for these quarrels, when inflicted — which was very rarely done — was not so prompt and terrible as for theft; but, to give the gambling community their due, their conduct was much more orderly and respectable than it is wont to be in other countries. This, however, was not so much a merit of their own possessing, as the effect of a strong public sentiment in favor of preserving order.

SAN FRANCISCO, FOUR MONTHS LATER

302  When I first landed in California, bewildered and amazed by what seemed an unnatural standard of prices, I formed the opinion that there would be before long a great crash in speculation. Things, it appeared then, had reached the crisis, and it was pronounced impossible that they could remain stationary. This might have been a very natural idea at the time, but the subsequent course of affairs proved it to be incorrect. Lands, rents, goods and subsistence continued steadily to advance in cost, and as the credit system had been meanwhile prudently contracted, the character of the business done was the more real and substantial. Two or three years will pass, in all probability, before there is a positive abatement of the standard of prices. There will be fluctuations in the meantime, occasioning great gains and losses, but the fall in rents and real estate, when it comes, as it inevitably must in the course of two or three years, will not be so crushing as I at first imagined. I doubt whether it will seriously injure the commercial activity of the place. Prices will never fall to the same standard as in the Atlantic States. Fortunes will always be made by the sober, intelligent, industrious, and energetic; but no one who is either too careless, too spiritless or too ignorant to succeed at home, need trouble himself about emigrating. The same / gen- 303 eral rule holds good, as well here as elsewhere, and it is all the better for human nature that it is so.

The great want of San Francisco was 305 society. Think of a city of thirty thousand inhabitants, peopled by men alone! The like of this was never seen before. Every man was his own housekeeper doing, in many instances, his own sweeping, cooking, washing and mending. Many home-arts, learned rather by observation than experience, came conveniently into play. He who cannot make a bed, cook a beefsteak, or sew up his own rips and rents, is unfit to be a citizen of California. Nevertheless, since the town began to assume a permanent shape, very many of the comforts of life in the East were attainable. A family may now live there without suffering any material privations; and if every married man, who intends spending some time in California, would take his family with him, a social influence would soon be created to which we might look for the happiest results.

The severe weather occasioned a great 306 deal of sickness, especially among those who led an exposed life. The city overflowed with people, and notwithstanding buildings were continually growing up like mushrooms, over night, hundreds who arrived were obliged to lodge in tents, with which the summits of the hills were covered. Fever-and-ague and dysentery were the prevailing complaints, the great prevalence of which was owing undoubtedly to / exposure and an irregular habit of life. 307 An association was formed to relieve those in actual want, many of the wealthiest and most influential citizens taking an honorable part in the matter. Many instances of lamentable destitution were by this means brought to light. Nearly all the hospitals of the place were soon filled, and numbers went to the Sandwich Islands to recruit. The City Hospital, a large, well ventilated and regulated establishment, contained about fifty patients. The attending physician described to me several cases of nearly hopeless lunacy which had come under his care, some of them produced by disappointment and ill-luck, and others by sudden increase of fortune. Poor human nature!

308 The effect of a growing prosperity and some little taste of luxury was readily seen in the appearance of the business community of San Francisco. The slouched felt hats gave way to narrow-brimmed black beavers; flannel shirts were laid aside, and white linen, though indifferently washed, appeared instead; dress and frock coats, of the fashion of the previous year in the Atlantic side, came forth from trunks and sea-chests; in short, a San Francisco merchant was almost as smooth and spruce in his outward appearance as a merchant anywhere else. The hussar boot, however, was obliged to be worn, and a variation of the Mexican sombrero — a very convenient and becoming head-piece — came into fashion among the younger class.

309 The steamers which arrived at this time brought large quan-/tities of newspapers from all parts of the Atlantic States. The speculation which had been so successful at first, was completely overdone; there was a glut in the market, in consequence whereof newspapers came down to fifty and twenty-five cents apiece. The leading journals of New-York, New-Orleans and Boston were cried at every street-corner. The two papers established in the place issued editions "for the Atlantic Coast," at the sailing of every steamer for Panama. The offices were invaded by crowds of purchasers, and the slow hand-presses in use could not keep pace with the demand. The profits of these journals were almost incredible, when contrasted with their size and the amount of their circulation. Neither of them failed to count their gains at the rate of $75,000 a year, clear profit.

### SOCIETY IN CALIFORNIA

310 There are some features of society in California, which I have hitherto failed to touch upon in my narrative, but which deserve a passing notice before I take my final leave of that wonderful land. The direct effect of the state of things growing out of discovery of the placers, was to develop new qualities and traits of character, not in single individuals, but in every individual of the entire community — traits frequently most unlooked-for in those who exhibited them in the most marked degree. Society, therefore, was for the time cast into new forms, or, rather, deprived of any fixed form. A man, on coming to California, could no more expect to retain his old nature unchanged, than he could retain in his lungs the air he had inhaled on the Atlantic shore.

The most immediate and striking change which came upon the greater portion of the emigrants was an increase of activity, and proportionately, of reckless and daring spirit. It was curious to see how men hitherto noted for their prudence and caution took sudden leave of those qualities, to all appearance, yet only prospered the more thereby. Perhaps there was at bottom a vein of keen, shrewd calculation, which directed their seemingly heedless movements; certain it is, at least, that for a long time the rashest / speculators were the most 31 fortunate. It was this fact, no doubt, that seemed so alarming to persons newly-arrived, and gave rise to unnumbered predictions of the speedy and ruinous crash of the whole business fabric of San Francisco. But nothing is more contagious than this spirit of daring and independent action, and the most doleful prophets were, ere long, swallowed up in the same whirlpool against which they had warned others.

The emigrants who arrive in California, very soon divide into two distinct classes. About two-thirds, or possibly three-fourths of them are active, hopeful and industrious. They feel this singular intoxication of society, and go to work at something, no matter what, by which they hope to thrive. The remaining portion see everything "through a glass, darkly." Their first bright anticipations are unrealized; the horrid winds of San Francisco during the dry season, chill and unnerve them: or, if they go to the placers, the severe labor and the ill success of inexperienced hands, completes their disgust. They commit a multitude of sins in the shape of curses upon every one who has written or spoken favorably of California. Some of them return home without having seen the country at all, and others, even if they obtain profitable situations, labor without a will. It is no place for a slow, an over-cautious, or a desponding man. The emigrant should be willing to work, not only at one business, but many, if need be; the grumbler or the idler had far better stay at home.

It cannot be denied that the very activity of California society created a spirit of excitement which frequently led to dangerous excesses. The habits of the emigrants, never, even at home, very slow and deliberate, branched into all kinds of wild offshoots, the necessary effect of the sudden glow and expansion which they experienced. Those who retained their health 12 seemed to revel in an / exuberance of animal spirits, which carried them with scarce a jar over barriers and obstacles that would have brought others to a full stand. There was something exceedingly hearty, cordial and encouraging in the character of social intercourse. The ordinary forms of courtesy were flung aside with a bluntness of good-fellowship infinitely preferable, under the circumstances. I was constantly reminded of the stories of Northern History — of the stout Vikings and Jarls who exulted in their very passions and made their heroes of those who were most jovial at the feast and most easily kindled with the rage of battle. Indeed, it required but little effort of the imagination to revive those iron ages, when the rugged gold-diggers, with their long hair and unshorn beards, were grouped around some mountain camp-fire, revelling in the ruddy light and giving full play to a mirth so powerful and profound that it would not have shamed the Berserkers.

The most common excesses into which the Californians run, are drinking and gambling. I say drinking, rather than drunkenness, for I saw very little of the latter. But a single case came under my observation while I was in the gold region. The man's friends took away his money and deposited it in the hands of the Alcalde, then tied him to a tree where they left him till he became sober. The practice of drinking, nevertheless, was widely prevalent, and its effects rendered more destructive by the large amount of bad liquor which was sent into the country. Gambling, in spite of universal public sentiment against it, grew and flourished; the disappointment and ruin of many emigrants were owing to its existence. The gamblers themselves were in many instances men who had led orderly and respectable lives at home. I have heard some of them frankly avow that nothing would induce them to acquaint their friends and families with the nature of their occupa-/tion, they would soon have enough, 313 they said, and then they would wash their hands of the unclean stain, and go home to lead more honorable lives. But alas! it is not so easy to wash out the memory of self-degradation. If these men have in truth any sentiment of honor remaining, every coin of the wealth they have hoarded will awaken a shameful consciousness of the base and unmanly business by which it was obtained.

In spite, however, of all these dissipating and disorganizing influences, the main stock of society was sound, vigorous and progressive. The rank shoots, while they might have slightly weakened the trunk, only showed the abundant life of the root. In short, without wishing to be understood as apologizing in any degree for the evils which existed, it was evident that had the Californians been more cool, grave and deliberate in their temperament — had they lacked the fiery energy and impulsive spirit which pushed them irresistibly forward — the dangers which surrounded them at the outset would have been far more imminent. Besides, this energy did not run at random; it was in the end directed by an enlightened experience, and that instinct of Right, which is the strength and security of a self-governed People. Hundreds of instances might be adduced to show that the worst passions of our nature were speedily developed in the air of California, but the one grand lesson of the settlement and organization of the country is of a character that ennobles the race.

The unanimity with which all united in this work — the frankness with which the old prejudices of sect and party were disclaimed — the freshly-awakened pride of country, which made every citizen jealously and disinterestedly anxious that .he should acquit herself honorably in the eyes of the Nation at large — formed a spectacle which must claim our entire admiration. In view 314 of / the splendid future which is opening for California it insures her a stable foundation on which to build the superstructure of her wealth and power.

After what has been said, it will appear natural that California should be the most democratic country in the world. The practical equality of all the members of a community, whatever might be the wealth, intelligence or profession of each, was never before thoroughly demonstrated. Dress was no gauge of respectability, and no honest occupation, however menial in its character, affected a man's standing. Lawyers, physicians and ex-professors dug cellars, drove ox-teams, sawed wood and carried luggage; while men who had been Army privates, sailors, cooks or day laborers were at the head of profitable establishments and not infrequently assisted in some of the minor details of Government. A man who would consider his fellow beneath him, on account of his appearance or occupation, would have had some difficulty in living peaceably in California. The security of the country is owing, in no small degree, to this plain, practical development of what the French reverence as an abstraction, under the name of *Fraternité*. To sum up all in three words, LABOR IS RESPECTABLE: may it never be otherwise, while a grain of gold is left to glitter in Californian soil!

# Franklin A. Buck

From *A Yankee Trader in the Gold Rush: The Letters of Franklin A. Buck.* Compiled by Katherine A. White. Boston (Houghton Mifflin Company), 1930.

    Franklin A. Buck arrived in San Francisco at about the same time as Bayard Taylor but the similarity ends here. Buck, a state-of-Mainer, and a graduate of Phillips Academy, Andover, Massachusetts, came to California to participate rather than to observe, albeit as a merchant rather than as a miner. Part of the charm of his letters to his sister, Mary Sewall Bradley, is that they are clearly personal and were not intended for publication. Buck emerges as a most interesting personality — inquisitive, optimistic, wryly humorous, and remarkably level-headed and self-contained, sometimes to the point of smugness. That he was a man of broad culture is evident from his tastes in music and in books. Buck is most instructive when he is commenting upon the social scene — dances, customs, entertainments, the role of minorities in the mining community, and problems of law and order. Unlike Taylor, whose visit was fleeting, Buck chose to remain in the West. The last letter in his collection, written in 1881, indicates that he had become a settled rancher and viticulturist in Napa Valley, California. Between the time of his arrival in 1849 and the 1881 letter Buck had tried his hand at storekeeping, lumbering, contracting, silver mining, and real estate.

*San Francisco, August 22, 1849*

As we entered this noble Bay, with a cracking breeze, the blue devils that had been haunting us for the last month left and every countenance was radiant. We sailed up about five miles and rounded a point and the City of San Francisco lay before us. We ran in among a forest of shipping, selected a good berth and after 195 days our anchor once more hooked into Uncle Sam's soil.

I found things here just as I had heard with some few exceptions. The town is growing very fast. You can see it grow every night. It already contains streets and / squares, several large hotels and any quantity of grog shops and gambling saloons. This is carried on with a perfect looseness, night and day. A large number of the houses and stores are merely frames covered with canvas, as it never rains, except in the rainy season, this answers very well.

The land rises up . . . into high hills back of the town. The whole country is yellow, not a green thing to be seen and not a tree. Right off the town lies the island of Yerba Buena and the shore inside sweeps around in the form of a horseshoe, making a beautiful harbor. There are lying here over 130 vessels, most of them large ships of all nations. The ship of the line Ohio, Steam Ship Mississippi and three other men of war.

The town contains over 5000 inhabitants. Business is brisk. There are thirty or forty new buildings going up. Land is higher than in New York. The most eligible rent for $500 per month and there is not one can be bought for less than $4000. The Parker House built by Bob Parker is *the* hotel, not much larger than yours at Bucksport. It rents for $175,000 per year. Board is $25 per week. Common laborers get one dollar an hour or six per day; mechanics, $16; carmen, $3 per load.

In spite of the immense quantities of goods brought here the prices of some still keep up. Tin pans are worth $5, saleratus $1.00 a lb, boots and shoes and hard ware are in good demand, but, alas for our fortunes, provisions are plentiful and cheap. Flour has come from Chili and it is only worth $7. They have glutted the market

57

and some are obliged to sell cargoes at auction to keep them from spoiling. This has ruined our prospects, for you know our cargo was wholly provisions. If we could have looked ahead and seen what to bring we could have made our fortunes. Lumber

47 is worth $300 per thousand. We had / on deck 4 houses, 14 by 28 feet, framed. They cost $147 apiece and we have sold them for $4000 *and got the dust.* I gave one dollar and a half for a tin pail to put it in.

There is plenty of gold here, no doubt of that. It is legal tender and worth $16 the oz. There is no spurious either. That is all humbug. You can't counterfeit it. When we landed our goods at the foot of Sacramento Street, a little ways from the water, our men washed out several grains of gold. It is found in little scales in the sand. This was right in the street. One man stuck to it all day and got five dollars.

The mines are on the forks of the Sacramento and San Joaquin rivers. The miners average about $16 per day but it is hard and just now hot and sickly. The cost of transportation is so great that it cost them four dollars a day to live. I have seen several of my friends who have returned from the mines, some of them with a thousand dollars, others with a great deal less. From what they have told me I have no desire to go to the diggings. I am satisfied with what I can make in trade. Land speculation is all the rage and men who bought lots here last winter find themselves rich. We have arrived too late to go into this.

New towns are being laid out every day. There is a large place at the head of navigation, Sacramento City. Another town at the mouth is called Benicia, the government is building a navy yard here. It is impossible to keep sailors here. They get perfectly crazy and are all off for the diggings. Sunday a boat's crew escaped from the Ohio. They fired on them but without effect. We have kept three of our men by promising to pay them off when the vessel is discharged. The Captain and myself had to take hold and work to land cargo but it's no disgrace here. . . .

I wish I could send you a *lump*. I have 48 seen some big pieces. The largest we have weighs 1½ oz, and that's nothing. I don't regret coming out at all and just as long as the gold mines last, business will be good.

The country is as quiet and peaceable as you can expect where there is no government, no police, no society and where every man does what is right in his own eyes. Sunday is respected but there is no church and no parson. There are more females here than I expected to see. A great many brought their wives but none whom I know.

*San Francisco, October 31st, 1849*
I arrived all safe on Saturday at this place 53 [From a trip to Sacramento]. It has grown much larger since I have been up the river. There is a perfect forest of shipping in the harbor. All the canvass houses have disappeared and handsome frame and brick buildings have taken their places. Several new saloons have been opened equal to the Broadway saloons and eating houses. A circus and theatre have been opened and the streets are as much blocked up with carts and people as New York.

The weather is fine; much warmer than when we were here in August. People look much more dressed here than up the river: more cityfied. There is more society. Ladies are quite plentiful as you may judge from the fact that there are two large handsome ballrooms in full blast. The city contains now over 20,000 people. It is bound to be a large city. The trade from China is coming in here fast and from all over the Pacific. . . .

. . . This country raises gold and they 54 have not begun to dig it up yet. If you had seen the heavy valises that came down the river when I came you would think there was some here, if not more. I know of three men who are going 'home' with $150,000. Samuel Brannan, one of the proprietors of Sac. City and who owns the city hotel there, has an income from his rents alone of $160,000 a year, besides a store here and at the place. He is a young man who came out here three years ago.

When mine amount to that I shall come home. . . .

Politics begin to be agitated. A mass meeting was held the other evening in the square and a governor and a delegate to congress were nominated and will be elected soon. Next congress this will be made a *state*.

*Sacramento City, November* 25, 1849

I am in possession of a letter dated in 55 August from you. . . . I am glad / to know that you are all alive and well and hope you will continue so for some years, at least until I come home which I intend doing at some future time — when, the Lord only knows. I have not come 20,000 miles to turn around and go right back again like some persons who have been here and gotten homesick. I prophesy that they will be sick to come back here again when they hear of the prosperity of this great and growing country. I finished your letter from San Francisco, as you will see if you ever get it.

Shortly after, I returned to this place on the steamer 'Senator.' It really seemed like travelling again to sit on a sofa in her splendid saloon. . . .

Upon our arrival at Sacramento City we were greeted with the firing of cannon and the cheers of the inhabitants. She now runs regularly three times a week, through by day light, fare $25, meals $2. She must coin money.

56 . . . We have fitted up the upper part of our store: clothed it with sheeting, carpeted it with Chinese mats, furnished it with chairs and tables and live in luxury for this country. The heaviest bill was for the cookstove, $100 was the lowest cent we could get one for and a common one at that. . . . We have a parlor and kitchen and begin to live like rational beings again. It costs us about $10 a week and you can't board at any place less than $20.

. . . The rain does not stop the place from going ahead. Two large hotels are being erected and a city hospital. The city contains over 800 framed buildings, besides the tents. In the *election* last held, over 1800 votes were thrown. This will give you some idea of this 'right smart place.'

Trade has fallen off some since the rainy weather but week before last we sold out of our little store $1500 worth of goods. All cash trade in one day. Tell Joseph to beat that. We make a percentage here, too. The flour that I bought in San Francisco for $18 per sack (200 lbs) we sold for $44 and are all out. Flour is a little cheaper now. We sold at the top of the market and for once were *lucky*, for great quantities are arriving from Chile. It is now worth $35 here and $2 a lb in the mines. It costs 75¢ a pound to transport goods from here to the mines and our merchant from Weaver Creek, 50 miles from here, whose team we loaded, paid $1000 for having one load hauled. This is on account of the muddy roads.

So much for California. It has gotten to 57 be an old story to me. The first dust that I received, $2800, on our selling two houses in San Francisco, made my eyes sparkle and my heart beat rather quickly as I spooned it into a two quart pail. But now, I receive it and weigh it out with as little feeling as I would so much sand.

*Sacramento City, February* 12, 1850

During the rainy season business has 58 been very dull. As all the roads to the mines are impassable all the transportation has been by water.

I have learned a great deal about the country — one thing in particular — that the valley of the Sacramento was originally and is now during the greater part of the rainy season, a part of the Pacific Ocean. You have probably heard ere this of the flood at this place — almost equal to the one in which Noah figured. . . .

About the 10th of January we had warm weather that melted the snow on the mountains, followed by a heavy south east rain storm. The water in the river was nearly to the top of the bank at the time. At 12 o'clock (noon) it boiled over the bank of the American Fork and came down on the city. The bank of the Sacramento is higher than the country back. That night the Sacramento / flowed over also and about dark the water was up to the floor of our store.

We piled the dry barrels upon the wet ones and on the counter and took part of our stock up stairs. At 9 o'clock the water was over the counter.

Boats were taking people out of one story buildings. A large adobe bakery close to us fell in with a tremendous crash. The water kept rising and things began to look serious. We had no boat and began to calculate how long it would be before we should float. . . .

About 12 o'clock it stopped rising. The next morning there were three feet ten inches in our store and five feet in the street in front. We got into a whale boat and went down to the shipping. There were about 25 vessels lying at the bank. They were crowded with sick people and women and children.

The scene in the city was curious. It was a second Venice. A great quantity of merchandise floated off and was either stolen or lost. We lost over $500 worth of rice, besides dried fruits and other things damaged, though most of our goods we had taken upstairs.

We lived just as comfortably as before. Rigged a side ladder out of the chamber window, built a flat boat and paddled over the country extensively. Instead of the people wearing long faces as you would suppose, the city never was more lively. The streets were filled with boats and everybody was for having a frolic.

The prairie where I used to ride last summer as far as / you see, was covered with water. All the cattle on the plains were drowned. It was a hard sight to see them swimming about or lying dead in heaps on some little hill. There must be an immense quantity of them lost. . . .

*Sacramento City, April 25, 1850*

We have built a new store, one of the handsomest in Sacramento City: twenty

feet wide by fifty eight long, two stories with an elegant front and balcony. The upper part will make a fine residence.

The great excitement here now is the grand soiree to come off tomorrow night at the opening of the new theatre. White vests have gone up and kids are in great demand. One of the committee told me that they had issued invitations to *one hundred ladies.* So you see the / *sex* are not so few and far between here as you might suppose. I have no doubt by fall they will glut the market, as is the case with lumber. The theatre is a very handsome one with parquet and boxes and larger than the Olympic at New York. 'Mary Taylor' is engaged and will soon be here to play. Why, we had three concerts last week from 'Hertz.' I can't keep up with this country. It goes ahead of me.

The Panama arrived Monday and I have been reading the speech of D. Webster. We have papers to March 15th. I should think there was quite an excitement in Congress but it's no use for the South to try to crowd slavery into this country. There are too many Northern people here for this ever to become a slaveholding state. Liberty in its largest sense reigns here.

*Hermitage Rancho, February 24, 1852*

Last night the aristocracy of Marysville had a Grand Ball at the U. S. Hotel. I have not heard the particulars but suppose it was a grand affair as people throw themselves on such occasions here. Perhaps you will think it strange that I do not mix in these brilliant assemblies. Well, in the first place I 'hain't got no clothes' and I don't think the fun equal to the expense. I had a very pressing invite to go to a Ball at Parkhurst and Arnold's Ranch on the Sacramento River. Parkhurst promised me some fine sport as he had nine Pike Co. girls engaged; but this was too far (30 miles). The only dancing I have indulged in was at a fandango at the Sonorian Camp, three miles from here. It is a regular Mexican town, some 3000 people and about 40 houses and a number of Mexican families engaged in packing mules. They patronise our Rancho and most all know me and I take every opportunity to learn Spanish and can converse pretty well now as it is of great service here.

Well, I heard of the fandango and I went. It was held in a good-sized room with a bar on one side, of course, and crowded with men and women, all smoking. The orchestra consisted of two fiddles and guitars and made pretty good music. The men were dressed in sky-blue velvet pants, open at the sides and rows of buttons, with /
97 white drawers, red sash and a fancy shirt. The Senoritas, with white muslin dresses, stretched so stiffly that you could not get very near, and silk stockings, looked very pretty. We had cotillions and waltzes and one Senorita danced a fancy dance and made more noise with her little feet and slippers than I could with thick boots. . . . Their cotillions are the same as ours except that the last figure is 'all promenade to the Bar,' where you and your fair partner imbibe.

The Fandango went off well. I was very much amused and came away without being stabbed, which was lucky as such things often happen.

*Weaverville, June* 9, 1852
I have settled down once more and intend to stay settled if the town I have selected does not die out as a great many places do in this mushroom country, but I suppose the locality of this place is unknown to you. Look on the map and find Shasta. On the head waters of the Sacramento and forty miles north, ten miles from Trinity River, is Weaverville. It is situated in a beautiful valley, surrounded by mountains. Those on the north are still covered with snow. This is the best mining country in California as the dirt all pays from the surface in most places.

The town contains about forty buildings and 1200 inhabitants in the vicinity. We have rented a good store and arrived with our goods last week. It costs 13¢ per lb /
98 to get goods here from Sacramento City,

150 miles by steamboat, 275 by wagon and 40 on the backs of mules. Articles are not quite as cheap as in Bucksport, but we board for $15 per week. Our trade is better than I expected and think we shall do well. We started on what we got for our house in Sacramento City, $2000, and of course had to begin small; but we have already sold quite an amount of goods and Cole goes down today for more. So now you know what I am doing and what I intend to do for the next two years, if nothing extraordinary takes place.

On our way up we pass through Colusa, 99 on the Sacramento River. Here we leave the steamboat and take the stage. This is the loveliest spot in California. The prairies at this season were covered with flowers. The town is built under the large oaks and is completely shaded. There is a large rancheria of Indians here and, in fact, there are more Indians than whites in the place. The weather was awfully hot and I was very strongly reminded of the Islands, to see the whole tribe in swimming in the river, an example we followed as it was the only way to keep cool. In the afternoon we had a horse race and 'there was a sound of revelry by night.' Music arose from the rancheria and we lit our cigars and strolled out to see what was the row. We found out that there was a wedding going on.

The evening was fine, with a full moon, and seated around in a circle were one or two hundred Indians with goose wings in their hands to keep time with. The leader gave a grand flourish with his wing and then sang a solo. Then with another grand flourish, he brought in the whole chorus. They kept good time and made no discords and the whole effect was not bad. After singing sometime there was a loud call for cheunnek (food) and large baskets of acorn bread and dried salmon were emptied. Then another concert.

At twelve I went to bed and the last sound I heard was the sacred order, for it sounded like 'chevova.' These are the best specimens of the Diggers to be seen in the country. They are all clothed and the men

work discharging the boats and the girls are
100 employed as servants in the / Public Houses
and they do first-rate. At Hall's Ranch they
wait on the table and are clean and neat . . .
ask you whether you will have tea or coffee.
The Mountain Diggers are another race,
perfectly wild and untamable. You never
see one and war to the knife exists between
them and the whites. They waylay and
murder all they can and the whites shoot
every Indian that shows himself. A short
time ago they killed a Mr. Anderson from
this place, close by town. A party of men
went out, discovered the rancheria, surrounded it and killed 140 Indians. They
brought in one squaw and a little boy.
Their destiny is to be exterminated.

*Weaverville, July 6th,* 1852
. . . Trade is slow and will not be right
brisk until the rainy season on account of
scarcity of water, but we do a very good
business and increasing every day. Some
of the claims will pay very well. Last
Saturday night, four men came into the
store and weighed their gold that they had
dug that week $1960.00. This is very good
wages. But they don't all pay at that rate.
Our town is now built up with good buildings as we have a saw mill and plenty of
lumber.

As to the society — it is decidedly bad,
gambling, drinking, and fighting being the
amusements of the miners in their leisure
hours. Saturday night is usually celebrated
by such hideous yells and occasionally a
volley from their revolvers which makes it
rather dangerous to be standing around.
At least a poor inoffensive jackass found it
so the other night. I am glad to be able
to say that the majority of the people are
101 from Pike Co., although there / are quite
a number from Maine. . . .

Last Sunday was the glorious 4th of July,
and in this country people get most glori-
ously drunk generally. But in this place we
had an awful tragedy in the morning which
tended to sober people a little. You will
probably see reports of it in the papers, but
as it took place opposite our store, and I

was an eye witness, I will give you the facts.
A certain Doctor Horton built a large saloon
and public house called the American. He
kept a woman called Eliza, Vanderburg
family from New Orleans. He was sued
for a debt contracted in San Francisco and
made his house over to the woman. This
was decided to be a fraud and the Sheriff
ordered to take possession and sell the
property by Judge Lake of San Francisco.
On application of the woman, Judge Williams of this district granted an injunction.
The Sheriff wrote to Judge Lake to know
whom he should obey. He ordered him to
go on and sell as Judge Williams had no
authority to grant the injunction having
previously assisted to sell the property. The
Sheriff proceeded on Sunday morning to
take possession. Horton and the woman
armed with revolvers drove him from the
house. Now Diggon, the Sheriff is game to
the backbone. He summoned a possee of
four or five men / and went in and showed 102
his authority and ordered a man to nail up
the doors. Horton told the woman to 'shoot
his head off.' Diggon says, 'If you shoot
you are a dead man.' She fired at the man
and missed. Horton fired at the Sheriff and
shot him in the groin. The crowd rushed
out of the house leaving the Sheriff and his
men and Horton and the woman to fight
it out. Some fifteen or twenty shots were
heard and then all was still. I went over
and went in and saw Horton and the
woman lying side by side riddled with balls.
In five minutes both were dead. The Sheriff
were all of the party that was hit and he
had strength to walk to the house. He will
probably recover. This put a damper on the
Fourth and people were quiet all day. Mr.
Allen called the people together and related
the facts of the suit and most of them think
that the Sheriff was right. According to
the California Code if one man strikes
another without provocation he has a perfect right to shoot him down. Everyone
goes armed and at the least quarrel at a
gambling saloon out come the revolvers.
Someone sings out, 'Don't shoot,' the crowd
surge back, and they blaze away. A man's

life is but little thought of. Sunday these two persons were killed; yesterday buried; and today almost forgotten.

In the midst of this ungodly community Mr. Hill, a Baptist minister, preaches every Wednesday evening. Standing on the steps of a house he preaches to the whole town. He is a good preacher, but the fruit has not appeared as yet. The Indians steal a mule now and then, but no one has been hurt by them lately.

*Weaverville, October 5, 1852*

08  Since my last letter the Indian Chiefs from the South Fork have come in and
09  sued for peace and the people have / had so much business on hand that mining has been neglected.

King 'Tulas' was accompanied by eight warriors and a large crowd assembled to hear him tell his story. A young man who has resided some years among them acted as interpreter. A stand was erected and the old chief mounted the rostrum without the slightest embarrassment and talked like a book. He was greeted with hearty cheers and his appearance was interesting. We dressed him up in white pants and shirt, two coats and a beaver hat and *white kids,* which he felt very proud of. The language is not as rough as I supposed and his gestures were natural. Of course we had great sport: 'Now he's on internal improvements,' says one. 'Ask him if he goes for Scott,' says another. But old Tulas talked right to the point. He promised to eat no more mules if he could be allowed to come on to the river and fish, and said 'he was glad to see we had such good houses and plenty of blankets and he would come over this winter and live with us.'

The Treaty was drawn up and signed and afterwards we had a war dance. A large ring was formed and lighted with candles and the crowd at last *sat down in front* and order was restored. There must have been at least a thousand persons present. The Indians dressed in all their finery with their bows and arrows came bounding into the ring and were received with thundering applause. They sang and yelled and danced after the most approved style probably. . . .

The Indians went back very pleased with their visit and I don't think it will be their fault if the Treaty is / broken, as the wrong 110 in most all cases is first on the side of the whites. The poor Indians have been treated with great cruelty, I always thought, by our forefathers at home, but they have been killed off in this State like some wild animals, without the slightest cause and driven to actual starvation. Moreover, these Indians in the mountains are not so mean a race as those in the valley. They are larger and possess more intelligence and are easier civilized than any other Indians I have ever seen. There are five boys in town who are as bright and smart as any white boys. Enough said about the Diggers.

While we were in the midst of the Treaty a man by the name of Holt, who started to go to Shasta, was found shot about 2 miles from town. Suspicion immediately fell on an Irishman: Michael Grant, who was seen in company with him close by the spot where he was found. He was arrested and from the facts which soon came out, the sovereign people: i.e. a mob, held a meeting and resolved to take him. He was taken and the question put to the people whether he should be tried by the people or by the legal tribunal. The Judge was asked how long it would be before he could be tried by the Court and he stated that the Court could not sit until next January and as there is no jail nor money in the treasury to keep him and the credit of the County good for nothing, it was decided that it would save time and money and be altogether better to try him and hang him right off.

A Judge was appointed, a jury impaneled and he was tried and found guilty. After the sentence was read a dispute arose as to whether he should be hung right up the next morning or have ten days. Although a majority of the people voted for ten days the minority held on to hang him the next day. High words ensued. Pistols were drawn and I thought for sometime that half a dozen more lives would be lost in discussing

111 this point. But finally the / few blood-thirsty scoundrels (who will probably be hung themselves) were ruled down and ten days were given him. The time expired to-day and at eleven o'clock to-day a wagon on which he was standing was driven out from under which caused his death by strangulation. He had a Catholic Priest to attend on him, which he said was a great consolation and died perfectly resigned to his lot. He was about 25 years of age.

Although no one has the slightest doubt as to his guilt and I think he suffered justly, yet I say Heaven preserve me from falling into the hands of an excited people. It is a hard tribunal and if circumstances are against you, however innocent you may be, you stand no chance. Give me a dungeon in the Tombs and all the police of New York first.

*Weaverville, December* 18, 1852

In my last letter I wrote you about the snow on the mountains and I really had an 112 idea of going up just to / roll in it. Since then I have been saved the trouble for the last four days we have had an incessant snow storm and it now lays about two feet deep all over the country and from four to six feet on the mountains a little way out of town. . . .

Owing to this long spell of weather there is a right smart chance of a famine. No mule trains can get through and we are reduced to beef and some of us are fortunate enough to have a few potatoes. There is no flour nor meal nor beans. I have sold everything in the shape of eatables but the pickles and sardines and the sardines are going fast. I was fortunate enough to buy of a man on the river just before the snow set in, 2200 lbs of potatoes. We saved a few to eat and I sold the rest in one day for 37½¢ per lb (made $250 easy). Flour has been selling at 75¢ per lb. This is awful business for the miners but owing to the rise in everything, we have made more than in all the previous summer and if we had had the money to have laid in a large stock of flour we could have made a fortune.

Another chance slipped by, you see. I am content, however. . . .

. . . All the / hotels in town failed when 11. the prices advanced so much, but two. They still keep open at $1.50 a meal.

Doctor Winston and Mr. McKenzie, next door neighbors, and engaged in the butcher business and one or two more of us have formed a mess. The Doctor has a negro boy he brought to this country who cooks. We call our hotel the Metropolitan and have lived first-rate at a cost of about $12 per week each. But one thing after another has disappeared from our table until, if you will analyze any dish, you will find it composed principally of beef. But we don't fall away any and the Doctor and I sing and chant by way of soup and smoke our pipes and tobacco for a dessert. We also have hot whisky toddy and brandy peaches for the evening while the class, as we term the five or six men who generally come in and sit with us of an evening, listen to the Doctor's discourse on scientific subjects. There are a few fine whole-souled men here who have travelled and are well informed on all subjects. The Doctor and McKenzie are from Jefferson City Missouri, and are an exception to the people from that State generally. Beckett from New York, has travelled all over Canada and England. Williams from New Orleans and Blanchard from Kentucky, are the Southern representatives. So we have all the different characters in the Union and there is a vast difference. We all have different pronunciations and use different words to express the same ideas. One is sensitive on some points which we in New England wouldn't notice, but we all agree that there are *gentlemen* from all parts.

I have met with all kinds of people and from my experience from what I have seen of Southern and Western character, I am not ashamed to hail from Yankee Land, but I am hardly ever taken for a Yankee. So I expect I have lost some of the characteristics or adopted some others. I can in nine cases out of ten name the State a / man is from 11. after observing him a little. You know very little about the people that compose this vast Republic by travelling in New England.

*Weaverville, January* 18, 1853

Provisions are still very high, but will soon go down. I am selling flour, sugar, salt, beans and rice for *one dollar per lb*. I have five mules packing from Shasta and have been doing very well, but some part of the time we have been entirely out. For one week we had nothing in town but barley. Saturday a drove of cattle arrived and they sold out six in one day at 40¢ per lb.

At Yreka, 125 miles north, things are worse than here. Salt is $10 a pound; no flour at any price; nothing but venison. This will injure this part of the country. A great many of the people have left but we are 115 about as / well off as any part of the country. Sacramento has been overflowed again and provisions all over the mines are high. If the weather holds good we shall soon have a full supply.

Well, we have had some sensible pleasure here. On New Year's eve we had a ball. I was one of the managers. We endeavored to get it up in good shape; so elected the best men for managers and invited only *respectable ladies* (you have to cull them out here). We found thirty two in town and vicinity and had twenty four at the ball. It went off first-rate. I was afraid there 116 would be a row of / some kind but every one behaved themselves with propriety and enjoyed it much.

Clothes were in great demand and it was fun to see men whom we had always seen in a red shirt, sporting a dress coat and white vest. I was introduced to all the ladies. They were all married but three, but their husbands were very obliging and we all danced. Every one dances in this country and a party would be a dry one without it. Most of the ladies were young, just married and come out here and were glad of this chance to get acquainted with each other. One, Mrs. Carr from Wisconsin, is very lady-like and genteel and has evidently moved in the first circles. Mrs. Harper put

on more airs than anyone. She waltzes rather better than I would want my wife to. Some of them were rotten, on the backwoods order, but I found a much better sample of ladies than I expected to up here.

Weaverville has had much the appearance of a quiet country village lately. McGee, the great shooting character, has left town and we have not had a shot fired for a month. Gambling is dull, the miners having as much as they can do to buy something to eat. Checkers and backgammon are more in play than monte and faro.

John Chinaman (frequently multiplied) is one of my best customers. There are thirty or forty of them and today they have come to town in force. One of them wrote me a sign in Chinese.

*Weaverville, March* 18, 1853

Our business is fair and increasing and 117 if the mines pay well we shall come out ditto, as last winter I was obliged to trust a good deal and in spite of all my precautions we have $1800 credited, but I think most of it is good. The law in this country is good for collecting debts. I have several times been obliged to sue in this country until I have gotten to be quite a lawyer. I have never lost a case yet. I made out the papers today and saved $85 by sueing a note that I have.

I am getting tired of this kind of life and have fully made up my mind that when I do leave I will go into a civilized community for a short time at least, and, by the way, in order to civilize our town we want a school marm. There are ten or fifteen children running about the streets, growing up perfectly savage and their parents would be glad to pay some one well to train them I have told several that where I come from the market is stocked with school mistresses and that I would write and order one immediately. Now, if you know of anyone (a young girl preferred, of course) who wants to make her board and one hundred dollars per month, here is a splendid opening — great chances to marry, too. Now, without joking, the parents here do want one very much and there are lots of little Diggers, bright little boys, owned by men who would be ready to send them if there was an 118 op-/portunity. You ought also, when you are giving money to send missionaries to the Kanakas and the Africans, remember that we are here without any religion, no Sunday, no church, no minister — with a dozen families of children growing up ignorant of anything but Monte and learning to swear. Truly we are a curious state of society and the millennium seems far off.

*Weaverville, April 23, 1853*

120    Our city is growing and filling up with people fast. Within the last month, over 500 Chinamen and as many Americans have arrived here and the cry is 'Lice! Lice!' (rice). They prefer it to flour and we can't keep enough on hand. It sells 3 lbs for a dollar, flour, 4 lbs. We are doing a good business, own a mule train and the store we occupy; so our expenses are light and I hope at last 'Something has turned up.' Business below is dull and goods cheap. This is all the better for us as we get just as good prices as when they are high.

For amusement we have had a cock fight and two horse races lately and the grand ball of the season comes off Monday night at the new Union Hotel. Ladies are expected from Shasta and all along the road and we have twenty five in town. . . .

*Weaverville, June 5, 1853*

122    You spoke of the Chinese in your last letter. We have lots of them about and they are among our best customers and certainly the best foreigners we have. They buy lots of provisions, chiefly rice, flour, lard, codfish, tea, etc; drink whisky and smoke like other people. I rode down to the river yesterday. There are three hundred of them 123 / on one bar that has been worked out by our people and they are perfectly satisfied if they make two or three dollars per day.

Besides these we have all nations and here, while I write, I can hear Dutch, French, Spanish, English and that rich Irish brogue (I hate the whole Irish race), all at once.

You who live under the Maine Liquor law can have no idea of the immense quantity of liquor consumed in one of these mining towns. There are fourteen bar rooms in this little town and I only wonder that there is not more drunkenness than there is. Although we all drink, the 'getting drunk' is done by very few and no man of any standing in the town ever thinks of doing such a thing.

*San Francisco, July 12th, 1853*

This city is *the city* of the *Pacific* — 124 crowded with people of all nations and the buildings will vie with those of New York. Everything: hotels, theatres, saloons, carriages and horses, men and women, are on a scale with any city in the States. Of course I am having a fine time. I always have here. This is my vacation and I let myself out loose you would think at home, probably, but don't be alarmed I have a well-balanced mind; reason is always on her throne. I like to have a good time as well as anybody but in a decent genteel way, of course.

I sent my train of mules to Colusa and shall buy enough goods to load them there and go up Wednesday and once more return to the shades of private life as a *Country Merchant*, not considered as honorable an occupation as an 'honest miner' but I like it better.

*Weaverville, September 18, 1853*

Our success in business stopped about the 1st of July. Since that time we have done scarcely nothing. The water dried up and business has been poor. No money and the hardest kind of work to collect debts. With a great many I am afraid we never shall collect. We have a Celestial for a clerk and he is very successful in trading with his countrymen. These Chinese are the greatest traders in the world. They lay over the genuine Yankee even in buying and selling. All of them appear to be well

educated in their language and can calculate how much a bill of goods comes to in
29 their heads quicker than I can. / 'Ahyung,' who is with us, speaks good English and is very industrious. They are first-rate cooks. I wish you had one for a servant.

It has rained every month this year and lately we have had heavy rains and thunder showers frequently. The rivers and creeks have risen from four to six feet, to the great damage of the miners at work fluming them. Since I wrote you the community here has been very quiet. We have had our election and been beaten by the great unwashed Democracy, of course, although it is still doubtful whether Bigler or Waldo is governor. But here in our own County the Democratic ticket has all been elected. If ever I entended to figure in political affairs or wanted office I should have come out a Democrat long since. They stick to their party and vote the regular ticket no matter if the Devil himself heads it. They never bolt. The Whig Party, besides being in a minority, split up and vote for all their friends. There never will be another such a chance to elect a Whig governor again but it shows what a state of discipline the Democratic Party is in in this State.

The landlord of the Miners Hotel struck a man on the head with a club, from the effects of which he died that night. The man was drunk and disorderly. The Sheriff arrested a gambler. While conveying him to his office he drew a bowie knife and got away. The Sheriff drew a revolver and ordered him to surrender. He refused and he shot him through the heart and all the people cried Amen. This is all the remarkable events that have transpired in Weaverville lately.

*Weaverville, May 22, 1854*
133   Our village is very lively now and has improved this Spring. The lower part is all occupied by Chinese. They have four stores, four gambling saloons and a restaurant. They bid fair to outnumber the Americans in a short time. There are probably 1000 in

town and in the vicinity, also four women. One of them has a Celestial baby, the first Chinese child I ever saw. Some of these China gamblers and merchants have plenty of money and actually lay over us a long way in fine clothes and high living. They eat chickens and eggs, two articles that are eaten only by the aristocracy here, for at a restaurant two eggs are furnished for $1.25. You can imagine what it would cost me for a dinner at this rate.

They have rented the Golden Gate Saloon and have seventeen gambling tables in one room. They have no bar but a side table with tea and paper cigars. The game I cannot describe very well, but it is played with coins one of which I enclose. A lot of these are shuffled together and then covered with a tin cover. After the bets are made the cover is removed and the checks counted out by fours, and the game appears to be odd and even. When these tables are surrounded by two or three hundred Chinamen, all talking at once, the noise is equal to that made by a cotton mill in full blast. They are fast becoming a / nuisance. 134 Several of them are in jail for stealing, etc., and if it were not for the sums collected from them for mining, four dollars per month, which helps the county officers out, they would not be allowed to stay among us I think.

*Weaverville, June 29, 1854*
Since I wrote we have had the first 135 temperance lecture delivered in town. Miss Pellet has been here. She came in town Sunday and lectured in front of the hotel. When she took her stand on a dry goods box and commenced talking everybody ran. The saloons and stores were deserted. No dog fight ever drew together such a crowd. Perhaps you have seen Miss Pellet, as she hails from Maine. She is not bad looking, dresses in the Quaker style, has a fine voice and a great flow of language. Did I say flow? It is a perfect torrent. She talked for an hour and never stopped to draw breath. The noon arrived. We drew a long breath

when she got through and thanked our stars we were not tied to her for life.

In the evening she took the theatre and 136 spoke for two / hours, all on temperance. At the close a collection was taken up to defray her expenses. She got seventy one dollars — pretty good days work. As she is travelling all over the country at this rate she must have a pretty good thing. Great country for women, isn't it? What an opening this state presents for a woman of genius . . . while we poor men have to work at least three days in the week to get a living.

I believe it is a great event at home to have a new minister. Well, we have a young man among us who says he was sent here by the Methodist Conference and that he is a preacher. He preaches in the Court House twice Sundays and is a very pleasant young man though not much of a sermonist. He has quite a large audience and will remain for a year. A paper was taken around town and $200 a month was subscribed to support the Gospel — $2400 a year. How much do you give your minister? How I would like to ask you and Father and the Congregational Church generally, why it is that no minister of that denomination ever finds his way here? There is not one in the State north of Marysville, while the Methodist are sending theirs into every mining town, steadily gaining every year. I know that more than one half of the people here have been in the habit of attending this and the Presbyterian Church and would give two dollars when they give one, if we had an educated minister. While you are sending out men to preach to the Hindoos and the Hottentots (?) you are forgetting this country settled with your own sons and daughters, where a minister could be well supported and a Church built at once. At the next monthly concert I wish you would ask a report from the northern part of California.

*Weaverville, Monday, November 13th* 1854 146   Miss Goodenow sang Saturday and Sunday night. Last night she had a crowd of five or six hundred, most of them hardfisted, red-shirted miners who had not heard a woman sing since they left home. They sat with mouths open and drank in every word and brought her out every time. They would all pay a dollar just to look at her and she sang songs that pleased them very much. Such as: Sweet Home; Comin' thro the Rye; The Old Folks at Home, etc. Her voice appears to have failed. She can't touch a high note, but I like her style. . . .

A fellow from Steubenville, Ohio, sat near me. He raised up in his seat when she commenced and hardly / breathed. When 147 she finished he sank back perfectly exhausted and says: 'That's good. I like to see her throw her upper jaw back and let it come.' The remarks by the audience are as amusing to me as the performance. I wonder if she hails from Maine? She substituted the *Kennebec* for the Swannee River in the song.

The District Court is in session and a man will be sentenced to be hung tomorrow. He will probably have about thirty days allowed him to make his peace with God. The Presiding Elder, Mr. Arnold, preached yesterday afternoon in the street in front of the Diana Saloon. The audience would have been considered a motly one at home — consisting of men of all nations, including Chinese, Diggers and pack mules. He took for his text the whole Book of Jonah and likened himself unto Jonah and Weaverville unto Nineveh. Not a bad comparison except that he has never been swallowed by a fish and Weaver is not quite so large as Nineveh was. He told us that he had travelled and had visited a great many places and never had seen a place where wickedness of all kinds stalked abroad as it did here and exhorted us to repent before the besom of destruction should sweep us away. He preached more sensibly and to the point than any minister I have ever heard in California. He has a fine voice and sang the old Methodist tunes with great unction. I hope it may have a good effect for he told us some plain truths in a plain way.

If he thinks the town such a wicked place now I wonder what he would have thought two years ago. We have been congratulating ourselves that we have reformed and got to be a decent people, but our standards of morality as compared with towns at home, I expect, is very low.

*Weaverville, March 19, 1855*

48   . . . I have been mining for the past month, about two miles below town and have only been in town Sundays. I have gone back to first principles again. There are five of us living together. We have built a large log house with a splendid fire place and live the free and easy life of California miners. The claim has not paid much yet. In four days last week we made fifty one dollars, but we hope for better things when we get farther into the hill.

I am tired of *store keeping* where there is not business enough to keep me employed half the time and feel much better contented to be at work. Most men who have been here since '49 and have at some former time worked at mining find it very hard to go back to the old style of life: a cabin, cooking, etc., but I enjoy it yet. I very soon got accustomed to the pick and shovel again and if you can only make a dollar or two a day over expenses, it is such an independent life: paid in hard cash every night, no business matters, bad debts, etc., to bother your head about.

*Weaverville, May 6, 1855*

49   Summer is in full bloom with us and the old idea that gold exists only in barren countries is exploded, for every day we are sluicing off whole banks of flowers in our claim. I often wish when looking at them that the seeds I sent you had grown. . . .

I am working for passage money now, but I don't think I shall get it in time to go home this summer, although the past week we did very well. The four of us made $226.00. This is Congress wages and a little more. Certainly we ought to be satisfied, but when we wash out the little pile at night — forty, fifty or one day sixty

two dollars — we exclaim why can't there be a thousand. I / have been here so long 150 I ought to make a thousand a day for some time to get even. But don't dream any such dreams. Such cases are rare, I might say almost out of date now. I believe, however, that mining, with ordinary success, is the best business yet in the country. Not one farmer, merchant or banker makes money and *keeps it* out of fifty. Most of them are sold out by the Sheriff. It is some consolation to me when I meet my old friends of '49, who were once the Merchant Princes of San Francisco, Sacramento or Marysville, to find them (as most of them are) dead broke, communing in some mining town and trying to make the fortune they once had over again. Well, I never had any to lose. There has been what the papers term a *crisis* in California, which means that those people who for the last few years have been doing an immense business on somebody else's money at five per cent per month, living at fashionable hotels, keeping fast horses and fast women, have failed — frizzled out — bust up. People have come to the conclusion that the rate of interest and rents and lots in cities are too high. These things will all come down to their proper level by and by and then we shall have better times.

All this I look upon and read from the papers with the same interest as the man who looked at the bear and dog fight. Don't care a damn which is whipped as long as the claim pays. We get our pay every night in an article which the market doesn't affect.

We have plenty of reading matter: Harpers Magazine every month, the best in the world, I believe; and all the papers and around our table in the evenings we discuss the fate of nations, the siege of Sebastapole, the probabilities of a war with Spain, and how to fix our sluice boxes with false bottoms and ingenuous riffles so as to catch the most gold.

*Saw Mill, June 1st, 1856*

I was at Weaverville last Sunday. Wea- 159 verville is advancing in civilization and the fine arts very fast. They have built a good school house. Gambling has been entirely stopped. The theatre has been enlarged and beautified. At last we have a performance worth looking at. Instead of Miss Mowbray and Pebby, we have a star actress: Estelle Potter and 'Box and Cox,' etc. have been succeeded by the 'Hunchback,' 'The Lady of Lyons,' etc. The house is crowded and the audience *cry* for they have fine feelings, these rough miners, and it only requires talent to have them appreciate it. I saw her play 'Lucretia Borgia' and it was as good acting as I ever saw.

They have a dancing school also in full feather, only think of that for the mines. Mr. Wilson and Miss Burbank (the 'Divine Lizzie') guide them through the mazes of the waltze and schottiche. After ten o'clock the school closes and anyone paying one dollar for the music has the right to pitch in. The night I attended there were about forty gents and twenty ladies, quite a ball. Don't you think Weaverville has changed since I wrote to you in the year '52?

*North Fork, July 12th, 1856*

160 I went to Weaverville to spend the Glorious Fourth. Quite a large crowd came in to this place. There was an oration, etc., at the theatre and there was ice cream brandy smashes and all sorts of fancy drinks at the saloons. Ice is plentiful at only five cts per lb this year and these summer drinks are a luxury. The Sons of Temperance languish about this time of year. There was also a picnic for the Sabbath School children. There are thirty children here and on the increase. This is exclusive of babies in arms.

Following the current of events and determined to have all the fun, I dressed myself with an entire new rig and attended to all these things. Was fortunate enough to get into a private box at the theatre with two married women and fanned the baby with my hat. I went to the picnic, ate some of the fixins, didn't address the children; took dinner at the French Restaurant at four o'clock with Feast and others. But *the*

event of the day was the ball at night. As we didn't go to bed until the next day at noon we'll call it all day. The ball was given at Chauncey's Hotel, about two miles below town. Just before dark all the buggies (three), wagons, horses and mules were put in requisition and away we went at a race for the house. The ball room was a fine one and there was a good band of music. There were about 250 persons present, 50 ladies. We had ten sets of cotillions at once.

The Dancing School has improved the men and they could all go through a cotillion without making a botch of it. I found myself behind the times when they called a schottische a waltz, not having paid as much attention to this as to the saw mill lately.

Well, the supper was spread in an arbor. Plenty to eat and drink and they took in a thousand dollars at the bar and still there was no one drunk in the ball room and everything went off smoothly.

We quit at sunrise and scrub raced it 161 back to town. Miss Burbank's horse fell going about 2.40, through an old bed of a stream. She went about fifteen feet over his head and landed in a soft muddy place, with all her ball fixins on. Some gents along with her washed off the thickest of the mud and got her home in a buggy.

Mrs. Todd broke down the seat in a wagon and created considerable confusion as she weighs about 200. She lost $75 worth of jewelry.

Taking it all together it was the greatest affair of the kind that has ever come off here and we had lots of fun.

I see by the papers from the States that the American people are 'spiling for a fight.' What a pity that England will not pitch into us about this time. It would heal up all the difficulties in Kansas, stop the fighting in the Senate and put an end to the Vigilance Committee. Give us war, by all means, or we shall have two or three civil wars in a few years.

Fortunately for me, we are busy making lumber. We sold 25,000 feet the last fortnight and have orders for 25,000 more.

We keep the saw running day and night. If it would only last this way all the year round we could make something.

*North Fork, September* 21, 1856

162    We have made our County and State nominations. There are but two political parties in this Country: American and Democratic. You know where to find me. Fremont stands a poor show in this state. The fact is he is known too well. I am disgusted when I read from the Northern papers the account of the doings of this man and no doubt the people there all swallow it down. The New York Tribune makes him out the Conqueror of California, when it is well known here that he never was in a single fight. Kearny and Stockton conquered the country before he got here. I have seen him and know men who were with him on the plains. He is a Gigantic Humbug. I am also taken all aback to hear that a great many old Whigs will support him in preference to Fillmore. I do hope that Father is not one of these, although I do not suppose Fillmore has much show. Yet, he is my man and beyond all doubt the best man for the office. We are all going up to Weaverville to hear Governor Foote on the 30th. I have not heard a political speech yet.

*Weaverville, January* 22, 1860

This place is getting so civilized that 182 really I have nothing to write. We are getting settled down like a New England village. A fight is a rare occurrence; gambling does not attract any attention as people are not so flush with money as they used to be and stay at home evenings instead of spreeing around town. The women mind their own business. No scandal or elopements — the doctor says it is distressingly healthy, owing to people drinking less whisky and keeping better homes.

# Frank Marryat

From *Mountains and Molehills or Recollections of a Burnt Journal*. New York (Harper and Brothers), 1855.

Frank Marryat (1826–1855) was the son of Captain Frederick Marryat, English author of maritime adventure stories such as *Mr. Midshipman Easy*. The son's first published work, *Borneo and the Indian Archipelago* (1848) was the product of three years of cruising and sketching in the Orient and established the name of Frank Marryat as both writer and artist. Soon after, the word reached London of the discovery of gold in California and before long Marryat was off for the diggings via the Panama route arriving in San Francisco in the spring of 1850. Two years later he left for England but returned to San Francisco with his bride in the spring of 1853. This visit was brief for, weakened with yellow fever contracted on the passage over, the couple soon returned to England where Marryat began to put together the book from which the following excerpts are taken. He wrote largely from memory for the original notes and sketches were lost in one of the fires that swept San Francisco during the gold rush era. In *Mountains and Molehills* which appeared early in 1855 in both a London and a New York edition, Marryat records the California scene in graceful prose laced with wry humor and enlivened by anecdote. The book was enthusiastically received, but Frank Marryat did not live to savor success. He died in London, August 12, 1855.

## June, 1850

36 **T**HE STRANGER in San Francisco at this time is at once impressed with the feverish state of excitement that pervades the whole population; there is no attention paid to dress, and every one is hurried and incoherent in manner. Clubs, reading-rooms, and the society of women are unknown; and from the harassing duties of the day's business, there is nothing to turn to for recreation but the drinking-saloons and gambling-houses, and here nightly all the population meet. Where the commerce engaged in fluctuates with every hour, and profit and loss are not matters of calculation, but chance — where all have hung their fortunes on a die, and few are of that class who bring strong principles to 37 bear upon conduct that / society does not condemn — the gambling-tables are well supported, and the merchant and his clerk, and perhaps his cook, jostle in the crowd together, and stake their ounces at the same table.

Drinking is carried on to an incredible extent here; not that there is much drunkenness, but a vast quantity of liquor is daily consumed.

From the time the habitual drinker in San Francisco takes his morning gin-cocktail to stimulate an appetite for breakfast, he supplies himself at intervals throughout the day with an indefinite number of racy little spirituous compounds, that have the effect of keeping him always more or less primed. And where saloons line the streets, and you can not meet a friend, or make a new acquaintance, or strike a bargain, without an invitation to drink, which amounts to a command; and when the days are hot, and you see men issuing from the saloons licking their lips after their iced mint juleps; and where Brown, who has a party with him, meets you as he enters the saloon, and says, "Join us!" and where it is the fashion to accept such invitations, and rude to refuse them, what can a thirsty man do? The better description of drinking-bars are fitted up with great taste, and at enormous expense. Order and quiet are preserved within them during the day; they are generally supplied with periodicals and newspapers, and business assignations are made and held in them at all hours. Every body in the place is generous and lavish of money; and perhaps one reason for so many drinks being consumed is in the fact that there is ever some liberal soul who is not content until he has ranged some twenty 38 of his acquaintances / at the bar; and when each one is supplied with a "drink," he says, "My respects gentlemen!" and the twenty heads being simultaneously thrown back, down go "straight brandies," "Queen-Charlottes," "stone-fences," "Champagne-cocktails," and "sulky sangarees," while the liberal entertainer discharges the score, and each one hurries off to his business. There is no one in such a hurry as a Californian, but he has always time to take a drink. There is generally a sprinkling of idlers hanging about these saloons, waiting for any chance that may turn up to their benefit; and particularly that of being included in the general invitation of "drinks for the crowd," which is from time to time extended by some elated gentleman during the day. These hangers-on are called "loafers." There is a story told of an old judge in the southern part of the country, who was an habitual frequenter of the bar-room, and who, with his rich mellow voice, would exclaim, "Come, let's all take a drink!" Gladly the loafers would surround the bar, and each would call for his favorite beverage; but when all was finished, the judge would observe, *"And now let's all pay for it!"* which the loafers would sorrowfully do, and then retire wiser men.

Perhaps in no other community so limited could one find so many well-informed and clever men — men of all nations, who have added the advantages of traveling to natural abilities and a liberal education. Most of these are young, and are among the most reckless, perhaps, just now; but by-and-by, when this fever of dissipation has given 39 way to better impulses, these / men will gladly abjure a life which has been entailed more upon them by circumstance than choice, and will be the first to help to elevate society to a standard adapted to their real qualities and tastes.

The banks of San Francisco are naturally important, as being the depositories of the wealth that thousands are hourly accumulating on the rich "placer" fields. These buildings are of brick, and have fireproof cellars; and although at the time they were erected the outlay was enormous, both for material and labor, it was a mere trifle in comparison with the profits of their owners. The banks line one side of Montgomery Street, the principal thoroughfare of the city; and as the space on all sides has been entirely cleared for some distance by the fire, this row of buildings stands alone just now and solitary, like the speculative "Terrace" with "extensive marine view," that fronts an unpopular watering-place in England. At the corner of a street is Burgoyne's Bank; you enter and find it very crowded, and full of tobacco-smoke. Instead of the chinking of money, you hear a succession of thumps on the counter, as the large leathern bags of gold-dust come down on it. Some of the clerks are weighing dust, some are extracting the black sand with a magnet, and others are packing it in bags and boxes. The depositors are, generally speaking, miners who have come down from the diggings — fellows with long beards and jack-boots, and of an unwashed appearance, for the most part. However, many of these are not, by any means, what they seem. They have just arrived, perhaps, from a toilsome, dusty journey, and deposit their gold as a first / precaution; and before 40 the evening they will have been metamorphosed into very respectable-looking members of society, and will remain so until they return again to the diggings. Large blocks of quartz lie about the room, in all of which are rich veins of gold. These have been sent down from the mountains to be assayed; and the rich yield that these solitary specimens afforded, led, some time afterward, to a great deal of very ruinous speculation; for it had been represented that these specimens were average samples of great veins; and it was only when money had been expended in large sums, that it was discovered that these rich morsels were merely accidental deposits of gold, and by no means indicated the value of the veins. A few rich lumps were brought to England, and, by a little judicious handling, and a few public dinners, were turned to good account; and nothing but the bungling stupidity of some of those who were sent here to *pull the wires* prevented the consummation of some of the greatest swindles that ever were imposed upon the English public. I feel sore upon this point; for the dishonesty thus practiced produced an ill feeling against the country which was undeserved, and the stigma of fraud and dishonesty was unjustly cast upon the whole population.

There are no public lamps in the town, at this time, so that the greater part of it is admirably adapted for that portion of the population who gain their livelihood by robbery, and *murder* in those cases where people object to being robbed. But Commercial Street, which is composed entirely 41 of saloons, is / a blaze of light, and resounds with music from one end to the other. No expense is spared to attract custom: the bar-keepers are "artists" in their profession; rich soft velvet sofas and rocking-chairs invite the lounger; but popular feeling runs strongest in favor of the saloon that contains a pretty woman to attend the bar. Women are rarities here; and the population flock in crowds and receive drinks from the fair hands of the female dispenser, while the fortunate proprietor of the saloon realizes a fortune in a week — and only has that time to do it in, for at the end of that period the charmer is married! A French ship arrived during my stay, and brought as passengers a large number of very respectable girls, most of whom were tolerably well looking; they were soon caught up by the saloon proprietors as waiting-women at salaries of about £50 each month, and after this influx the public became gradually inured to female attendance, and looked upon it as a matter of no moment.

Near the centre of the town is a square, which, in common with many other things in the country, retains its Spanish appellation, and is called the "Plaza;" two sides of this are occupied by brick buildings, devoted solely to gambling. We have the "Veranda," "El Dorado," "Parker House," "Empire," "Rendezvous," and "Bella Union," in one row. Most of these establishments belong to companies, for the amount of capital required is very large. One or two of the houses are under French superintendence; companies having been formed in Paris, who openly avowed their object in the pro-/ spectus they issued. On entering one of 42 these saloons the eye is dazzled almost by the brilliancy of chandeliers and mirrors. The roof, rich with giltwork, is supported by pillars of glass; and the walls are hung with French paintings of great merit, but of which female nudity forms alone the subject. The crowd of Mexicans, Miners, Niggers, and Irish bricklayers, through which with difficulty you force a way, look dirtier (although there is no need of this) from contrast with the brilliant decorations. Green tables are scattered over the room, at each of which sit two "monte" dealers surrounded by a betting crowd. The centres of the tables are covered with gold ounces and rich specimens from the diggings, and these heaps accumulate very rapidly in the course of the evening, for "monte," as played by these dexterous dealers, leaves little chance for the staker to win. The thin Spanish cards alone are used, and although the dealer is intently watched by a hundred eyes, whose owners, in revenge for having lost, would gladly detect a cheat, and fall upon him and tear him to pieces, yet are these eyes no match for his dexterous fingers, and the savage scrutiny with which he is assailed as his partner rakes in the stakes produces no emotion on his pale unimpassioned face. The duty of a "monte" dealer is one of great difficulty; although surrounded by a clamorous crowd, and the clang of music, his head is occupied by intricate calculations, his eyes are watch-fully (though apparently carelessly) scanning the faces that surround his table, yet they appear to be riveted to his cards; he has, in the presence of vigilant observers, to execute feats, the detection of / which 45 would cost him his life — nightly almost he draws his revolver in self-defense; and through all this he must never change a muscle of his face, and must be ready at all times to exercise a determined courage in resenting the mere suspicion of dishonesty on his part, if such is expressed incautiously by those about him.

There is no limit to the introductions one is subjected to in a Californian crowd. If the "monte" dealer rises from his chair, you will probably be introduced to him, and I had the honor of shaking hands with a murderer quite fresh from his work, who had been acquitted a day or two previously by bribing the judge, jury, and the witnesses against him. I should have declined the honor had I learnt his profession with his name, but custom insists on your shaking hands on being introduced to a fellow-mortal; and to refuse to do so is tacitly to deny one of the great principles of the model republic, which holds that "one man is as good as another;" and, as I heard a democratic Irishman observe, "*a d — d sight better!*"

Amidst all the din and turmoil of the crowd, and the noisy music that issues from every corner, two or three reports of a pistol will occasionally startle the stranger, particularly if they should happen to be in his immediate vicinity, and a bullet should (as is not uncommon) whistle past his head, and crack the mirror on the other side of him. There is a general row for a few moments; spectators secure themselves behind pillars and under the bar; there is a general exclamation of "don't shoot," which means, of course, "don't shoot till we get out of the way;" but after the first discharges 46 the excitement settles down, and / the suspended games are resumed. A wounded man is carried out, but whether it is a "monte" dealer who has shot a player, or one gentleman who has drawn on another gentleman, in the heat of altercation, one does not learn that night, but it will appear in the morning paper; if the former, it will be headed "*Murderous affray;*" if the latter, "*Unfortunate difficulty.*" There are differ-

ent names for the same thing, even in a democratic colony! The climate of California is very healthy; there is a tendency in it to intermittent fever and ague in some parts of the mountains; but in the mines, sickness has generally resulted from imprudent exposure, and the drinking of the worst possible description of ardent spirits. On the sea coast and at San Francisco, the weather is very changeable during the summer months. When the sun rises and clears away the fog that hangs over the Bay, the air is as pure and transparent as that of Naples; by noon the glass is at 90°, and then the sea breeze sets in, and would be welcome, but that it does not fan one gently like other sea breezes, but bursts on you with the force of a hurricane, blows off a bit of the roof of your house, and sends the fine dust in whirling clouds along the street, in such a way that the people would profit by lying down flat on their stomachs, as they do in a regular Simoom![1] As the sun goes down the "doctor" subsides, after having done a great deal of good in airing the town, which as yet is unprovided with sewers. Then there creeps in steadily a heavy, fat fog, which takes up its quarters in the Bay every night, and disappears as before mentioned when the sun rises — under whose / influence it doesn't melt like 49 other fogs, but goes out to sea, and watches the town gloomily, until it is time to come in again.

These varieties of temperature during some months are methodically regular, but are not productive of sickness of any kind. The front of the city is extending rapidly into the sea, as water-lots are filled up with the sand-hills which the steam excavators remove. This has left many of the old ships, that a year ago were beached as storehouses, in a curious position; for the filled-up space that surrounds them has been built on for some distance, and new streets run between them and the sea, so that a stranger puzzles himself for some time to ascertain how the "Apollo" and "Niantic" became perched in

[1] A sort of dust storm

the middle of a street; for although he has heard of ships being thrown up "high and dry," he has probably sufficient nautical experience to observe that the degree of "height" and "dryness" enjoyed by the "Apollo" and "Niantic" resulted from some other cause than the "fury of the gale." Leaving San Francisco for the present, to return to it again by-and-by and watch its growth and improvement, I got all ready for a start for Benicia, a little town on the Bay, from whence I intended to travel leisurely to Russian River. I had chosen this district as it abounded in game; and was in quite an opposite direction to the diggings — a visit to which I postponed until the ensuing summer, my object for the present being to encamp myself in some snug place in the mountains, and there live upon my gun, in all the enjoyment of a free life and the pleasures of the chase. . . .

*Spring,* 1851

134 It was now spring, and I started alone, on foot, for San Francisco, where business required my presence. . . .

*April,* 1851

155 On landing at San Francisco, I found so many changes on every side, that my knowledge of locality was at fault; wharves extended on all sides into the sea, and the spot where I last had landed was scarcely recognizable, it was now so far inland; the steam-paddy had worked incessantly, and the front of the town still advanced into the bay.

The winter had been (compared with that of 1849) a dry one, and some of the streets having been graded and planked, the town was, under the worst circumstances, navigable for jack-boots.

What first struck me, among the many changes of a few months, was that the inhabitants generally were less eccentric in dress. When first I arrived, the people were most capricious in this respect; they wore, in fact, whatever pleased them, long hair and beards included; sobered down by circumstances, however, they had now quietly relapsed into the habits of ordinary mortals. . . .

[After an interlude of coyote and bear hunting in the vicinity of Vallejo, Frank Marryat was drawn back to San Francisco by a fire only to find that his belongings including notes and sketches of the country had been destroyed. He and a friend, the victim of similar misfortune, determined to visit the northern mines to recoup their fortunes.]

*July,* 1851

210 We reached the Salmon Fall diggings about noon, and, without halting, crossed a wooden bridge that had been built here on the north fork of the American River; we paid five dollars toll to its enterprising owner, and ascended the opposite hill. The road here became so uneven that we got out of the wagon in preference to being pitched out, and we were kept very busy in locking the wheels when it went down hill, and pushing behind when it went up. We passed no houses now, but trails led off on either side, while occasionally we encountered solitary miners "prospecting" near the road. "Prospecting" is the term applied to a pursuit of knowledge under difficulties,

that is, searching for gold where no trace of it is apparent on the surface. There are plenty of "prospectors" in the mines, but the profession scarcely pays, for the "prospector" is the jackal who must search for many days, and, when he has found, the lion, in the shape of the old miner, steps in and reaps the benefit. So that there is something to be learnt in the diggings, for undoubtedly one of the first princi- / ples in 211 life is to look on while others work, and then step in and cry "halves." . . .

At noon, having reached the ridge of the 212 mountain, we had an extended view of the gold country as it stretched away for miles beyond us in a succession of steep red hills; through these the American Fork rushed impetuously, and huge masses of redwoods clothed the highest mountains; while, in the distance, the white peaks of the Sierra Nevada were perceptible; those famous mountains of which the reputed wealth is still as much the Dorado of the Californian diggers, as were the placer fields before me once the dream of the Mexicans of the sixteenth century. "Prospectors" visit these cheerless snows never to return; but, like the discontented squirrel of the fable, who would ascend the sun-lit hills that looked so much like gold, reach them, utter a moral, and die.

213    A turn of the road presented a scene of mining life, as perfect in its details as it was novel in its features. Immediately beneath us the swift river glided tranquilly, though foaming still from the great battle which, a few yards higher up, it had fought with a mass of black obstructing rocks. On the banks was a village of canvas that the winter rains had bleached to perfection, and round it the miners were at work at every point. Many were waist-deep in the water, toiling in bands to construct a race and dam to turn the river's course; others were intrenched in holes, like grave-diggers, working down to the "bed rock." Some were on the brink of the stream washing out "prospects" from tin pans or wooden "batteas," and others worked in company with the long-tom, by means of water-sluices artfully conveyed from the river. Many were coyote-ing in subterranean holes, from which from time to time their heads popped out, like those of squirrels, to take a look at the world, and a few with drills, dissatisfied with nature's work, were preparing to remove large rocks with gunpowder. All was life, merriment, vigor, and determination, as this part of the earth was being turned inside out to see what it was made of.

The air was so still and clear that the voices rose to us with startling distinctness, and when a head appeared from a distant pit, and its owner vociferated, "How are you, Frank?" I thought at first he meant me, and was on the point of replying, "Well

and hearty, thank him. How was he?"

Small patches of garden surrounded the village, which bore so palpably the stamp of cheerfulness and / happy industry, that 214 I was disappointed on learning that its name was "Murderer's Bar;" though the appellation was justly conferred in memory of a brutal murder that had been committed among its earliest settlers.

Had all the diggings been named in accordance with the circumstances that ushered them individually into public notice, there would be more Murderer's Bars than the traveler would well know what to do with, unless they were numerically arranged like the John Smiths in the muster-roll of a marching regiment.

The name is unpleasantly candid; there are plenty of "diggings" that can record their tales of blood much more forcibly than Murderer's Bar, but under such peaceful titles as "Diamond Springs," or "Happy Valley," they bring no shudder to the traveler. So that we learn another thing at the diggings, which is, that it is ridiculous to be a Publican and make a clean breast of it to every stranger, when such great immunity is gained under the garb of the Pharisee.

One would ask how it is that Murderer's Bar, despite its name, is a peaceable village, where each man's wealth, in the shape of ten feet square of soil, is virtuously respected by his neighbor; it is not because there is enough for all, for every paying claim has long ago been appropriated, and the next comer must go further on. There is a justice of the peace (up to his arms in the river just at present), and there is a constable (who has been "prospecting" a bag of earth from the hill, and been rewarded with a gold flake of the value of three cents); these two, one would suppose, could scarcely control two or three hundred men, / with 215 rude passions and quick tempers, each of whom, as you observe, carries his revolver even while at work. But these armed, rough-looking fellows themselves elected their judge and constable, and stand, ever ready, as "specials," to support them.

If a man wanted a pickax or a shovel, and thought to help himself to one of those that lie about at all times at Murderer's Bar, he would find it inconvenient if discovered; for, as there is no extenuating clause of hunger or misery in the diggings, theft is held to be a great crime; in all probability the offender would be whipped at the tree; and this brings us again to the perplexing subject of Lynch law as relating to the miners.

I venture to say that it will puzzle the theorist to determine how far the roving population of the mining regions in California have been justified in taking measures to eject the bad and worthless from among them; for all rules and precedents fall before the strong argument of self-preservation. When Christian and his shipmates landed at Pitcairn's Island and made laws for the regulation of their small colony (happily little needed), they acted as much upon the principle of Lynch law as did the miners; for these latter were equally without the reach of the laws under which they had been born. Where, after all, was the great difference in the first trial by jury and the Lynch execution among a colony of men living far from civilization? Was the peace of a community of honest men to be disturbed by crime and bloodshed, unpunished, when, from circumstances, the law of their country was unable to protect them? 216 These / and similar questions would form the basis of the argument in defense of Lynch law in the mountains.

On the other hand, the opponent would point to the fearful instances on record of men being hurried to eternity without preparation — victims to the overwrought feelings of an excited mob. The defense of self-constituted law is untenable, yet there are instances in which small communities have seemed to me justified in enforcing, by the only means at their command, the order so necessary in such a state of society as that of the mountain gorges of California.

But when we see this law "subverting law" in a city like San Francisco, then we are forced sweepingly to condemn, once and for all, all that bears the name of Lynch, and we feel loth to admit that in any case the end can ever justify the means. Still it is a question, taken from first to last, that one may split straws on, when we see how peacefully Murderer's Bar progresses, not under the *execution,* but under the *fear* of Lynch law. In most mining villages public indignation has been confined to ordering men to "leave the camp" in twenty-four hours, or otherwise take the consequences; and after being thus warned, the nefarious digger invariably "slopes."

The mining population have been allowed to constitute their own laws relative to the appointment of "claims," and it is astonishing how well this system works. Had the Legislature, in ignorance of the miner's wants, interfered and decided that a man should have so much, and no more, of the soil to work on, all would have been anarchy and confusion.

Whereas now, every "digging" has its fixed rules / and by-laws, and all disputes 217 are submitted to a jury of the resident miners; excepting in those instances where twenty men or so are met by twenty men, and in these cases there is first a grand demonstration with fire-arms, and eventually an appeal to the district court. The by-laws of each district are recorded in the Recorder's Office of the county, and these laws are stringent although self-constituted; ill-defined at first, and varying as they did, they were conflicting and troublesome, but though they have been jumbled as it were in a bag, they have come out like Mr. Crockett, "right side up."

I have had my claim in the digging more than once, of ten feet square; if a man "jumped" it, and encroached on my boundaries, and I didn't knock him on the head with a pickax, being a Christian, I appealed to the "crowd," and my claim being carefully measured from my stake and found to be correct, the "jumper" would be ordered to confine himself to his own territory, which of course he would do with many oaths.

It is customary to leave your mining tools

in your claim, to indicate to all new-comers that it is occupied, and as this rule is recognized, it saves a great deal of unnecessary explanation; but it has often struck me that if in the quiet and virtuous hamlet of Little Pedlington, a market gardener were to leave his spade outside as a sign of occupancy, he would not detect that implement in the morning, in spite of the vigilance of the one policeman, who guards that blissful retreat. . . .

18    The gold is found here in coarse flakes, and the bank washings, from all accounts, average five or six dollars a day per man.

The days had passed when diggings were abandoned, so soon as they ceased to reward a day's toil with less than an ounce or two of gold, and "chunks" and "big strikes" were now exceptions to the rule; but the days had passed, also, when to obtain these prizes men labored painfully under the influence of fever, produced by bad food and poisonous spirits, to die at last, perhaps, disgorging every hard-earned flake of gold to some attendant quack.

Much happier the miner, when, as at Murderer's Bar, his toil is regularly rewarded with a smaller gain, for his health is no longer impaired by feverish excitement and drink, and the necessaries of life 19 are placed / within his reach, at prices that enable him to save his gold scales as well as his constitution, for the "rainy day," that in one form or the other comes to all at last.

Leaving the village and passing some hills, the sides of which were overgrown with the white azalia, we reached another part of the river, where was a ferryboat, and here we found our wagon. On the opposite side of the river the ascent was very steep, and would have been impracticable for wagons, had not the owner of the ferry excavated a portion of the mountain, and otherwise constructed a road.

For this outlay of capital the ferryman was reaping a rich harvest; having thus opened the only practicable trail at this time to the more northern mines, he had secured to himself the toll of every wagon passing to or from those regions, and these tolls amounted in one year to sixty thousand dollars (£12,000). The original capital was, I understood, the result of successful digging; and I mention this circumstance, as it proves two things; first, that fortunes in the mines are not dependent on the discovery of little nests of gold, as some suppose, but on the judicious application in a new country of the small capital which a little steady work with the pick-ax will insure to any industrious and healthy man; and, secondly, that a large portion of the gold amassed in mining regions is expended upon the permanent improvement of the country; so that the export of the "dust" is no criterion of the yield.

Bridges, ferries, roads, water-courses, dams, hotels, and stage-coaches, have nearly all been started by means of the capital obtained from the soil over which / they 220 run, or on which they are constructed. No one knows what a wagon will undergo until he has mastered Californian trails and gulches. The worst places are the steep descents that skirt the base of a mountain, where the road has an inclination of about thirty degrees toward the precipice beneath.

In such places you may fasten a rope to the axle of the wagon, and passing the other end round a tree or rock as a check, you may let her "slide," which she will do without any further trouble on your part.

*September*, 1851

So many reports had reached San 224 Francisco at this time of the discovery, in various parts of the mining regions, of auriferous veins of quartz of immense wealth, that all that portion of the population who were in waiting for something to turn up, had already departed for the mountains in search of gold rock.

Although not exactly belonging to this class, it was my destiny to hear from one Joe Bellow an account of a certain mineral district, a portion of which, it appeared, had been showered by Fortune into his lap. His description was resistless. His natural volubility, trained as it had been by his professional duties as an auctioneer, overcame all obstacles that I could raise, and I succumbed to his earnest entreaty that I would visit the mine in question and feast my eyes, as he had feasted his, on the glittering wealth which nature had here exposed to view, and of which he extracted a specimen from his pocket of the most satisfactory description.

The mine was situated in the vicinity of 225 Sonora, / the chief town of the southern mines; and as, independently of my curiosity to inspect it, I wished to visit that section of the country, we started at four o'clock one evening in a small river boat called the "Jenny Lind," bound to Stockton, a town situated on the San Joaquin River.

On starting from San Francisco for the mines, it was but natural to bid adieu to cleanliness and comfort for the time being; and having so fortified myself, I was better able to withstand the intolerable filth of the "Jenny Lind." She has since "blown up," which is about the only thing that could have purified her.

At daylight we arrived at Stockton, which I shall allude to more fully by-and-by, and at once landed and secured our places in the stage then about to start for the town of Sonora.

The stage-coach was of American manufacture, and of the class known as "Concord" coaches. It carried nine inside and two out. Our driver was a colonel, and his name was Reed. He was one of the best of whips, and, as proprietor of the line by which we were now traveling, he was making money very fast. Having been forestalled in the box seat by a very hairy miner, I completed, in company with Mr. Joe Bellow, the complement inside, after paying the gallant colonel an "ounce" for passage money. This was a "reduced fare," occasioned by an opposition having lately made its appearance on the Sonora road; the bare mention of this emulative vehicle raised the colonel's "dander." With a crack of the whip we started at a good pace behind four well-/ 226 built, active beasts, not over-groomed, or "turned out" very expensively as to harness,

but famous goers, and good for ten miles an hour over the plain.

Lines of stages now traverse the country in every direction, and there is scarcely a canvas mining village that is debarred from communication in this way with the principal towns. The horses used by these lines are of the best quality; for a Yankee stage-driver knows wherein true economy lies; but the capital required to start a line is very considerable, and as soon as the profits begin to "tumble in pretty freely," as Colonel Reed remarked, up starts an opposition — for stage-driving is a favorite speculation! Our inside passengers consisted of a young Canadian woman, who traveled under the protection of an ill-looking dog, a kind of Irish Yankee, who was very quarrelsome and bumptious, and carried his revolver in a very prominent position. We had two or three miners, who, as a matter of course, brought their rifles and blankets with them into the coach, and who squirted their juice at passing objects on the road with astonishing accuracy. We had, however, one decided character. This was a man who, as he gratuitously informed us, was professionally a bear-hunter, bear-trapper, and bear-fighter; who, in fact, dealt generally in grizzly bears. When he shot bears — and it appeared he lived in the mountains — he sold the meat and cured the skins; but when he was fortunate enough to trap a fine grizzly alive, a rich harvest generally awaited him. The grizzly was immediately transferred, bound head and foot, to a large and strong cage; and this being mounted on the bed / of a 227 wagon, the animal was dispatched to some large mining town in the vicinity, where notice was given, by means of handbills and posters, that "on the Sunday following the famous grizzly bear, 'America,' would fight a wild bull, etc., etc. Admission, five dollars."

A bull and bear fight is, of all exhibitions of this description, the most cruel and senseless. The bear, cramped in his limbs by the strict confinement that his strength and ferocity have rendered necessary, is placed in the arena; and attached to him by a rope is a bull, generally of fine shape and courage, and fresh from the mountains. Neither animal has fair play, and, indeed, in most instances, each one avoids the other. The bull's power of attack is weakened by the shortness of the tether, while the bear, as above mentioned, has scarcely the free use of his muscles.

The bull invariably commences the attack, and the immense power of the bear's fore-arm is then exemplified; for, raising himself on his hams, he meets the coming shock by literally boxing the bull's ears; but this open-handed blow saves his entrails, and the bull swerves half stunned, while his horns graze Bruin's skin. But if the bull approaches in a snuffing, inquisitive kind of manner, the bear will very probably seize his enemy's nose, and half suffocate him in his grip. The fight generally ends without much damage on either side, for the simple reason that neither of the combatants means mischief. . . .

Dinner over, we mounted a strong spring wagon in exchange for our covered coach, which had too much top hamper for the 231 mountain trail we had be-/fore us. We had now six horses, all American, good sound cattle, that had come to California across the plains, and were well broken in to crossing gulches and mud-holes. We were soon in a different style of country. Hitherto we had been crossing a level track across the Stockton plain, interrupted by an occasional dive into a dry gulch; now we commenced at once to ascend the hilly country which first indicates the approach to the mining regions. The road to Sonora, as indeed to most places in this country, has never been laid out by Government, but is, in fact, a natural trail or path marked out by the first pioneer wagons that passed that way, deviated from, from time to time, as experience indicated a shorter cut; receiving no assistance from the hand of man, and encountering a vast number of obstacles from the hand of nature. . . .

It was dark when we entered Sonora; 235 and as the habits of the people here are nocturnal, the evening may be said to have commenced as we alighted. It certainly had commenced, for Greenwich Fair might be spoken of as a sober picture of domestic life, compared to the din and clamor that resounded through the main street of Sonora. On either side were gambling-houses of large dimensions, but very fragile structure, built of a fashion to invite conflagration, though offering little of value to the devouring element when the invitation was accepted, which it was about every other night or so. In most of these booths and barns the internal decorations were very glittering; chandeliers threw a brilliant light on the heaps of gold that lay piled on each monté table, while the drinking-bars held forth inducements that nothing mortal is supposed to be able to resist. On a raised platform is a band of music, or perhaps some Ethiopian serenaders, or, if it is a Mexican saloon, a quartet of guitars; and in one house, and that the largest, is a piano, and a lady in black velvet who sings in Italian and accompanies herself, and who elicits great admiration and applause on account of the scarcity of the fair sex in this region.

Each gambling-house is full; some are 236 crowded; and the streets are full also, for it is Saturday, a night on which the miners flock into Sonora, with the avowed intention of purchasing necessaries for the ensuing week, and returning the same night; but, seduced by the city's blandishments, they seldom extricate themselves from its temples of pleasure until very early on the ensuing Monday morning, when they return to their *camps* and *long-toms,* and soothe their racking headaches by the discovery of chunks of gold.

The Mexican population preponderates in Sonora and its vicinity, and nearly every thing is stamped with their nationality. The gambling-tables are surrounded by them; and, dirty fellows as they are, they are very picturesque at a distance with their slouch

hats and long serapes. The American population, between whom and the Mexicans a rooted hatred exists, call the latter "Greasers," which is scarcely a complimentary sobriquet, although the term "Greaser camp," as applied to a Mexican encampment, is truthfully suggestive of the filth and squalor the passing traveler will observe there. Sonora has a large French population, and to this Gallic immigration is attributable the city's greatest advantages; for where Frenchmen are, a man can dine, which is very important. The *"Trois Frères Provençaux,"* has its namesake here, where good cooking and excellent light wines are at all times to be relied on; but where Frenchmen are, there are also good bakers; and there is, moreover, a great deal of sing-
237 ing, and gayety, and good-humor, / which is a pleasant contrast to the coarser hilarity of a generally very drunken population. . . .

*September,* 1851

241    Early the next morning I proceeded on horseback with Joe Bellow and an engineer to the mine, which was situated near a mining village called Tuttle-Town. To reach this spot we had to cross a table mountain, so covered with the débris of former volcanic eruptions, that it was a perfect cinderheap upon a large scale. The ground reverberated as we passed over concealed craters, and for two or three miles we were confined to a foot pace, as we picked our way through the rough boulders that lay half buried in the earth, like a field of winter turnips.

The Tuttletonians were not actively employed at the time of our arrival, principally from the fact that the diggings had "given out."

The quartz vein, however, was there, and after a day's inspection, I was satisfied that in external appearance at least it bore out the report that Joe Bellow had given of it. To the man who wants more money than he has (and few of us are free from that craving), the sight of massive veins of rock, peppered with specks of gold, is a trying spectacle.

As he sits upon a boulder on the outcrop, 24 and extracts a piece of pure metal with the point of a knife, he is subject to a thrill which I am afraid is indicative of the sordid ideas of his nature — when he descends the shaft, and by the aid of a candle still beholds the specks of gold, he draws a long breath, in mental contemplation of the wondrous wealth before him; then when the wealthy seam is placed at his service, on terms so easy that it appears quite thrown away, in all probability he will do as I did, swallow the bait, hook and all. The opinion of the engineer was highly satisfactory, as engineers' opinions generally are; we therefore returned to Sonora, where I plunged at once into the subject of mining statistics. I remember now how ridiculously plain the whole matter appeared; here was the gold — you could see it and feel it — well, all you had to do was to get it out! Argument would have been wasted upon any thickheaded fellow who looked upon the matter in any other light. But none such existed — all Sonora was quartz-mine mad — and although no machinery had as yet reached this region, shafts were being sunk, and adits cut, in every hill around the town. One mine, which extended from the rear of the principal hotel, was owned entirely by Cornish miners; these had sunk two deep shafts, and connected them by a gallery, by which means two or three hundred yards of the vein were laid bare.

This vein was called the "Englishmen's mine," and it had not only the merit of being sufficiently rich to all appearance to justify the erection of machinery, but it was about the only lode that had been scien- / tifically opened by miners, and 24? which was ready without further expense to supply any amount of ore. But up to the time of my leaving the country, the owners of this vein, although Englishmen, had not been able to exert sufficient interest to get it "looked at," and if this incident should be read by any victim who has had two and twopence returned to him in exchange for the sovereign he invested in California Mining Companies, let him not, as he contemplates his "small returns," lay the blame on the quartz rock of the country, for I assure him that the cause of failure is much nearer home; but of this I shall speak in its proper place.

Sonora is dependent for existence on the surrounding mining population; it is a town with a resident population of about three thousand souls, but with accommodation on the corral principle for about ten thousand more. Sonora is advantageously situated in one respect, inasmuch as it is irresponsible for the morals and conduct of its floating population; if Sunday is desecrated in Sonora by five thousand pleasure-seeking miners, Sonora washes its hands of that.

Sonora is one large house of entertainment for bonâ-fide travelers; and although nearly every one makes a point of traveling thither on a Saturday, to have a "burst" on Sunday, and return in penitence on Monday, Sonora washes its hands of that — otherwise I should say that Sonora in 1851 was as loose a community as was that of San Francisco in 1849.

No church bells here usher in the Sab-
244 bath; but / auction bells arouse the inhabitants equally to a full sense of the duties before them — the sun shines for Sonora on this day alone, and in accordance with wise maxims, the population commences early to make hay.

The miners prefer buying every thing at auction, and although I imagine the purchasers suffer in the long run by this principle, the "loafers" gain by it; for (supposing you are a loafer) you have only to mix with the crowd of bidders, and take out your clasp-knife; you can then make an excellent meal from the samples exposed to view, presuming always that your constitution will stand a mixture of salt butter, Chinese sugar, pickles, and bad brandy....

*October,* 1851
272  The diggings in our immediate vicinity were not actively worked, as their was not sufficient water for the purpose; this, however, was shortly to be remedied, for companies composed of miners were at work in

every direction, conducting water from the rivers to the dry diggings; and at this moment new plots of auriferous soil are daily being added to the area of "paying ground" in the mines by the artificial introduction of the water which nature has denied to them. Most of these companies have received handsome returns; the charge to each miner supplied with water being about two shillings a day.

This affords another instance of the successful employment of capital originally procured by gold digging; and if you wanted a few shares in one of these young companies, you could procure them without money, for by taking your coat off and helping to cut the ditch, you could in six months work yourself into a very respectable stockholder. I suppose each traveler who returns to his home from California, whether he is an Englishman or ⸺awich Islander, is questioned on all sides as to whether the "diggings" are / nearly ex- 273 hausted? This is easy to answer in the negative, but then follows a query far more difficult to reply to, viz., "When will they be?" Conjecture must necessarily have much weight in determining this problem, statistics of the past or present yield of the placers being almost valueless for that purpose. Yet this should be a question of very great financial importance, and not alone as regards the probable duration of the twelve million sterling now annually exported from California. For we must consider how far we are sustained by facts in presuming that the present yield of this country will be doubled, nay, quadrupled annually before the surface-soil is left again, as once no doubt it was, valueless in gold. Of course, the gold mines must some day be exhausted; let us see, then, how far we are justified in supposing this day to be, comparatively speaking, distant as regards California. . . .

Mormon Gulch was the name of a ravine 274 that was about a hundred yards from my tent, it was reported to have been the wealthiest digging in the mines, and according to rumor, half an hour's work with a clasp knife or tin spoon had invariably enriched any of the fortunate Mormons who first discovered it in 1848. Since those days, however, the earth, or stones rather, for these preponderate, had been turned over again and again, each time yielding less, until the soil ceased to return sufficient remuneration to the only process of labor that could be at that time applied to it. But before now water has been conducted there, and by the more wholesale process of sluice-washing, the gulch claims are again up in the market.

By-and-by we shall hear of the sluice-washing companies having deserted the gulch, and perhaps for a short period the red stony gravel will lie idle; but soon steam-engines and some process of securing the gold by amalgamation with quicksilver, will brighten up old Mormon Gulch again, and there is no knowing how remote the day is, when its red banks shall for once and all, finally and for the twentieth time, be reported to have "given out."

The history of Mormon Gulch, and the future I have sketched for it, is applicable 275 to every ravine in / the country, so far as this, that each auriferous flat or gulch will be subjected to certain processes, until at last the appliances of steam and science shall have robbed every square foot of earth of the treasure it contains.

Now, if all the gold territory of this country had been seized upon and worked at the time that Mormon Gulch was first discovered, we might form some estimate of the time when machinery should be brought to bear generally upon the placers; but as yet we can not ascertain the amount of gold-bearing soil that exists; for not only are fresh diggings still brought to light, in the vicinity of the original discoveries, but we have ample proof that plenty lies beyond in the direction of the Sierra Nevada, which now, from the presence of hostile Indians, can not be disturbed, and indeed, for the present, is not wanted.

The number of those who are now actually collecting gold by mining in California, may be computed at about one hundred and forty thousand men.

The obstacles that are alike presented by the extremes of the wet and dry seasons, will not admit, probably, of these miners working for more than two hundred days in the year, and the average daily sum amassed by each man, may be fairly quoted at three and a half dollars, or fifteen shillings.

This will give an annual yield of twenty-one millions sterling from California, and I have no reason to doubt that this sum is obtained, although it does not (for many reasons) appear in the reported exports of specie from the country.

Now, if this sum can be annually real- 276 ized by the exertions of comparatively so small a body of men, who have even at the latest dates no better plan of securing the gold than by a rude system of washing, what may we expect when machinery is employed, and labor concentrated?

Those portions of the placer fields that would reward manual labor with less than one or two dollars a day, are as yet unmolested, for as yet the ruling rates of wages in the mines is higher, being guided by the average yield. Therefore it is difficult to place a limit on the amount of auriferous earth that now, rejected by the miner, will, by the proper application of machinery and the reduction of labor, eventually produce a vast return. There is scarcely a hillside but gives evidence of the existence of gold, but although this soil will not at present repay manual labor, no one can suppose that the metal will be allowed to rest there undisturbed.

The distribution of gold in the soil is most eccentric, and this is attributable probably to three causes: firstly, that for the most part it was disintegrated from the matrix during the stupendous volcanic action to which all the gold territory of California has been subjected; secondly, that it has been carried to and fro by vast masses of water, the result of heavy rains, or more probably of heavy falls of snow in the mountains, that have suddenly melted and carried all before them; finally, from the land-slips and accumulations of upper soil that must necessarily result where steep / 77 hills of gravel have been for ages subjected to the sudden transitions of wet and dry seasons. . . .

Wherever gold is discovered in California, particles of quartz are found adhering to it more or less; this quartz, even when found at great depths, is generally rounded by the action of water, for quartz, when detached by violent action, is naturally angular, and inclined to splinter, and from its hardness it must require ages to give it the form of a pebble, by the slow process of grinding it receives in a comparatively dry mountain gorge. This, taken in conjunction with the facts that the gold is found now on the surface, and now low down resting on the bed rock, here forced into clefts of granite, and again in clusters of small pear-shaped nuggets, as if the metal had been ejected by intense heat, and had dripped from the volcanic boulders that lie scattered around; tends to bear out the supposition that disintegrated gold has been cast into places that time and accident alone can reveal, and that the original opinion that the gold was on the surface only no longer holds good.

Tunneling has already been applied to rich hills in the mines with great success, 278 and this fact alone is / of great importance, in so far that it leaves us powerless to place a limit on the amount of auriferous soil that is imbedded in the small round hillocks that extend over a space of nearly four hundred miles, north and south. . . .

*January,* 1852

332 I have written favorably, it will be perceived, as regards the reward held out by the gold-fields of California, to those who *having arrived there* have seized properly the advantages that surrounded them, and I have no hesitation in saying, that to the industrious, healthy, and temperate man, a comfortable livelihood is certain; beyond this much will depend upon his energy and ability, and as regards grand results, I may add *speculative feeling.* I find it impossible to place in proper shape any remarks that could be adapted to the intending emigrant, but I will attempt to lay down a few broad facts that will apply equally to all gold countries.

It has appeared to me that a great number of those who fail, must attribute their ill success to not having previous to starting laid down the course they intended to pursue.

The emigrant, of whatever class, should 333 have something definite in view; for, like a ship of discovery, he has before him, as it were, an unnavigated sea, and unknown rocks and shoals will cause him often to deviate from his track, but it should be only to return by a circuitous route to the prosecution of his journey. But if he leaves home on the broad principle of "trying his luck," he will not only be the easier cast down by adverse circumstances, but he will stand the least chance of any of becoming eventually successful. The truth of this was exemplified in the case of the English officers whom I found watering cabbages at Napa; they had not even decided then what they should do, or how they should turn their ability to account.

It is a great drawback to the laboring emigrant to a gold country that he generally lands without capital, and is obliged at once to work where and how he may. This, however, may be said to him — that Californian experience shows that, in the long run, the man does best who, having prudently amassed some money at the diggings, turns his capital and abilities to the channel into which they were originally directed at home: thus, if he has been an agricultural laborer, let him farm so soon as he has saved something; if a tailor, let him turn back to the mining city, with his nuggets in his pockets, and there set up in trade: for the diggings will be replenished by newcomers, and high prices, whether for potatoes or trowsers, will still (unless peculiarly affected by over-shipment) be maintained in a fair proportion to the yield of gold; 334 and it stands to reason that, if all / labor in the diggings is compensated proportionately with that of the digger, it is better for a working man to labor at the trade he understands. The uncertainty of the miner's life is thus avoided, and if the profits are sometimes smaller, that is more than compensated for by regularity; for it is an extraordinary fact that, let the diggings fall off as they will, the miners will still require *bread* and *breeches,* and will find the money to pay for them.

When gold-fields are first discovered the profits of professional labor are proportionately great with the rate of wages, and it would appear, at the first glance, that a fine field was opened at these times for the emigration of professional young men; but I find that those occupations which combine at first large profits with comparatively easy labor, have soon so many aspirants that the markets become glutted, and the large profits are short-lived. Thus, in California the proportion of lawyers is very great, and it would be a sad thing for that country if every legal man there could live by his profession. Therefore it would seem that a man of education should more than all shape his course before he starts; and I think it would be wise for every emigrant, let his ability be what it may, to consider what he is fit for, to *fall back upon* in event of his finding his profession profitless.

It is requisite for an emigrant of superior class that he should possess at least three qualifications independent of his abilities; viz., a small amount of capital, a good constitution, and an absence of all pride but that which nerves a man to accomplish all 335 that / he undertakes honestly, be it what it may! Such a man is an acquisition to a colony, and if his fortunes are adverse he is an exception to the rule.

The reader may observe that my own failures scarcely bear out this remark, and this is true; but my efforts were of an experimental nature, and, as I observed elsewhere, Fortune has ever snubbed me, but the jade does it so gently that I forgive her.

The emigrating reader may try farming, housebuilding, or quartz-mining with perfect security for all that bears upon the case in my experience, unless indeed my narrative serves to point out to him the folly of embarking in what one does not understand; and I would rather, if he pleases, attribute my failures to that cause, for I thereby bring to his notice a golden rule he can never keep too much in view. But this much is borne out by the histories of California and Australia, that gold countries increase permanently in wealth and prosperity; therefore the emigrant need not be downcast by present misfortune, he has but still to strive, and, in common with all, he will reap eventually the fruits of the great blessings which the Creator has been pleased to shower on these lands. He needs no better assurance than that he carries health, industry, and patience to a colony that is in a state of rapidly progressing improvement; and if, in those countries he may visit, as much care has been taken as in California to provide hospitals for the sick, and asylums for the destitute, *free of charge,* why he may land, if it so happens, shattered in mind and body, and be yet turned out a good man and true, to aid by his pickax or his plow the general / prosperity of the state that provides with so 336 much forethought for the casualties that may beset him.

Something has been said already, and with good purpose, to aid the emigrant in preserving his health under the influence of a new climate, and I will introduce a few remarks that have resulted from my own experience, which has not been confined entirely to the adventures herein related.

I would strongly advise every man to wear flannel or woven stuff next his skin, and let him never remove that which encases the upper part of the body but of a morning, when he bathes himself from head to foot; flannel on the chest and abdomen is more requisite perhaps by night than by day to those who are subjected to exposures.

Dispense with what is termed a medicine-chest, but which is, generally speaking, a box of rubbish, and even if well fitted is a dangerous thing to have by you.

Certain merchant vessels, which do not carry "an experienced surgeon," are supplied with medicine-chests and an accompanying book of reference. It is related that one tarry fellow once applied to his captain for relief; his complaint was "that he had something on his stomach." Under these circumstances the skipper turned over his pharmacopœia, and at once prescribed two teaspoonfuls of No. 15 (the drugs being numerically arranged); on an inspection of the "chest" it was found that No. 15 had "given out," and for the moment it seemed that Jack was likely to die from want of medical assistance; but the skipper had a forethought. There was plenty of No. 8 — 337 plenty of / No. 7; seven and eight make fifteen, says the captain, and Jack, to whom this calculation seemed quite natural, took two teaspoonfuls of the joint mixture, and with so much benefit as this, that whatever *was* "on his stomach" came up with a rapidity that would have astonished the Royal College of Surgeons. Although the intelligent emigrant would not make so great a blunder as this, he might make a greater, and kill himself, even while strictly following out his medicine book. For self-doctoring becomes a mania, and, as with some men, you must keep the bottle away if you would have them sober, so with others, you must deprive them of calomel and opium if you would have them healthy. I have met many infatuated fellows, who, on the first symptom of fever, have salivated themselves, from an inherent faith in the efficacy of mercury; and to see a man in the rainy season in a canvas tent, lying on a damp floor and in damp blankets, bolting calomel pills, is a sight that soon becomes very sad, and yet is very common. American emigrants are very prone to carry with them a preparation of mercury, called "blue mass;" fortunately for them there is more clay and rubbish than any thing else in the composition. I shall carry with me, when I next start for a region where doctors are not, half a gallon of castor-oil in a tin bottle, a few trifles for the cure of wounds, mustard, and *quinine;* if the emigrant can afford it, this latter should always form part of his stock. As regards castor-oil, I can only say that it was the sole medicine I took when attacked by malignant yellow fever, and that I was the only survivor of the passengers of the steamer "Dee" that were attacked.

When first arrived at his new home the 338 emigrant should avoid exposure to the midday sun or night air; but if he be a digger in the gold-fields, let him make this rule, that so soon as he feels the first symptom of illness, he will *lay by* for twenty-four hours. Premonitory fever can be arrested very easily by rest and quiet, but in nearly every instance it is aggravated to a dangerous pitch by a feeling of pride that will not allow a man to surrender; and the fear of the jeers of his healthier companions will often cause a man to continue work, when prudence would dictate an opposite course. When headaches and sickness attack you, *then* you may give in. A dose of medicine and a little rest will restore you, and shortly you will become acclimated; but if you fight against feverish symptoms, you may recover, but will probably be a wreck for life. There is an inclination to bathe when fever first appears; avoid that. I became very ill from bathing in the Chagres river one evening, to relieve, as I thought, the headache consequent on exposure to the heat, and Barnes nearly succumbed to a fever produced by the same cause; and although they are not mentioned in this narrative in their proper places, several cases of intermittent fever have from time to time appeared among my party, otherwise I should not presume to lay down any rule for the guidance of others; nor would I now, but that I have seen so many lose their lives from a want of the most ordinary precaution. I would advise the emigrant to the gold-fields to encumber himself as little as possible with what is called an "outfit." Flannel clothing, thick socks, and the best highlows that can be made for money, he should

339 select with care. Let him / take also good blankets. There is no better protection for a man in wet seasons than a blanket with a hole cut in the middle for his head to come through: the body is free, the perspiration is unconfined, and you can't wear the blanket out. India-rubber I can not recommend; it is, I believe, more productive of ague than any thing else, for it confines the perspiration, and subjects the wearer to a sudden check when it is removed. An India-rubber counterpane is useful, but should be placed over, not under, for it absorbs the moisture at all seasons, and makes a point of sending the rheumatism into your back if you lie on it. An India-rubber cap, with a curtain to protect the neck, is very useful in rainy weather, but should be lined with flannel or felt. If you intend to dig, have one or two pickaxes and crowbars made under your own supervision; exported tools are too often made of very inferior iron, and it is money well spent to pay something over the market price for a pickax that won't turn its nose up at you the instant you drive it into the hillside.

After one of the San Francisco fires an intelligent blacksmith bought up a quantity of "burnt-out" gun-barrels; these were filled up to give weight, and the breach of each was fashioned to the shape of a crowbar. These instruments sold very well; but if ever there is a calendar of saints in California, that enterprising blacksmith will not be one of them! or if he is, he will have been sworn at more than a saint by right should be.

I have said all that occurs to me would 34● be of service to the emigrant: it is little enough, and may have been said before; but if it only corroborates the experience of others, it answers fully the end I have in view. And I have no hesitation in submitting these remarks, for the great advantage of one man falling into a pit is that he can show thousands how to avoid it. I have plunged headlong into many such holes, and as I would myself avoid them for the future, so I would that others should. And although in the form that this is published it will not probably meet the eye of the poor man; still, if those who through the journals they conduct so bravely cheer and assist the emigrant, see any thing in these remarks that may save him from unnecessary expense or sickness, they will, I know, too gladly in their own way extend the aid which I intend. Above all, I would that the emigrant who has a little money should be impressed with the necessity of carrying as much of his fund out with him as he can. The best ten pounds a poor man can spend is that which enables him on his arrival in a new country to look about him for a day or two before he begins his work.

# Dame Shirley
## (Louise Amelia Knapp Smith Clappe)

From *The Pioneer; or, California Monthly Magazine*. Edited by Ferdinand C. Ewer. San Francisco (W. H. Brooks and Company), January, 1854 – December, 1855. Vols. I, II, III, IV.

Dame Shirley (Louise Amelia Knapp Smith Clappe) came to San Francisco with her physician husband in 1849. However, the fog and dampness in this region forced him to seek another climate. Dr. Clappe found the atmosphere of the northern mines at the north fork of the Feather River favorable to his health and set up his practice at Rich Bar in 1851. "Shirley" joined him late in the summer of that year. During the thirteen months that made up their stay in the mining areas, she was to write twenty-three letters to her sister Molly in "the States." Written in the detailed style of a woman writing to another woman, these letters present a fine portrait of life in this early mining camp — at its beginnings, during its boom, and at the dissolute end of its short career. In an endeavor to put forth a complete picture of the period, Dame Shirley has included the pleasant and the unpleasant, the richer and the poorer sides of the life that was going on around her. This intention of presenting all sides of the story, augmented by her keen perception and a lively literary style, make for one of the most complete and most sensitively written accounts of the California mining towns in the early days of the Gold Rush. The letters, commonly called "The Shirley Letters," appeared in *The Pioneer; or California Monthly Magazine*.

After her stay in the mining regions, Shirley went for a time to San Francisco where she resumed her occupation of teaching school. In later years the former New Jersey girl moved back East. She died in her native state in 1906 at the age of 87. Bret Harte, among others, drew heavily upon her recorded experiences for his tales of old California.

*Rich Bar, September* 13, 1851

ON MONDAY the eighth of September, I seated myself in the most excruciatingly springless wagon that it was ever my lot to be victimized in, and commenced my journey in earnest. I was the only passenger. For thirty miles the road passed through as beautiful a country as I had ever seen. Dotted here and there with the California oak, it reminded me of the peaceful apple orchards and smiling river meadows of dear old New England. As a frame to the graceful picture, on one side rose the Buttes, that group of hills so piquant and saucy; and on the other tossing to Heaven the everlasting whiteness of their snow wreathed foreheads, stood, sublime in their very monotony, the glorious Sierra Nevada.

We passed one place where a number of Indian women were gathering flower-seeds, which, mixed with pounded acorns and grasshoppers, forms the bread of these miserable people. The idea, and the really ingenious mode of carrying it out, struck me as so singular, that I cannot forbear attempting a description. These poor creatures were entirely naked with the exception of a quantity of grass bound round the waist and covering the thighs midway to the knees perhaps. Each one carried two brown baskets, (which, I have since been told, are made of a species of osier,) woven with a neatness which is absolutely marvellous, when one considers that they are the handiwork of such degraded wretches. Shaped like a cone, they are about six feet in circumference at the opening, and I should judge them to be nearly three feet

89

in depth. It is evident by the grace and care with which they handle them, that they are exceedingly light. It is possible that my description may be inaccurate, for I have never read any account of them, and merely give my own impressions as they were received, while the wagon rolled rapidly by the spot at which the women were at work. One of these queer baskets is suspended from the back and is kept in place by a thong of leather passing across the forehead. The other they carry in the right hand, and wave over the flower seeds, first to the right and back again to the left alternately, as they walk slowly along, with a motion as regular and monotonous as that of a mower. When they have collected a handful of the seeds, they pour them into the basket behind, and continue this work until they have filled the latter with their strange harvest. The seeds thus gathered are carried to their *rancherias* and stowed away with great care for winter use. It was, to me, very interesting to watch their regular motion, they seemed so exactly to keep time with each other; and with their dark shining skins, beautiful limbs and lithe forms, they were by no means the least picturesque feature of the landscape.

Ten miles this side of Bidwell's Bar, the road, hitherto so smooth and level, became stony and hilly. . . .

I,45 Soon Table Mountain became visible, extended like an immense dining board for the giants, its summit, a perfectly straight line pencilled for more than a league against the glowing sky. And now we found ourselves among the Red Hills, which look like an ascending sea of crimson waves, each crest foaming higher and higher, as we creep among them, until we drop down suddenly, into the pretty little valley called Bidwell's Bar.

I arrived there at three o'clock in the evening where I found F—— in much better health than when he left Marysville. As there was nothing to sleep *in* but a tent, and nothing to sleep *on* but the ground, and the air was black with the fleas hopping about in every direction, we concluded

to ride forward to the Berry Creek House, a ranch ten miles farther on our way, where we proposed to pass the night. . . .

Oh Mary! it makes me *shudder* when I I,9 think of the mad joy with which I saw that *rancho!* Remember that with the exception of three or four hours the night before, we had been in the saddle for nearly twenty-four hours, without refreshment. . . .

Every one that we met, congratulated us, upon not having encountered any Indians; for the paths which we followed were Indian trails, and it is said, they would have killed us for our mules and clothes. A few weeks ago, a Frenchman and his wife were murdered by them. I had thought of the circumstances when we camped, but was too sick to care what happened. They generally take women captive, however, and who knows how narrowly I escaped becoming an Indian chieftainess, and / feeding I,9 for the rest of my life upon roasted grasshoppers, acorns, and flower-seeds? By the way, the last mentioned article of food, strikes me as rather *poetical* than otherwise. . . .

Soon after we alighted, a *herd* of Indians, consisting of about a dozen men and squaws, with an unknown quantity of pappooses, the last, naked as the day they were born, crowded into the room to stare at us. It was the most amusing thing in the world, to see them finger my gloves, whip, and hat, in their intense curiosity. One of them had caught the following line of a song, "Oh! carry me back to old Martinez," with which he continued to stun our ears all the time we remained; repeating it over and over, with as much pride and joy, as a mocking bird will exhibit when he has learned a new sound.

On this occasion, I was more than ever struck, with what I have often remarked before, the extreme beauty of the *limbs* of the Indian women of California. Though for haggardness of expression, and ugliness of feature, they might have been taken for a band of Macbethian witches, a bronze statue of Cleopatra herself, never folded more beautifully rounded arms above its dusky bosom, or poised upon its pedestal, a slenderer ankle, or a more statuesque foot, than those which gleamed from beneath the dirty blankets of these wretched creatures. There was one exception, however, to the general hideousness of their faces. A girl of sixteen perhaps; with those large, magnificently lustrous, yet at the same time, soft eyes, so common in novels, so rare in real life, had shyly glided, like a dark, beautiful spirit into the corner of the room. A fringe of silken jet swept heavily upward from her dusky cheek, athwart which, the richest color came and went like flashes of lightning. Her flexible lips curved slightly away from teeth like strips of cocoanut meat, with a mocking grace infinitely bewitching. She wore a cotton chemise, disgustingly dirty, I must confess, girt about her slender waist with a crimson handkerchief; while over her night black hair, carelessly knotted beneath the rounded chin, was a purple scarf of knotted silk. Her whole appearance was picturesque in the extreme. She sat upon the ground, with her pretty, brown fingers languidly interlaced above her knee "round as a *period*," (as a certain American poet has so funnily said of a similar limb in his Diana,) and smiled up into my face, as if we were the dearest friends. . . .

I happened to take out of my pocket a paper of pins when all the women begged for some of them. This lovely child still remained silent in the posture of exquisite grace which she had so unconsciously assumed, but nevertheless, she looked as pleased as any of them, when I gave her also a row of the much coveted treasures. But I found I had got myself into business; for all the men wanted pins too; and I distributed the entire contents of the papers, ,93 which I happened to have in / my pocket, before they were satisfied; much to the amusement of F., who only laughs at what he is pleased to call my absurd interest in these poor creatures. But you know M——, I always *did* "take" to Indians; though it must be said, that those who bear that name here, have little resemblance to the glorious

forest heroes that live in the Leather Stocking Tales; and in spite of my desire to find in them something poetical and interesting, a stern regard for truth, compels me to acknowledge, that the dusky beauty above described, is the only even moderately *pretty* squaw that I have ever seen. . . .

I wish I could give you some faint idea I,94 of the majestic solitudes through which we passed; where the pine trees rise so grandly in their awful height, that they seem looking into Heaven itself. . . .

Sometimes we were compelled to cross broad plains, acres in extent, called *chaparrals*, covered with low shrubs which, leafless and barkless, stand like vegetable skeletons along the dreary waste. You cannot imagine what a weird effect these eldritch bushes had upon my mind. Of a ghastly whiteness, they at first reminded me of a plantation of antlers, and I amused myself by fancying them a herd of crouching deer; but they grew so wan and ghastly, that I began to look forward to the creeping across a *chaparral*, — (it is no easy task for the mules to wind through them,) with almost a feeling of dread.

But what a lovely sight greeted our enchanted eyes, as we stopped for a few moments on the summit of the hill leading into Rich Bar. Deep in the shadowy nooks of the far down valleys, like wasted jewels dropped from the radiant sky above, lay half a dozen blue-bosomed lagoons, glittering and gleaming and sparkling in the sunlight, as though each tiny wavelet were formed of rifted diamonds. It was worth the whole wearisome journey, danger from Indians, grizzly bears, sleeping under the stars, and all, to behold this beautiful vision. . . .

The hill leading into Rich Bar is five miles long, and as steep as you can imagine. Fancy yourself riding for this distance, along the edge of a frightful precipice, where should your mule make a misstep, you would be dashed hundreds of feet into the awful ravine below. . . .

We are boarding at present at the "Em- I,95 pire," — a huge shingle palace in the centre of Rich Bar, — which I will describe in my next letter.

*Rich Bar, East Branch of the North Fork*
*of Feather River, September 15, 1851*

I,174    Dear M. — I believe that I closed my last letter by informing you that I was safely ensconced — after all the hair-breadth escapes of my wearisome, though at the same time, delightful journey — under the magnificent roof of the "Empire," which, by the way, is *the* hotel of the place; not but that nearly every other shanty on the Bar claims the same grandiloquent title. Indeed, for that matter, California herself might be called the Hotel State, so completely is she inundated with taverns, boarding-houses, &c. The Empire is the only two-story building in town, and absolutely has a live "up-stairs." Here you will find two or three glass windows, an unknown luxury in all the other dwellings. It is built of planks of the roughest possible description; the roof, of course, is covered with canvas, which also forms the entire front of the house, on which is painted in immense capitals, the following imposing letters: "THE EMPIRE!" I will describe, as exactly as possible, this grand establishment. You first enter a large apartment, level with the street, part of which is fitted up as a bar-room, with that eternal crimson calico, which flushes the whole social life of the "Golden State," with its everlasting red — in the centre of a fluted mass of which, gleams a really elegant mirror, set off by a back-ground of decanters, cigar vases and jars of brandied fruit; the whole forming a *tout ensemble* of dazzling splendor. A table covered with a green cloth, — upon which lies a pack of monte cards, a backgammon board, and a sickening pile of "yellow kivered" literature, — with several uncomfortable looking benches, complete the furniture of this most important portion of such a place as "The Empire." The remainder of the room does duty as a shop; where velveteen and leather, flannel shirts and calico ditto — the latter starched to an appalling state of stiffness — lie cheek by jowl with hams, preserved meats, oysters and other groceries, in hopeless confusion. From the bar-room you ascend by four steps into the parlor, the floor of which is covered by a straw carpet. This room contains quite a decent looking-glass, a sofa fourteen feet long, and a foot and a half wide, painfully suggestive of an aching back — of course covered with red calico, (the sofa, *not* the back,) — a round table with a green cloth, six cane-bottom chairs, red calico curtains, a cooking stove, a rocking chair, *and* a woman and a baby, of whom more anon — the latter wearing a scarlet frock, to match the sofa and curtains. A flight of four steps leads from the parlor to the upper story; where, on each side of a narrow entry, are four eight feet by ten bed-rooms, the / floors of which are covered by straw I,175 matting. Here your eyes are again refreshed with a glittering vision of red calico curtains, gracefully festooned above wooden windows, picturesquely lattice-like. These tiny chambers are furnished with little tables covered with oil-cloth, and bedsteads so heavy that nothing short of a giant's strength could move them. Indeed, I am convinced that they were built, piece by piece, on the spot where they now stand. The entire building is lined with purple calico, alternating with a delicate blue, and the effect is really quite pretty. The floors are so very uneven, that you are always ascending a hill or descending into a valley. The doors consist of a slight frame, covered with dark blue drilling, and are hung on hinges of leather. As to the kitchen and dining-room, I leave to your vivid imagination to picture their primitiveness, merely observing, that nothing was ever more awkward and unworkmanlike than the whole tenement. It is just such a piece of carpentering as a child two years old, gifted with the strength of a man, would produce, if it wanted to play at making grown-up houses. And yet this impertinent apology for a house, cost its original owners more than eight thousand dollars. This will not be quite so surprising, when I inform you that at the time it was built, every thing had to be packed from Marysville, at a cost of forty cents a pound. Compare this with the price of freight on the railroads at home, and you will easily make an estimate of the immense outlay of money necessary to collect the materials for such an undertaking at Rich Bar. It was built by a company of gamblers, as a residence for two of those unfortunates, who make a trade — a thing of barter — of the holiest passion, when sanctified by *love*, that ever thrills the wayward heart of poor humanity. To the lasting honor of *miners* be it written, the *speculation* proved a decided failure. . . . These unhappy members of a class, to one of which, the tenderest words that Jesus ever spake, were uttered — left in a few weeks, absolutely driven away by public opinion. The disappointed gamblers sold the house to its present proprietor for a few hundred dollars. . . .

*Rich Bar, East Branch of the North Fork of Feather River, September* 20, 1851

21   I intend to-day, dear M., to be as disagreeably statistical and as praiseworthily matter-of-factish as the most dogged utilitarian could desire. I shall give you a full, true and particular account of the discovery, rise and progress of this place, with a religious adherence to *dates*, which will rather astonish your unmathematical mind. . . .Imagine a tiny valley, about eight hundred yards in length and, perhaps, thirty in width, [it was measured for my especial information,] apparently hemmed in by lofty hills, almost perpendicular, draperied to their very summits with beautiful fir trees; the blue-bosomed "Plumas," or Feather River I suppose I must call it, undulating along their base, and you have as good an idea as I can give you of the *locale* of "Barra Rica," as the Spaniards so prettily term it. . . .

22   Through the middle of Rich Bar runs the street, thickly planted with about forty tenements; among which figure round tents, square tents, plank hovels, log cabins, &c., — the residences, varying in elegance and convenience from the palatial splendor of "The Empire," down to a "local habitation," formed of pine boughs, and covered with old calico shirts.

To-day I visited the "Office;" the only one on the river. I had heard so much about it from others, as well as from F., that I really *did* expect something extra. When I entered this imposing place, the shock to my optic nerves was so great that I sank, helplessly, upon one of the benches which ran, divan-like, the whole length (ten feet!) of the building, and laughed till I cried. There was, of course, no floor; a rude nondescript in one corner, on which was ranged the medical library, consisting of half a dozen volumes, did duty as a table. The shelves, which looked like sticks snatched hastily from the wood-pile and nailed up without the least alteration, contained quite a respectable array of medicines. The white canvas window stared everybody in the face, with the interesting information painted on it, in perfect grenadiers of capitals, that this was Dr. ——'s office. . . .

During my call at the office, I was introduced to one of the *finders* of Rich Bar — a young Georgian, who afterwards gave me a full description of all the facts connected with its discovery. This unfortunate had not spoken to a woman for two years; and in the elation of his heart at the joyful event, he rushed out and invested capital in some excellent champagne, which I, on Willie's principle of "doing in Turkey as the Turkies do," assisted the company in drinking to the honor of my own arrival. I mention this, as an instance, that nothing can be done in California without the sanctifying influence of the *spirit*; and it generally appears in a much more "questionable shape" than that of sparkling wine. Mr. H. informed me, that on the twentieth of July, 1850, it was rumored at Nelson's Creek — a mining station situated at the Middle Fork of the Feather River / about eighty miles from Marysville — that one of those vague "Somebodies" — a near relation of the "They Says" — had discovered mines of a remarkable richness in a north-easterly

I,223

direction, and about forty miles from the first-mentioned place. Anxious and immediate search was made for "Somebody," but, as our western brethren say, he "wasn't thar!" But his absence could not deter the miners when once the golden rumor had been set afloat. A large company packed up their goods and chattels, generally consisting of a pair of blankets, a frying-pan, some flour, salt pork, brandy, pick-axe and shovel, and started for the new Dorado. They "traveled, and traveled, and traveled," as we used to say in the fairy stories, for nearly a week in every possible direction, when one evening, weary and discouraged, about one hundred of the party found themselves at the top of that famous hill, which figures so largely in my letters, whence the river can be distinctly seen. Half of the number concluded to descend the mountain that night, the remainder stopping on the summit until the next morning. On arriving at Rich Bar, part of the adventurers camped there, but many went a few miles further down the river. The next morning two men turned over a large stone, beneath which they found quite a sizable piece of gold. They washed a small panful of the dirt, and obtained from it two hundred and fifty-six dollars. Encouraged by this success, they commenced staking off the legal amount of ground allowed to each person for mining purposes; and, the remainder of the party having descended the hill, before night the entire bar was "claimed." In a fortnight from that time, the two men who found the first bit of gold had each taken out six thousand dollars. Two others took out thirty-three pounds of gold in eight hours; which is the best day's work that has been done on this branch of the river; the largest amount ever taken from one panful of dirt was fifteen hundred dollars. In little more than a week after its discovery, five hundred men had settled upon the bar for the summer. — Such is the wonderful alacrity with which a mining town is built. Soon after was discovered on the same side of the river — about half a mile apart, and at nearly the same distance from this place — the two

bars, "Smith" and "Indian," both very rich; also another, lying across the river, just opposite Indian, called "Missouri Bar." There are several more, all within a few miles of here, called "Frenchman's," "Taylor's," "Brown's," "The Junction," "Wyandott" and "Muggin's." But they are at present of little importance as mining stations.

Those who worked in these mines during the fall of 1850 were extremely fortunate; but, alas! the Monte fiend ruined hundreds! Shall I tell you the fate of two of the most successful of these gold hunters? From poor men, they found themselves at the end of a few weeks, absolutely rich. Elated with their good fortune, seized with a mania for Monte, in less than a year, these unfortunates, — so lately respectable and intelligent, — became a pair of drunken gamblers. One of them at this present writing, works for five dollars a day and boards himself out of that; the other actually suffers for the necessaries of life, — a too common result of scenes in the mines.

There were but few that dared to remain [1,2] in the mountains during the winter for fear of being buried in the snow; of which at that time they had a most vague idea. I have been told that in these sheltered valleys it seldom falls to the depth of more than a foot, and disappears almost invariably within a day or two. Perhaps there were three hundred that concluded to stay; of which number, two-thirds stopped on Smith's Bar, as the labor of mining there is much easier than it is here. Contrary to the general expectation, the weather was delightful until about the middle of March; it then commenced storming, and continued to snow and rain incessantly for nearly three weeks. Supposing that the rainy season had passed, hundreds had arrived on the river during the previous month. The snow, which fell several feet in depth on the mountains, rendered the trail impassable and entirely stopped the pack trains; provisions soon became scarce, and the sufferings of these unhappy men were, indeed, extreme. Some adventurous spirits, with true Yankee hardihood, forced their way through the snow to the Frenchman's ranch, and packed flour *on their backs,* for more than forty miles! The first meal that arrived sold for three dollars a pound. Many subsisted for days on nothing but barley, which is kept here to feed the pack-mules on. One unhappy individual who could not obtain even a little barley, for love or money, and had eaten nothing for three days, forced his way out to the Spanish rancho fourteen miles distant, and in less than an hour after his arrival, had devoured *twenty-seven* biscuits and a corresponding quantity of other eatables, and, of course, drinkables to match. Don't let this account alarm you. There is no danger of another famine here. They tell me that there is hardly a building in the place that has not food enough in it to last its occupants for the next two years; besides, there are two or three well-filled groceries in town.

*Rich Bar, East Branch of the North Fork*
*of Feather River, September 22, 1851*
. . . I have just returned from the funeral of poor Mrs. B., who died of peritonitis, (a common disease in this place) after an illness of four days only. . . .

Her funeral took place at ten this morning. The family reside in a log-cabin at the head of the Bar; and, although it had no window — all the light admitted, entering through an aperture where there *will* be a door when it becomes cold enough for such a luxury — yet I am told, and can easily believe that it is one of the most *comfortable* residences in the place. I observed it particularly, for it was the first log-cabin that I had ever seen. Everything in the room, though of the humblest description, was exceedingly clean and neat.

On a board, supported by two butter-tubs, was extended the body of the dead woman, covered with a sheet; by its side stood the coffin of unstained pine, lined with white cambric. You, who have alternately laughed and scolded at my provoking and inconvenient deficiency in the power of observing, will, perhaps, wonder at the minuteness of my descriptions; but I know how deeply you are interested in everything relating to California, and therefore I take pains to describe things exactly as I *see* them, hoping that thus you will obtain an idea of life in the mines, *as it is.*

The bereaved husband held in his arms a sickly babe ten months old, which was moaning piteously for its mother. The other child, a handsome, bold-looking little girl six years of age, was running gaily around the room, perfectly unconscious of her great bereavement. A sickening horror came over me, to see her every few moments, run up to her dead mother, and peep laughingly under the handkerchief, that covered her moveless face. Poor little thing! It was evident that her baby-toilet had been made by men; she had on a new calico dress, which, having no tucks in it, trailed to the floor, and gave her a most singular and dwarf-womanly appearance.

About twenty men, with the three women of the place, had assembled at the funeral. An *extempore* prayer was made, filled with all / the peculiarities usual to 1,348 that style of petition. Ah! how different from the soothing verses of the glorious burial service of the church.

As the procession started for the hill-side grave-yard — a dark cloth cover, borrowed from a neighboring monte-table, was flung over the coffin. Do not think that I mention any of these circumstances in a spirit of mockery; far from it. Every observance, usual on such occasions, that was *procurable,* surrounded this funeral. All the gold on Rich Bar could do no more; and should I die to-morrow, I should be marshaled to my mountain grave beneath the same monte-table cover pall, which shrouded the coffin of poor Mrs. B.

I almost forgot to tell you, how painfully the feelings of the assembly were shocked by the sounds of the nails — there being no screws at any of the shops — driven with a hammer into the coffin, while closing it. It seemed as if it *must* disturb the pale sleeper within. . . .

From our Log Cabin, Indian Bar,
October 7, 1851

II,91    You will perchance be surprised, dear M.,
to receive a letter from me dated Indian,
instead of Rich Bar; but as many of F's most
intimate friends reside at this settlement,
he concluded to build his log cabin here.

Solemn council was held upon the ways
and means of getting "Dame Shirley" to
her new home. The general opinion was,
that she had better mount her fat mule and
ride over the hill, as all agreed it was very
doubtful whether she would be able to cross
the logs and jump the rocks, which would
bar her way by the water-passage. But that
obstinate little personage, who has always
been haunted with a passionate desire to
do every thing which people said she could
*not* do, made up her wilful mind immediately to go by the river. Behold then, the
"Dame" on her winding way, escorted by a
deputation of Indian Barian's, which had
come up for that important purpose.

It is impossible, my sister, for any power
of language over which I have command,
to convey to you an idea of the wild grandeur and the awful magnificence of the
scenery in this vicinity. This Fork of the
Feather river, comes down very much "as
the water does at Lodore;" now gliding
along with a liquid measure, like a river in
a dream, and anon bursting into a thousand
glittering foam-beads over the huge rocks,
which rise dark, solemn and weird-like, in
its midst. The crossings are formed of logs,
often moss-grown. Only think how charm-
ingly picturesque, to eyes wearied with the
costly masonry, or carpentry of the bridges
at home. At every step gold diggers or their
operations greet your vision. Sometimes in
the form of a dam; sometimes in that of a
river, turned slightly from its channel, to
aid the indefatigable gold hunters in their
mining projects. Now, on the side of a hill
you will see a long-tom, — a huge machine
invented to facilitate the separation of the
ore from its native element; or a man busily
engaged in working a rocker, — a much
smaller and simpler machine, used for the
same object; or more primitive still, some

solitary prospecter, with a pan of dirt in his
hands, which he is carefully washing at the
water's edge, to see if he can "get the color,"
as it is technically phrased, which means
literally the smallest particle of gold.

As we approached Indian Bar, the path
led several times fearfully near deep holes,
from which the laborers were gathering
their yellow harvest; and "Dame Shirley's"
small head swam dizzily as she crept shud-
deringly by.

The first thing which attracted my attention, as my new home came in view, was
the blended blue, red and white of the
American banner, / undulating like a many-  II
colored snake amid the lofty verdure of the
cedars which garland the brown brow of
the hill behind our cabin. This flag was
suspended on the Fourth of July last, by a
patriotic sailor, who climbed to the top of
the tree to which he attached it, cutting
away the branches as he descended, until it
stood among its stately brethren, a beautiful
moss-wreathed Liberty pole, flinging to the
face of Heaven the glad colors of the Free.

When I attempt, dear M., to describe one
of these spots to you, I regret more than
ever, the ill-health of my childhood, which
prevented my obtaining any degree of ex-
cellence in sketching from Nature. Had it
not been for that interruption to my artistic
education, I might, with a few touches of
the pencil or the brush, give you the place
and its surroundings. But alas! my feeble
pen will convey to you a very faint idea of
its savage beauty.

This bar is so small, that it seems impossible that the tents and cabins scattered over
it can amount to a dozen; there are, however, twenty in all, including those formed
of calico shirts and pine boughs. With the
exception of the paths leading to the different tenements, the entire level is covered
with mining holes, on the edges of which
lie the immense piles of dirt and stones
which have been removed from the excavations. There is a deep pit in front of our
cabin and another at the side of it; though
they are not worked, as when "prospected,"
they did not "yield the color."

Not a spot of verdure is to be seen on this place; but the glorious hills rising on every side vested in foliage of living green, make ample amends for the sterility of the tiny level upon which we camp. The surrounding scenery is infinitely more charming than that of Rich Bar. The river in hue of a vivid emerald — as if it reflected the hue of the fir trees above, — bordered with a band of dark red, caused by the streams flowing into it from the different sluices, ditches, long-toms, etc., which meander from the hill just back of the Bar, wanders musically along. Across the river and in front of us, rises nearly perpendicularly, a group of mountains, the summits of which are broken into many beautifully cut conical and pyramidal peaks. At the foot and left of these eminences, and a little below our Bar, lies Missouri Bar, which is reached from this spot by a log bridge. Around the latter, the river curves in the shape of a crescent and singularly enough, the mountain rising behind this bend in the stream, outlines itself against the lustrous Heaven, in a shape as exact and perfect as the moon herself in her first quarter. Within one horn of this crescent, the water is a mass of foam sparkles, and it plays upon the rocks which line its bed an everlasting dirge suggestive of the "grand forever" of the ocean.

At present the sun does not condescend to shine upon Indian Bar at all, and the old settlers tell me that he will not smile upon us for the next three months; but he nestles lovingly in patches of golden glory, all along the brows of the different hills around us, and now and then stoops to kiss the topmost wave on the opposite shore of the Rio de las Plumas.

The first artificial elegance which attracts your vision, is a large rag / shanty, roofed, however, with a rude kind of shingles, over the entrance of which is painted in red capitals, ("to what base uses do we come at last,") the name of the great Humboldt spelt without the *d*. This is the only hotel in this vicinity, and as there is a really excellent bowling alley attached to it, and the bar-room has a floor upon which the

miners can dance, and, above all, a cook who can play the violin, it is very popular. But the clinking of glasses, and the swaggering air of some of the drinkers, reminds us that it is no place for a lady, so we will pass through the dining room and emerging at the kitchen, in a step or two reach our log cabin. Enter my dear; you are perfectly welcome; besides, we could not keep you out if we would, as there is not even a latch on the canvas door, though we really intend in a day or two to have a hook put on to it.

The room into which we have just entered is about twenty feet square. It is lined over the top with white cotton cloth, the breadths of which being sewed together only in spots, stretch gracefully apart in many places, giving one a birds-eye view of the shingles above. The sides are hung with a gaudy chintz, which I consider a perfect marvel of calico printing. The artist seems to have exhausted himself on *roses*; from the largest cabbage, down to the tiniest Burgundy, he has arranged them in every possible variety of wreath, garland, bouquet, and single flower; they are of all stages of growth, from earliest budhood up to the ravishing beauty of the "last rose of summer." Nor has he confined himself to the colors usually worn by this lovely plant; but, with the daring of a great genius soaring above nature, worshiping the ideal rather than the real, he has painted them brown, purple, green, black and blue. It would need a floral catalogue to give you the names of *all* the varieties which bloom upon the calico; but, judging by the shapes — which really are much like the originals — I can swear to moss roses, Burgundies, York and Lancaster, tea roses, and multifloras.

A curtain of the above described chintz, (I shall hem it at the first opportunity), divides off a portion of the room, behind which stands a bedstead that in ponderosity leaves the Empire couches far behind. But before I attempt the furniture let me finish describing the cabin itself.

The fireplace is built of stones and mud, the chimney finished off with alternate layers of rough sticks and this same rude mortar; contrary to the usual custom, it is built inside, as it was thought that arrangement would make the room more comfortable; and you may imagine the queer appearance of this unfinished pile of stones, mud and sticks. The mantle-piece — remember that on this portion of a great building, some artists, by their exquisite workmanship, have become world renowned — is formed of a beam of wood, covered with strips of tin procured from cans, upon which still remain in black hieroglyphics, the names of the different eatables which they formerly contained. Two smooth stones — how delightfully primitive — do duty as fire-dogs. I suppose that it would be no more than civil to call a hole two feet square in one side of the room, a window, although it is as yet guiltless of glass. F. tried to coax the proprietor of the Empire II,94 to let him / have a window from that pine and canvas palace; but he of course declined, as to part with it would really inconvenience himself; so F. has sent to Marysville for some glass, though it is the general opinion that the snow will render the trail impassable for mules before we can get it. In this case, we shall tack up a piece of cotton cloth, and should it chance at any time to be very cold, hang a blanket before the opening. At present the weather is so mild that it is pleasanter as it is, though we have a fire in the mornings and evenings, more, however, for luxury than because we really need it. For my part, I almost hope that we shall not be able to get any glass, for you will perhaps remember that it was a pet habit of mine, in my own room, to sit by a great fire in the depth of winter, with my window open.

One of our friends had nailed up an immense quantity of unhemmed cotton cloth — very coarse — in front of this opening, and as he evidently prided himself upon the elegant style in which he had arranged the drapery, it went to my heart to take it down, and suspend in its place some pretty blue linen curtains which I had brought from the valley. My toilet table is formed of a trunk elevated upon two claret cases, and

by draping it with some more of the blue linen neatly fringed, it really will look quite handsome, and when I have placed upon it my rosewood work-box, a large cushion of crimson brocade, some Chinese ornaments of exquisitely carved ivory, and two or three Bohemian glass cologne stands, it would not disgrace a lady's chamber at home.

The looking-glass is one of those which come in paper cases for doll's houses; how different from the full length Psyches so almost indispensable to a dressing-room in the States.

The wash-stand is another trunk covered with a towel, upon which you will see for bowl, a large vegetable dish, for ewer, a common sized dining pitcher; near this, upon a small cask, is placed a pail, which is daily filled with water from the river. I brought with me from Marysville a handsome carpet, a hair mattress, pillows, a profusion of bed linen, quilts, blankets, towels, &c., so that in spite of the oddity of most of my furniture, I am in reality as thoroughly comfortable here as I could be in the most elegant palace.

We have four chairs which were brought from the Empire. I seriously proposed having three-legged stools; with my usual desire for symmetry I thought that they would be more in keeping; but as I was told that it would be a great deal of trouble to get them made, I was fain to put up with mere chairs; so you see that even in the land of gold itself, one cannot have everything that she desires. An ingenious individual in the neighborhood, blessed with a large bump for mechanics and good nature, made me a sort of wide bench, which covered with a neat plaid, looks quite sofa-like. A little pine table with oil-cloth tacked over the top of it, stands in one corner of the room, upon which are arranged the chess and cribbage boards. There is a larger one for dining purposes, and as unpainted pine has always a most dreary look, F. went every where in search of oil-cloth for it, but there was none on any of the bars; at last "Ned," the Humboldt Paganini, remembered two old monte table covers, which had been thrown aside as useless. I received them 95 thankfully, and with my / planning and Ned's mechanical genius, we patched up quite a respectable covering; to be sure, the ragged condition of the primitive material, compelled us to have at one end an extra border, but that only agreeably relieved the monotony. I must mention that the floor is so uneven that no article of furniture gifted with four legs pretends to stand upon but three at once, so that the chairs, tables, etc., remind you constantly of a dog with a sore foot.

At each end of the mantle-piece is arranged a candlestick, not, much to my regret, a block of wood with a hole in the centre of it, but a real brittania-ware candlestick; the space between is gaily ornamented with F.'s meerschaum, several styles of clay pipes, cigars, cigaritos, and every procurable variety of tobacco; for you know the aforesaid individual is a perfect devotee of the Indian weed. If I should give you a month of Sundays you would never guess what we use in lieu of a bookcase, so I will put you out of your misery by informing you instantly that it is nothing more nor less than a candle-box, which contains the library, consisting of a bible and prayer-book, Shakespeare, Spenser, Coleridge, Shelley, Keats, Lowell's Fable for Critics, Walton's Complete Angler and some Spanish books — spiritual instead of material lights, you see.

There, my dainty Lady Molly, I have given you, I fear, a wearisomely minute description of my new home. How would you like to winter in such an abode? in a place where there are no newspapers, no churches, lectures, concerts or theaters; no fresh books, no shopping, calling nor gossiping little tea-drinkings; no parties, no balls, no picnics, no *tableaux*, no charades, no latest fashions, no daily mail, (we have an express once a month,) no promenades, no rides nor drives; no vegetables but potatoes and onions, no milk, no eggs, no *nothing*? Now I expect to be very happy here. This strange, odd life, fascinates me. As for churches, "the groves were God's first tem-

ples," "and for the strength of the hills, the Swiss mountains bless him;" and as to books, I read Shakespeare, David, Spenser, Paul, Coleridge, Burns and Shelley which are never old. In good sooth I fancy that nature intended me for an Arab or some other Nomadic barbarian, and by mistake my soul got packed up in a christianized set of bones and muscles. How I shall ever be able to content myself to live in a decent, proper, well-behaved house, where toilet tables are toilet tables, and not an ingenious combination of trunk and claret cases, where lanterns are not broken bottles, book cases not candle boxes, and trunks not wash-stands, but every article of furniture, instead of being a make-shift, is its own useful and elegantly finished self. I am sure I do not know, however, when too much appalled at the hum-drumish prospect, I console myself with the beautiful promises, "that sufficient unto the day is the evil thereof," and "as thy day is, so shall thy strength be," and trust that when it is again my lot to live amid the refinements and luxuries of civilization, that I shall endure them with becoming philosophy and fortitude.

*From our Log Cabin, Indian Bar,*
*November 25, 1851*

Nothing of importance has happened II,274 since I last wrote you, except that I have become a *mineress*; that is, if the having washed a pan of dirt with my own hands, and procured therefrom three dollars and twenty-five cents in gold dust, (which I shall inclose in this letter), will entitle me to the name. I can truly say, with the blacksmith's apprentice at the close of his first day's work at the anvil, that "I am sorry I learned the trade;" for I wet my feet, tore my dress, spoilt a pair of new gloves, nearly froze my fingers, got an awful headache, took cold and lost a valuable breastpin, in this my labor of love. After such melancholy self-sacrifice on my part, I trust you will duly prize my gift. I can assure you that it is the last golden handiwork you will ever receive from "Dame Shirley."

*Apropos,* of lady gold-washers in general, — it is a common habit with people residing in towns in the vicinity of the "Diggings," to make up pleasure parties to those places. Each woman of the company will exhibit on her return, at least twenty dollars of the *oro,* which she will gravely inform you she has just "panned out" from a single basinful of the soil. This, of course, gives strangers a very erroneous idea of the average richness of auriferous dirt. I myself thought, (now don't laugh,) that one had but to saunter gracefully along romantic streamlets, on sunny afternoons, with a parasol and white kid gloves, perhaps, and to stop now and then to admire the scenery, and carelessly rinse out a small panful of yellow sand, (without detriment to the white kids, however, so easy did I fancy the whole process to be), in order to fill one's workbag with the most beautiful and rare specimens of the precious mineral. Since I have been here, I have discovered my mistake, and also the secret of the brilliant success of former gold-washeresses.

The miners are in the habit of flattering the vanity of their fair visitors, by scattering a handful of "salt" (which, strange to say, is *exactly* the color of gold dust, and has the remarkable property of often bringing to light very curious lumps of the ore) through the dirt before the dainty fingers touch it; and the dear creatures go home with their treasures, firmly believing that mining is the prettiest pastime in the world.

I had no idea of permiting such a costly joke to be played upon me; so I said but little of my desire to "go through the motions" of gold washing, until one day, when, as I passed a deep hole in which several men were at work, my companion II,275 requested the owner to fill / a small pan, which I had in my hand, with dirt from the bedrock. This request was, of course, granted, and, the treasure having been conveyed to the edge of the river, I succeeded, after much awkward maneuvering on my own part, and considerable assistance from friend H., an experienced miner, in gathering together the above specified sum [$3.25].

All the diggers of our acquaintance say that it is an excellent "prospect," even to come from the bedrock, where, naturally, the richest dirt is found. To be sure, there are now and then "lucky strikes"; such, for instance, as that mentioned in a former letter, where a person took out of a single basinful of soil, two hundred and fifty-six dollars. But such luck is as rare as the winning of a hundred thousand dollar prize in a lottery. We are acquainted with many here whose gains have *never* amounted to much more than "wages"; that is, from six to eight dollars a day. And a "claim" which yields a man a steady income of ten dollars *per diem,* is considered as very valuable. . . .

*From our Log Cabin, Indian Bar,*
*December 15, 1851*

I little thought, dear M., that here, with II,3 the "green watching hills" as witnesses, amid a solitude so grand and lofty that it seems as if the faintest whisper of passion must be hushed by its holy stillness, I should have to relate the perpetration of one of those fearful deeds, which, were it for no other peculiarity than its startling suddenness — so utterly at variance with all *civilized* law — must make our beautiful California appear to strangers rather as a hideous phantom, than the flower-wreathed reality which she is. . . .

The facts in this sad case are as follows: Last fall, two men were arrested by their partners, on suspicion of having stolen from them eighteen hundred dollars in gold dust. The evidence was not sufficient to convict them, and they were acquitted. They were tried before a meeting of the miners — as at that time the law did not even *pretend* to wave its scepter over this place.

The prosecutors still believed them guilty, and fancied that the gold was hidden in a "coyote hole," near the camp from which it had been taken. They therefore watched the place narrowly while the suspected men remained on the Bar. They made no discoveries, however; and soon after the trial, the acquitted persons left the mountains for Marysville.

A few weeks ago, one of these men returned, and has spent most of the time since his arrival in loafing about the different bar-rooms upon the river. He is said to have been constantly intoxicated. As soon as the losers of the gold heard of his return, they bethought themselves of the "coyote hole," and placed about its entrance some brushwood and stones, in such a manner that no one could go into it without disturbing the arrangement of them. In the meanwhile the thief settled at Rich Bar, and pretended that he was in search of some gravel ground for mining purposes.

A few mornings ago, he returned to his boarding place — which he had left some hour earlier — with a spade in his hand, and as he laid it down, carelessly observed that he had "been out prospecting." The losers of the gold went, immediately after break-
,352 fast, as they had / been in the habit of doing, to see if all was right at the "coyote hole." On this fatal day, they saw that the entrance had been disturbed, and going in, they found upon the ground, a money belt which had apparently just been cut open. Armed with this evidence of guilt, they confronted the suspected person and sternly accused him of having the gold in his possession. Singularly enough, he did not attempt a denial, but said that if they would not bring him to a trial, (which of course they promised) he would give it up immediately. He then informed them that they would find it beneath the blankets of his *bunk*, — as those queer shelves on which miners sleep, ranged one above another, somewhat like the berths of the ship, are generally called. There, sure enough, were six hundred dollars of the missing money, and the unfortunate wretch declared that his partner had taken the remainder to the States.

By this time the exciting news had spread all over the Bar. A meeting of the miners was immediately convened, the unhappy man taken into custody, a jury chosen, and a judge, lawyer, etc., appointed. Whether the men, who had just regained a portion of their missing property, made any objec-

tions to the proceedings which followed, I know not; if they had done so, however, it would have made no difference, as the *people* had taken the matter entirely out of their hands.

At one o'clock, so rapidly was the trial conducted, the judge charged the jury, and gently insinuated that they could do no less than to bring in with their verdict of guilty, a sentence of *death!* Perhaps you know that when a trial is conducted without the majesty of the law, the jury are compelled to decide, not only upon the guilt of the prisoner, but the mode of his punishment also. After a few minutes' absence, the twelve men who had consented to burden their souls with a responsibility so fearful, returned, and the foreman handed to the judge a paper, from which he read the will of the *people*, as follows: "That William Brown, convicted of stealing, etc., should, in *one hour* from that time, be hung by the neck until he was dead."

By the persuasions of some men more mildly disposed, they granted him a respite of *three hours*, to prepare for his sudden entrance into eternity. He employed the time in writing in his native language (he is a Swede) to some friends in Stockholm; God help them when that fatal post shall arrive; for no doubt *he*, also, although a criminal, was fondly garnered in many a loving heart.

He had exhibited during the trial, the utmost recklessness and *nonchalance*, had drank many times in the course of the day, and when the rope was placed about his neck, was evidently much intoxicated. All at once, however, he seemed startled into a consciousness of the awful reality of his position, and requested a few moments for prayer.

The execution was conducted by the jury, and was performed by throwing the cord, one end of which was attached to the neck of the prisoner, across the limb of a tree standing outside of the Rich Bar grave-yard; when all, who felt disposed to engage in so revolting a task, lifted the poor wretch from the ground, in the most awk-

ward manner possible. The whole affair,
II,353 indeed, was a piece of cruel / butchery,
though *that* was not intentional, but arose
from the ignorance of those who made the
preparations. In truth, life was only crushed
out of him, by hauling the writhing body
up and down several times in succession,
by the rope which was wound round a large
bough of his green-leafed gallows. Almost
everybody was surprised at the severity of
the sentence; and many, with their hands
on the cord, did not believe even *then*, that
it would be carried into effect, but thought
that at the last moment, the jury would
release the prisoner and substitute a milder
punishment. . . .

The body of the criminal was allowed
to hang for some hours after the execution.
It had commenced storming in the earlier
part of the evening; and when those, whose
business it was to inter the remains, arrived
at the spot, they found them enwrapped in
a soft, white shroud of feathery snow-flakes,
as if pitying Nature had tried to hide from
the offended face of heaven, the cruel
deed which her mountain children had
committed.

I have heard no one approve of this
affair. It seems to have been carried on
entirely by the more reckless part of the
community. There is no doubt, however,
that they seriously *thought* they were doing
right, for many of them are kind and
sensible men. They firmly believed that
such an example was absolutely necessary
for the protection of this community. . . .

You must not confound this miner's
judgment with the doings of the noble
*Vigilance Committee* of San Francisco.
They are almost totally different in their
organization and manner of proceeding.
The Vigilance Committee had become
absolutely necessary for the protection of
society. It was composed of the best and
wisest men in the city. They used their
powers with a moderation unexampled in
II,354 his-/tory, and they laid it down with a calm
and quiet readiness which was absolutely
sublime, when they found that legal justice
had again resumed that course of stern,

unflinching duty which should always be
its characteristic. They took ample time for
a thorough investigation of all the circumstances relating to the criminals who fell
into their hands; and in *no* case have they
hung a man, who had not been proved
beyond the shadow of a doubt, to have
committed at least *one* robbery in which
life had been endangered, if not absolutely
taken. . . .

*From our Log Cabin, Indian Bar,*
*March 15, 1852*

All along the side of the hill, rising III,1
behind the Bar, and on the latter also,
glance spots of azure and crimson, in the
forms of blue and red-shirted miners,
bending steadily over pick-axe and shovel;
reminding one involuntarily of the muck-
gatherer in "Pilgrim's Progress." But, no,
that is an unjust association of ideas; for
many of these men are toiling thus wearily
for laughing-lipped children, calm-browed
wives, or saintly mothers, gathering around
the household hearth, in some far-away
country. Even among the few now remaining on the river, there are wanderers from
the whole broad earth; and, O! what a
world of poetic recollection is suggested by
their living presence! From happiest homes,
and such luxuriant lands, has the golden
magnet drawn its victims. From those palm-
girdled isles of the Pacific, which Melville's
gifted pen has consecrated to such beautiful
romance; from Indies, blazing through the
dim past with funeral pyres, upon whose
perfumed / flame, ascended to God, the III,2
chaste souls of her devoted wives; from the
grand old woods of classic Greece, haunted
by nymph and satyr, naiad and grace,
grape-crowned Bacchus and beauty-zoned
Venus; from the polished heart of artificial
Europe, from the breezy backwoods of
young America, from the tropical languor
of Asian Savannah; from *every* spot shining
through the rosy light of beloved old fables,
or consecrated by lofty deeds of heroism or
devotion, or shrined in our heart of hearts,
as the sacred home of some great or gifted
one, they gather to the golden harvest.

You will hear in the same day, almost at the same time, the lofty melody of the Spanish language, the piquant polish of the French, (which, though not a *musical* tongue, is the most *useful* of them all,) the silver, changing clearness of the Italian, the harsh gangle of the German, the hissing precision of the English, the liquid sweetness of the Kanaka, and the sleep-inspiring languor of the East Indian. To complete the catalogue, there is the *native* Indian, with his guttural vocabulary of twenty words! When I hear these sounds so strangely different, and look at the speakers, I fancy them a living polyglot of the languages, a perambulating picture gallery, illustrative of national variety in form and feature.

By the way, speaking of languages, nothing is more amusing, than to observe the different styles, in which the generality of the Americans talk *at* the unfortunate Spaniard. In the first place, many of them really believe, that when they have learned *sabe* and *vamos*, (two words which they seldom use in the right place,) *poco tiempo*, *si*, and *bueno*, (the last they will persist in pronouncing *whayno*,) they have the whole of the glorious Castilian at their tongue's end. Some, however, eschew the above words entirely, and innocently fancy, that by splitting the tympanum of an unhappy foreigner, in screaming forth their sentences in good solid English, they can be surely understood; others, at the imminent risk of dislocating their own limbs and the jaws of their listeners, by the laughs which their efforts elicit, make the most excruciatingly grotesque gestures, and think that *that* is speaking Spanish. The majority, however, place a most beautiful and touching faith in *broken English*, and when they murder it, with the few words of Castilian quoted above, are firmly convinced, that it is nothing but their "ugly dispositions" which makes the Spaniards pretend not to understand them. . . .

219  It is certainly most amusing, to hear of the different plans which the poor miners invented to pass the time during the trying season of rains. Of course, poker and euchre, whist and nine-pins, to say nothing of monte and faro, are now in constant requisition. But as a person would starve to death on *toujours des perdrix*, so a man cannot *always* be playing cards. Some *literary* bipeds, I have been told, reduced to the last degree of intellectual destitution, in a beautiful spirit of self-martyrdom, betook themselves to blue blankets, bunks and Ned Buntline's novels. And one day an unhappy youth went pen-mad, and in a melancholy fit of authorship wrote a thrilling account of our dreadful situation, which, directed to the editor of a Marysville paper, was sealed up in a keg and set adrift, and is at this moment, no doubt, stranded, high and dry, in the streets of Sacramento, for it is generally believed, that the cities of the plain have been under water during the storm. The chief amusement, however, has been the raffling of gold rings. There is a silversmith here, who, like the rest of the miserable inhabitants, having nothing to do, discovered that he could make gold rings. Of course every person must have a specimen of his workmanship, and the next thing was to raffle it off. The winner generally repeating the operation. Nothing was done or talked of for some days, but this important business.

I have one of these rings, which is really very beautifully finished, and, although, perhaps at home, it would look vulgar, there is a sort of massive and barbaric grandeur about it, which seems well-suited to our wild life of the hills. . . .

*From our Log Cabin, Indian Bar,*
*April 10, 1852*

I have been haunted all day, my dear M., III,305 with an intense ambition to write you a letter, which shall be dreadfully commonplace and severely utilitarian in its style and contents. . . .

In the first place, then, as to the discovery III,306 of gold. In California, at least, it must be confessed, that in this particular, science appears to be completely at fault; — or, as an intelligent and well-educated miner remarked to us the other day, "I maintain that science is the blindest guide that one could have on a gold-finding expedition. Those men, who judge by the appearance of the soil, and depend upon geological calculations, are invariably disappointed, while the ignorant adventurer, who digs just for the sake of digging, is almost sure to be successful." I suppose that the above observation is quite correct, as all whom we have questioned upon the subject repeat, in substance, the same thing. Wherever Geology has said that gold *must* be, there, perversely enough, it lies not; and wherever her ladyship has declared that it could *not* be, there has it oftenest garnered up in miraculous profusion the yellow splendor of its virgin beauty. It is certainly very painful to a well-regulated mind to see the irreverent contempt, shown by this beautiful mineral, to the dictates of science; but what better can one expect from the "root of all evil?" As well as can be ascertained, the most lucky of the mining Columbuses, have been ignorant sailors; and foreigners, I fancy, are more successful than Americans.

Our countrymen are the most discontented of mortals. They are always longing for "big strikes." If a "claim" is paying them a steady income, by which, if they pleased, they could lay up more in a month, than they could accumulate in a year at home, still, they are dissatisfied, and, in most cases, will wander off in search of better "diggings." There are hundreds now pursuing this foolish course, who, if they had stopped where they first "camped," would now have been rich men. Sometimes, a company of these wanderers will find itself upon a bar, where a few pieces of the precious metal III,307 lie / scattered upon the surface of the ground; of course they immediately "prospect" it, which is accomplished, by "panning out" a few basinsful of the soil. If it "pays," they "claim" the spot, and build their shanties; the news spreads that wonderful "diggings" have been discovered at such a place, — the monte-dealers, those worse than fiends, rush vulture-like upon the scene and erect a round tent, where,

in gambling, drinking, swearing and fighting, the *many* reproduce Pandemonium in more than its original horror, while a *few* honestly and industriously commence digging for gold, and lo! as if a fairy's wand had been waved above the bar, a full-grown mining town hath sprung into existence.

But first, let me explain to you the "claiming" system. As there are no State laws upon the subject, each mining community is permitted to make its own. Here, they have decided that no man may "claim" an area of more than forty feet square. This he "stakes off" and puts a notice upon it, to the effect that he "holds" it for mining purposes. If he does not choose to "work it" immediately, he is obliged to renew the notice every ten days; for without this precaution, any other person has a right to "jump it," that is, to take it from him. There are many ways of evading the above law. For instance, an individual can "hold" as many "claims" as he pleases, if he keeps a man at work in each, for this workman represents the original owner. I am told, however, that the laborer, himself, can "jump" the "claim" of the very man who employs him, if he pleases so to do. This is seldom, if ever, done; the person who is willing to be hired, generally prefers to receive the six dollars *per diem*, of which he is *sure* in any case, to running the risk of a "claim" not proving valuable. After all, the "holding of claims" by proxy is considered rather as a carrying out of the spirit of the law, than as an evasion of it. But there are many ways of *really* outwitting this rule, though I cannot stop now to relate them, which give rise to innumerable arbitrations, and nearly every Sunday, there is a "miners' meeting" connected with this subject.

Having got our gold mines discovered, and "claimed," I will try to give you a faint idea of how they "work" them. Here, in the mountains, the labor of excavation is extremely difficult, on account of the immense rocks which form a large portion of the soil. Of course, no man can "work out" a "claim" alone. For that reason, and also

for the same that makes partnerships desir-
able, they congregate in companies of four
or six, generally designating themselves by
the name of the place from whence the
majority of the members have emigrated;
as for example, the "Illinois," "Bunker Hill,"
"Bay State," etc., companies. In many
places the surface-soil, or in mining-phrase,
the "top dirt," "pays" when worked in a
"Long Tom." This machine, (I have never
been able to discover the derivation of its
name,) is a trough, generally about twenty
feet in length, and eight inches in depth,
formed of wood, with the exception of six
feet at one end, called the "riddle," (query,
why riddle?) which is made of sheet-iron,
perforated with holes about the size of a
large marble. Underneath this cullender-
like portion of the "long-tom," is placed
08 another trough, / about ten feet long, the
sides six inches perhaps in height, which
divided through the middle by a slender
slat, is called the "riffle-box." It takes several
persons to manage, properly, a "long-tom."
Three or four men station themselves with
spades, at the head of the machine, while
at the foot of it, stands an individual armed
"wid de shovel and de hoe." The spadesmen
throw in large quantities of the precious
dirt, which is washed down to the "riddle"
by a stream of water leading into the "long-
tom" through wooden gutters or "sluices."
When the soil reaches the "riddle," it is
kept constantly in motion by the man with
the hoe. Of course, by this means, all the
dirt and gold escapes through the perfora-
tions into the "riffle-box" below, one com-
partment of which is placed just beyond the
"riddle." Most of the dirt washes over the
sides of the "riffle-box," but the gold being
so astonishingly heavy remains safely at the
bottom of it. When the machine gets too
full of stones to be worked easily, the man
whose business it is to attend to them
throws them out with his shovel, looking
carefully among them as he does so for any
pieces of gold, which may have been too
large to pass through the holes of the
"riddle." I am sorry to say that he generally
loses his labor. At night they "pan out" the

gold, which has been collected in the "riffle-
box" during the day. Many of the miners
decline washing the "top dirt" at all, but
try to reach as quickly as possible the "bed-
rock," where are found the richest deposits
of gold. The river is supposed to have
formerly flowed over this "bed-rock," in the
"crevices" of which, it left, as it passed
away, the largest portions of the so eagerly
sought for ore. The group of mountains
amidst which we are living is a spur of the
Sierra Nevada; and the "bed-rock," (which
in this vicinity is of slate) is said to run
through the entire range, lying, in distance
varying from a few feet to eighty or ninety,
beneath the surface of the soil. On Indian
Bar, the "bed-rock" falls in almost perpendicular "benches," while at Rich Bar, the
friction of the river has formed it into large,
deep basins, in which the gold, instead of
being found, as you would naturally suppose, in the bottom of it, lies for the most
part, just below the rim. A good-natured
individual bored *me*, and tired *himself*, in
a hopeless attempt to make me comprehend
that this was only a necessary consequence
of the under-current of the water; but with
my usual stupidity upon such matters, I got
but a vague idea from his scientific explanation, and certainly shall not mystify *you*,
with my confused notions thereupon.

When a company wish to reach the bed
rock as quickly as possible, they "sink a
shaft," (which is nothing more nor less
than digging a well,) until they "strike" it.
They then commence "drifting coyote
holes" (as they call them) in search of
"crevices," which, as I told you before, often
pay immensely. These "coyote holes" sometimes extend hundreds of feet into the side
of the hill. Of course they are obliged to
use lights in working them. They generally
proceed, until the air is so impure as to
extinguish the lights, when they return to
the entrance of the excavation, and commence another, perhaps close to it. When
they think that a "coyote hole" has been
faithfully "worked," they "clean it up,"
which is done by scraping the surface of
the "bed / rock" with a knife, — lest by III,309

chance they have overlooked a "crevice," — and they are often richly rewarded for this precaution.

Now I must tell you how those having "claims" on the hills procure the water for washing them. The expense of raising it in any way from the river, is too enormous to be thought of for a moment. In most cases it is brought from ravines in the mountains. A company, to which a friend of ours belongs, has dug a ditch about a foot in width and depth, and more than three miles in length, which is fed in this way. I wish that you could see this ditch. I never beheld a NATURAL streamlet more exquisitely beautiful. It undulates over the mossy roots, and the gray, old rocks, like a capricious snake, singing all the time a low song with the "liquidest murmur," and one might almost fancy it the airy and coquettish Undine herself. When it reaches the top of the hill, the sparkling thing is divided into five or six branches, each one of which supplies one, two, or three "long-toms." There is an extra one, called the "waste-ditch," leading to the river, into which the water is shut off at night and on Sundays. This "race" (another and peculiar name for it) has already cost the company more than five thousand dollars. They sell the water to others at the following rates: Those that have the first use of it pay ten per cent. upon all the gold that they take out. As the water runs off from their machine, (it now goes by the elegant name of "tailings,") it is taken by a company lower down; and as it is not worth so much as when it was clear, the latter pay but seven per cent. If any others wish the "tailings," now still less valuable than at first, they pay four per cent. on all the gold which they take out, be it much or little. The water companies are constantly in trouble, and the arbitrations on that subject are very frequent.

I think that I gave you a vague idea of "fluming" in a former letter; I will not, therefore, repeat it here, but will merely mention, that the numerous "fluming" companies have already commenced their extensive operations upon the river.

As to the "rockers," so often mentioned in story and in song, I have not spoken of them since I commenced this letter. The truth is, that I have seldom seen them used, though hundreds are lying ownerless along the banks of the river. I suppose that other machines are better adapted to mining operations in the mountains.

Gold mining is Nature's great lottery scheme. A man may work in a claim for many months, and be poorer at the end of the time than when he commenced; or he may "take out" thousands in a few hours. It is a mere matter of chance. A friend of ours, a young Spanish surgeon from Guatemala, a person of intelligence and education, told us that, after "working a claim" for six months, he had taken out but six ounces.

It must be acknowledged, however, that if a person "work his claim" himself, is economical and industrious, keeps his health, and is satisfied with small gains, he is "bound" to make money. And yet, I cannot help remarking, that almost all with whom we are acquainted seem to have *lost*. Some have had their "claims" jumped; many holes which had been excavated, and prepared for working at a great / expense, caved in III, during the heavy rains of the fall and winter. Often after a company has spent an immense deal of time and money in "sinking a shaft," the water from the springs, (the greatest obstacle which the miner has to contend with in this vicinity) rushes in so fast, that it is impossible to work in them, or to contrive any machinery to keep it out, and for that reason only, men have been compelled to abandon places where they were at the very time "taking out" hundreds of dollars a day. If a fortunate or an unfortunate (which shall I call him?) *does* happen to make a "big strike," he is almost sure to fall into the hands of the professed gamblers, who soon relieve him of all care of it. They have not troubled the Bar much during the winter, but as the spring opens, they flock in like ominous birds of prey. Last week one left here, after a stay of four days, with over a thousand dollars of the hard-earned gold of the miners. But enough of these best-beloved of Beelzebub, so infinitely worse than the robber or murderer; — for surely it would be kinder to take a man's life, than to poison him with the fatal passion for gambling.

Perhaps you would like to know what class of men is most numerous in the mines. As well as I can judge, there are upon this river as many foreigners as Americans. The former, with a few exceptions, are extremely ignorant and degraded; though we have the pleasure of being acquainted with three or four Spaniards of the highest education and accomplishments. Of the Americans, the majority are of the better class of mechanics. Next to these, in number, are the sailors and the farmers. There are a few merchants and steamboat-clerks, three or four physicians, and one lawyer. We have no ministers, though fourteen miles from here there is a "Rancho," kept by a man of distinguished appearance, an accomplished monte-dealer and horse-jockey, who is *said* to have been — in the States — a preacher of the Gospel. I know not if this be true; but at any rate, such things are not uncommon in California.

I have spun this letter out until my head aches dreadfully. How tiresome it is to write *sensible* (?) things! But I have one comfort, — though my epistle may not be interesting, you will not deny, dear M., that I have achieved my ambition of making it both commonplace and utilatory.

,354

*From our Log Cabin, Indian Bar,*
*May 1, 1852*

,355  A few evenings ago, a Spaniard was stabbed by an American. It seems that the presumptuous foreigner had the impertinence, to ask very humbly and meekly that most noble representative of the stars and stripes, if the latter would pay him a few dollars which he had owed him for some time. His high mightiness, the Yankee, was not going to put up with any such impertinence, and the poor Spaniard received, for answer, several inches of cold steel in his breast, which inflicted a very dangerous wound. Nothing was done, and very little was said about this atrocious affair.

At Rich Bar they have passed a set of resolutions for the guidance of the inhabitants during the summer; one of which is to the effect that no foreigner shall work in the mines on that Bar. This has caused nearly all the Spaniards to immigrate upon Indian Bar, and several new houses for the sale of liquor etc., are building by these people. It seems to me that the above law is selfish, cruel and narrow-minded in the extreme.

When I came here, the Humboldt was the only public house on the Bar. Now there are the "Oriental," "Golden Gate," "Don Juan," and four or five others, the names of which I do not know. On Sundays, the swearing, drinking, gambling and fighting, which are carried on in some of these houses, are truly horrible.

It is extremely healthy, here; with the exception of two or three men who were drowned when the river was so high, I have not heard of a death for months. . . .

I should like to have visited the Indian III,35 encampment, which lies a few miles from the Junction, but was too much fatigued to attempt it. The Indians often visit us, and as they seldom wear anything but a *very* tight and *very* short shirt, they have an appearance of being, as Charles Dickens would say, all legs. They usually sport some kind of head-dress, if it is nothing more than a leather string, which they bind across their dusky brows in the style of the wreaths in Norma, or the gay ribbons garlanding the hair of the Roman youth in the play of Brutus. A friend of ours, who has visited their camp several times, has just given me a description of their mode of life. Their huts, ten or twelve in number, are formed of the bark of the pine — conically shaped, plastered with mud, and with a hole in the top, whence emerges the smoke, which rises from a fire built in the center of the apartment. These places are so low that it is quite impossible to stand upright in them, and are entered from a small hole in one side, on all fours. A large stone, sunk to its surface in the ground, which contains three or four pan-like hollows for the purpose of grinding acorns and nuts, is the only furniture which these huts contain. The women, with another stone, about a foot and a half in length, and a little larger than a man's wrist, pulverize the acorns to the finest possible powder, which they prepare for the table (?) in the following manner, viz: — Their cooking utensils consist of a kind of basket, woven of some particular species of reed, I should fancy, from the descriptions which I have had of them, and are so plaited as to be impervious to fluids. These they fill half full of water, which is made to boil by placing in it hot stones. The latter they drag from the fire with two sticks. When the water boils, they stir into it, until it is about as thick as hasty-pudding, the powdered acorns, delicately flavored with dried grasshoppers, and lo! dinner is ready. Would you like to know how they eat? They place the thumb and little finger together across the palm of the hand, and make of the other three fingers a spoon, with which they shovel into their capacious mouths this delicious compound.

There are about eighty Indians in all at this encampment, a very small portion of which number are women. A hostile tribe in the valley made a Sabine-like invasion upon the settlement, a few months since, and stole away all the young and fair *muchachas*, leaving them but a few old squaws. These poor, withered creatures, who are seldom seen far from the encampment, do all the drudgery. Their entire wardrobe consists of a fringe about two feet in length, which is formed of the branch or root — I cannot ascertain exactly which — of a peculiar species of shrub shredded into threads. This scanty costume they festoon several times about the person, fastening it just above the hips, and they generally appear in a startlingly unsophisticated state of almost entire nudity. They are very filthy in their habits; and my informant said that if one of them should venture out into the rain, / grass would grow on her neck and arms. The men, unhappy martyrs! are compelled to be a little more cleanly, from their custom of hunting and fishing, for the wind *will* blow off *some* of the dirt, and the water washes off more.

Their infants are fastened to a framework of light wood in the same manner as those of the North American Indians. When a squaw has anything to do, she very composedly sets this frame up against the side of the house, as a civilized housewife would an umbrella or broom.

Some of their modes of fishing are very curious. One is as follows: These primitive anglers will seek a quiet, deep spot in the river, where they know fish "most do congregate," and throw therein a large quantity of stones. This, of course, frightens the fish, which dive to the bottom of the stream, and Mr. Indian, plunging headforemost into the water, beneath which he sometimes remains several minutes, will presently reappear, holding triumphantly in each hand one of the finny tribe, which he kills by giving it a single bite in the head or neck with his sharp, knife-like teeth. . . .

It is impossible to conceive of anything more light and airy than the step of these people. I shall never forget with what enchanted eyes I gazed upon one of them, gliding along the side of the hill opposite / Missouri Bar. One would fancy that nothing but a fly or a spirit could keep its footing on the rocks along which he stepped so stately, for they looked as perpendicular as a wall. My friend observed that no white man could have done it. This wild creature seemed to move as a cloud moves on a quiet day in summer, and as still and silently. It really made me solemn to gaze upon him, and the sight almost impressed me as something superhuman.

Viewed in the most favorable manner, these poor creatures are miserably brutish and degraded, having very little in common with the lofty and eloquent aborigines of the United States. It is said that their entire language contains but about twenty words. Like all Indians, they are passionately fond of gambling, and will exhibit as much anxiety at the losing or winning of a hand-

III,3

1,359

ful of beans as do their paler brothers when thousands are at stake. Methinks, from what I have seen of that most hateful vice, the *amount* lost or won has very little to do with the matter. But let me not speak of this most detestable of crimes. I have known such frightful consequences to ensue from its indulgence, that I dare not speak of it, lest I use language, as perhaps I have already done, unbecoming a woman's lips. . . .

*From our Log Cabin, Indian Bar,*
*July 5, 1852*

V,24   About five o'clock, we arrived at home, just in time to hear some noisy shouts of "Down with the Spaniards;" "The great American People forever," and other similar cries, evident signs of quite a spirited fight between the two parties, which was, in reality, taking place at the moment. Seven or eight of the *elite* of Rich Bar, drunk with whisky and patriotism, were the principal actors in this unhappy affair, which resulted in serious injury to two or three Spaniards. For some time past, there has been a gradually increasing state of bad feeling exhibited by our countrymen (increased, we fancy, by the ill-treatment which our Consul received the other day at Acapulco,) towards foreigners. In this affair, our own countrymen were principally to blame, or, rather I should say, Sir Barley Corn was to blame, for many of the ringleaders are fine young men, who, when sober, are decidedly friendly to the Spaniards. It is feared that this will not be the end of the fracas, though the more intelligent foreigners, as well as the judicious Americans, are making every effort to promote kindly feeling between the two nations. This will be very difficult, on account of the ignorant prejudices of the low-bred, which class are a large proportion of both parties.

It is very common to hear vulgar Yankees say of the Spaniards, "Oh, they are half-civilized black men!" These unjust expressions naturally irritate the latter, many of whom are highly educated gentlemen of the most refined and cultivated manners.

We labor under great disadvantages, in the judgment of foreigners. Our peculiar, political institutions, and the prevalence of common schools, give to *all* our people an arrogant assurance, which is mistaken for the American *beau ideal* of a gentleman.

They are unable to distinguish those nice *shades* of manner, which as effectually separate the gentleman from the clown with *us*, as do these / broader lines, which mark  IV,25 these two classes among all other nations. They think that it is the grand characteristic of Columbia's children, to be prejudiced, opinionated, selfish, avaricious and unjust. It is vain to tell them, that such are not specimens of American gentlemen. They will answer, "They call themselves gentlemen, and you receive them in your houses as such." It is utterly impossible for foreigners to thoroughly comprehend and make due allowance for that want of delicacy, and that vulgar "I'm as good as you are," spirit, which is, it must be confessed, peculiar to the lower classes of our people, and which would lead the majority of them to —

"Enter a palace with their old felt hat on —
To address the King with the title of Mister,
And ask him the price of the throne he sat on."

The class of men who rule society (?) in the mines, are the gamblers, who, for the most part, are reckless, bad men, although no doubt there are many among them, whose only vice is that fatal love of play. The rest of the people are afraid of these daring, unprincipled persons, and when they commit the most glaring injustice against the Spaniards, it is generally passed unnoticed.

We have had innumerable drunken fights during the summer, with the usual amount of broken heads, collar bones, stabs, etc. Indeed, the sabbaths are almost always enlivened by some such merry event. Were it not for these affairs, I might sometimes forget that the sweet day of rest was shining down upon us.

Last week, the dead body of a Frenchman was found in the river, near Missouri Bar. On examination of the body, it was the general opinion that he had been murdered. Suspicion has, as yet, fallen upon no person.

*From our Log Cabin, Indian Bar,*
*August 4, 1852*

V,103 We have lived through so much of excitement for the last three weeks, dear M., that I almost shrink from relating the gloomy events which have marked their flight. But if I leave out the darker shades of our mountain life, the picture will be very incomplete. In the short space of twenty-four days, we have had murders, fearful accidents, bloody deaths, a mob, whippings, a hanging, an attempt at suicide, and a fatal duel. But to begin at the beginning, as according to rule one ought to do.

I think that even among these beautiful hills, I never saw a more perfect "bridal of the earth and sky," than that of Sunday the eleventh of July. On that morning, I went with a party of friends to the head of the "Ditch," a walk of about three miles in length. . . .

Shortly after our arrival, a perfectly deafening volley of shouts and yells elicited from my companion the careless remark, "that the customary Sabbath-day's fight was apparently more serious than usual." Almost as he spoke, there succeeded a death-like silence, broken in a minute after by a deep groan, at the corner of the cabin, followed by the words, "Why Tom, poor fellow, are you really wounded?" Before we could reach the door, it was burst violently open, by a person who inquired hurriedly for the Doctor—who, luckily, happened at that very moment to be approaching. The man who called him, then gave us the following excited account of what had happened.

,104 He said that in / a *melé* between the Americans and the foreigners, Domingo—a tall, majestic-looking Spaniard, a perfect type of the novelistic bandit of Old Spain—had stabbed Tom Somers, a young Irishman, but a naturalized citizen of the United States—and that at the very moment, said Domingo, with a *Mejicana* hanging upon his arm, and brandishing threateningly the long, bloody knife with which he had inflicted the wound upon his victim, was parading up and down the street unmolested. It seems that when Tom Somers fell, the Americans, being unarmed, were seized with a sudden panic and fled. There was a rumor, (unfounded, as it afterwards proved) to the effect, that the Spaniards had on this day conspired to kill all the Americans on the river. In a few moments, however, the latter rallied and made a rush at the murderer, who immediately plunged into the river and swam across to Missouri Bar; eight or ten shots were fired at him while in the water, not one of which hit him. He ran like an antelope across the flat, swam thence to Smith's Bar, and escaped by the road leading out of the mountains, from the Junction. Several men went in pursuit of him, but he was not taken, and without doubt, is now safe in Mexico.

In the meanwhile, the consternation was terrific. The Spaniards, who, with the exception of six or eight, knew no more of the affair than I did, thought that the Americans had arisen against them; and our own countrymen equally ignorant, fancied the same of the foreigners. About twenty of the latter, who were either sleeping or reading in their cabins at the time of the *emeute*, aroused by the cry of "Down with the Spaniards!" barricaded themselves in a drinking-saloon, determined to defend themselves as long as possible, against the massacre, which was fully expected would follow this appalling shout. In the bakeshop, which stands next door to our cabin, young Tom Somers lay straightened for the grave, (he lived but fifteen minutes after he was wounded,) while over his dead body a Spanish woman, was weeping and moaning in the most piteous and heart-rending manner. The Rich Barians, who had heard a most exaggerated account of the rising of the Spaniards against the Americans, armed with rifles, pistols, clubs, dirks, etc., were rushing down the hill by hundreds. Each one added fuel to his rage, by crowding into the little bakery, to gaze upon the blood-bathed bosom of the victim, yet warm with the life, which but an hour before it had so triumphantly worn. Then arose the most fearful shouts of "Down with the Spaniards!" "Drive every foreigner off the river!" "Don't let one of the murderous devils remain." "Oh, if you have a drop of American blood in your veins, it must cry out for vengeance upon the cowardly assassins of poor Tom." All this, mingled with the most horrible oaths and execrations, yelled up, as if in mockery, into that smiling heaven, which in its fair Sabbath calm, bent unmoved over the hell which was raging below. . . .

05    We three women, left entirely alone, seated ourselves upon a log, overlooking the strange scene below. The Bar, was a sea of heads, bristling with guns, rifles and clubs. We could see nothing, but fancied from the apparent quiet of the crowd, that the miners were taking measures to investigate the sad event of the day. All at once, we were startled by the firing of a gun, and the next moment, the crowd dispersing, we saw a man led into the log cabin, while another was carried, apparently lifeless, into a Spanish drinking-saloon, from one end of which, were burst off instantly several boards, evidently to give air to the wounded person. . . .

It seems that an Englishman, the owner of a house of the vilest description, a person, who is said to have been the primary cause of all the troubles of the day, attempted to force his way through the line of armed men which had been formed at each side of the street. The guard very properly refused to let him pass. In his drunken fury, he tried to wrest a gun from one of them, which being accidentally discharged in the struggle, inflicted a severe wound upon a Mr. Oxley, and shattered in the most dreadful manner the thigh of Señor Pizarro, a man of high birth and breeding, a *porteño* of Buenos Ayres. This frightful

accident recalled the people to their senses, and they began to act a little less like madmen, than they had previously done. They elected a Vigilance Committee, and authorized persons to go to the Junction and arrest the suspected Spaniards.

The first act of the Committee was to try a *Mejicana,* who had been foremost in the fray. She has always worn male attire, and on this occasion, armed with a pair of pistols, she fought like a very fury. Luckily, inexperienced in the use of fire-arms, she wounded no one. She was sentenced to leave the Bar by day-light, a perfectly just decision, for there is no doubt that she is a regular little demon. / Some went so far  IV,106 as to say, she ought to be hung, for she was the *indirect* cause of the fight. You see always, it is the old, cowardly excuse of Adam in Paradise: "The *woman* tempted me, and I did eat." As if the poor, frail head, once so pure and beautiful, had not sin enough of its own, dragging it forever downward, without being made to answer for the wrong-doing of a whole community of men.

The next day, the Committee tried five or six Spaniards, who were proven to have been the ringleaders in the Sabbath-day riot. Two of them were sentenced to be whipped, the remainder to leave the Bar that evening; the property of all to be confiscated to the use of the wounded persons. Oh Mary! imagine my anguish when I heard the first blow fall upon those wretched men. I had never thought that I should be compelled to hear such fearful sounds, and, although I immediately buried my head in a shawl, nothing can efface from memory the disgust and horror of that moment. I had heard of such things, but heretofore had not realized, that in the nineteenth century, men could be beaten like dogs, much less that other men, not only could sentence such barbarism, but could actually stand by and see their own manhood degraded in such disgraceful manner. One of these unhappy persons was a very gentlemanly young Spaniard, who implored for death in the most moving terms. He appealed to his judges in the most eloquent manner — as gentlemen, as men of honor; representing to them that to be deprived of life, was nothing in comparison with the never-to-be-effaced stain of the vilest convict's punishment — to which they had sentenced him. Finding all his entreaties disregarded, he swore a most solemn oath, that he would murder every American that he should chance to meet alone, and as he is a man of the most dauntless courage, and rendered desperate by a burning sense of disgrace, which will cease only with his life, he will doubtless keep his word.

Although in my very humble opinion and in that of others more competent to judge of such matters than myself, these sentences were unnecessarily severe, yet so great was the rage and excitement of the crowd, that the Vigilance Committee could do no less. The mass of the mob demanded fiercely the death of the prisoners, and it was evident that many of the Committee took side with the people. I shall never forget how horror-struck I was (bombastic as it *now* sounds) at hearing no less a personage than the Whig candidate for representative say, "that the condemned had better fly for their lives, for the Avenger of Blood was on their tracks!" I am happy to say, that said very worthy, but sanguinary individual, "The Avenger of Blood!" represented in this case by some half dozen gambling rowdies, either changed his mind or lost scent of his prey; for the intended victims slept about two miles up the hill, quite peacefully until morning.

The following facts, elicited upon the trial, throw light upon this unhappy affair: Seven miners from Old Spain, enraged at the cruel treatment which their countrymen had received on the "Fourth," and at the illiberal cry of "Down with the Spaniard," had united for the purpose of taking revenge on seven Americans whom they believed to be the originators of their insults. All well armed, they came from / the Junction, where they were residing at the time, intending to challenge each one

IV,107

his man, and in fair fight, compel their insolent aggressors to answer for the arrogance which they had exhibited more than once towards the Spanish race. Their first move on arriving at Indian Bar was to go and dine at the Humboldt, where they drank a most enormous quantity of champagne and claret. Afterwards, they proceeded to the house of the Englishman, whose brutal carelessness caused the accident which wounded Pizarro and Oxley, when one of them commenced a playful conversation with one of his countrywomen. This enraged the Englishman, who instantly struck the Spaniard a violent blow, and ejected him from the shanty. Thereupon ensued a spirited fight, which, through the exertion of a gentleman from Chili, a favorite with both nations, ended without bloodshed. This person knew nothing of the intended duel, or he might have prevented, by his wise counsels, what followed. Not suspecting for a moment anything of the kind, he went to Rich Bar. Soon after he left, Tom Somers, who is said always to have been a dangerous person when in liquor, without any apparent provocation, struck Domingo, (one of the original seven) a violent blow, which nearly felled him to the earth. The latter, a man of "dark antecedents" and the most reckless character, mad with wine, rage and revenge, without an instant's pause, drew his knife and inflicted a fatal wound upon his insulter. Thereupon followed the chapter of accidents which I have related.

On Tuesday following the fatal Sabbath, a man brought the news of the murder of a Mr. Bacon, a person well known on the river, who kept a ranch about twelve miles from Rich Bar. He was killed for his money, by his servant, a negro, who not three months ago was our own cook. He was the last one anybody would have suspected capable of such an act.

A party of men, appointed by the Vigilance Committee, left the Bar immediately in search of him. The miserable wretch was apprehended in Sacramento and part of the gold found upon his person. On the following Sunday he was brought in chains to Rich Bar. After a trial by the miners, he was sentenced to be hung at four o'clock in the evening. All efforts to make him confess proved futile. He said, very truly, that whether innocent or guilty, they would hang him; and so he "died and made no sign," with a calm indifference, as the novelists say, "worthy of a better cause." The dreadful crime and death of "Josh," who having been an excellent cook, and very neat and respectful, was a favorite servant with us, added to the unhappiness which you can easily imagine that I was suffering under all these horrors.

On Saturday evening about eight o'clock, as we sat quietly conversing with the two ladies from the hill — who, by the way, we found very agreeable additions to our society, hitherto composed entirely of gentlemen — we were startled by the loud shouting, and rushing close by the door of the cabin, which stood open, of three or four hundred men. Of course, we feminines, with nerves somewhat shattered from the events of the past week, were greatly alarmed.

08 We were soon informed that Henry Cook, *vice* "Josh" had, in a fit of delirium tremens, cut his throat from ear to ear. The poor wretch was alone when he committed the desperate deed, and in his madness, throwing the bloody razor upon the ground, he ran part of the way up the hill. Here he was found almost senseless, and brought back to the Humboldt, where he was very nearly the cause of hanging poor "Paganini Ned" — who returned a few weeks since from the valley, — for his first act on recovering himself, was to accuse that culinary individual of having attempted to murder him. The mob were for hanging our poor "Vatel" without judge or jury, and it was only through the most strenuous exertions of his friends, that the life of this illustrious person was saved. Poor Ned! it was forty-eight hours before his cork-screws returned to their original graceful curl; he threatens to leave us to our barbarism and no longer to waste his culinary talents upon an un-

grateful and inappreciative people. He has sworn "war to the knife" against Henry, who was formerly his most intimate friend, as nothing can persuade him that the accusation did not proceed from the purest malice on the part of the suicide.

Their majesties the mob, with that beautiful consistency which usually distinguishes those august individuals, insisted upon shooting poor Harry — for said they, and the reasoning is remarkably conclusive and clear, "a man so hardened as to raise his hand against his *own* life, will never hesitate to murder another!" They almost mobbed F. for binding up the wounds of the unfortunate wretch and for saying that it was possible he might live. At last, however, they compromised the matter, by determining, that if Henry should recover, he should leave the Bar immediately. Neither contingency will probably take place, as it will be almost a miracle if he survives.

On the day following the attempted suicide, which was Sunday, nothing more exciting happened than a fight and the half-drowning of a drunken individual in the river, just in front of the Humboldt.

On Sunday last, the thigh of Señor Pizarro was amputated; but alas, without success. He had been sick for many months with chronic dysentery, which after the operation returned with great violence, and he died at two o'clock on Monday morning with the same calm and lofty resignation which had distinguished him during his illness. When first wounded, believing his case hopeless, he had decidedly refused to submit to amputation, but as time wore on he was persuaded to take this one chance for his life, for the sake of his daughter, a young girl of fifteen, at present at school in a convent in Chili, whom his death leaves without any near relation. I saw him several times during his illness, and it was melancholy indeed, to hear him talk of his motherless girl who, I have been told, is extremely beautiful, talented and accomplished.

The state of society here has never been

so bad as since the appointment of a Committee of Vigilance. The rowdies have formed themselves into a company called the "Moguls," and they parade the streets all night, howling, shouting, breaking into houses, taking wearied miners out of their beds and throwing them into the river, and in short, "murdering sleep," in the most IV,109 remorseless manner. Nearly / every night they build bonfires fearfully near some rag shanty, thus endangering the lives, (or I should rather say the property — for as it is impossible to sleep, lives are emphatically safe) of the whole community. They retire about five o'clock in the morning; previously to this blessed event posting notices to that effect, and that they will throw any one who may disturb them into the river. I am nearly worn out for want of rest, for truly they "make night hideous" with their fearful uproar. Mr. O——, who still lies dangerously ill from the wound received, on what we call the "fatal Sunday," complains bitterly of the disturbance; and when poor Pizarro was dying, and one of his friends gently requested that they would be quiet for half an hour and permit the soul of the sufferer to pass in peace, they only laughed and yelled and hooted louder than ever, in the presence of the departing spirit, for the tenement in which he lay, being composed of green boughs only, could of course shut out no sounds. Without doubt if the "Moguls" had been sober, they would never have been guilty of such horrible barbarity as to compel the thoughts of a dying man to mingle with curses and blasphemies; but alas! they were intoxicated, and may God forgive them, unhappy ones, for they knew not what they did. The poor, exhausted miners, for even well people cannot sleep in such a pandemonium, grumble and complain, but they — although far outnumbering the rioters — are too timid to resist. All say "It is shameful; something ought to be done; something *must* be done," etc. and in the mean time the rioters triumph. You will wonder that the Committee of Vigilance does not interfere; it is said that some

of that very Committee are the ringleaders among the "Moguls."

I believe I have related to you everything but the duel — and I will make the recital of this as short as possible, for I am sick of these sad subjects, and doubt not but you are the same. It took place on Tuesday morning at eight o'clock, on Missouri Bar, when and where that same Englishman who has figured so largely in my letter, shot his best friend. The duelists were surrounded by a large crowd, I have been told, foremost among which stood the Committee of Vigilance! The man who received his dear friend's fatal shot, was one of the most quiet and peaceable citizens on the Bar. He lived about ten minutes after he was wounded. He was from Ipswich, England, and only twenty-five years of age, when his own high passions snatched him from life. In justice to his opponent, it must be said, that he would willingly have retired after the first shots had been exchanged, but poor Billy Leggett, as he was familiarly called, insisted upon having the distance between them shortened, and continuing the duel until one of them had fallen.

There, my dear M., have I not fulfilled my promise of giving you a dish of horrors? And only think of such a shrinking, timid, frail thing, as I *used* to be "long time ago," not only living right in the midst of them, but almost compelled to hear if not see the whole. I think that I may without vanity affirm, that I have "seen the elephant." "Did you see his tail?" asks innocent Ada J., in her mother's letter. Yes, sweet Ada, the "entire Animal" has been exhibited to my view. / "But you must remember, that this IV is California," as the new comers are so fond of informing *us!* who consider ourselves "one of the oldest inhabitants" of the golden State.

*From our Log Cabin, Indian Bar,*
*Nov. 21, 1852*

To our unbounded surprise, we found, IV on our return from the American Valley, that nearly all the fluming companies had failed — contrary to every expectation, on arriving at the bed-rock, no gold made its appearance. But a short history of the rise, progress, and final fate of one of these associations, given me in writing by its own Secretary, conveys a pretty correct idea of the result of the majority of the remainder:

"The thirteen men, of which the 'American Fluming Company' consisted, commenced getting out timber in February. On the fifth of July, they began to lay the flume. A thousand dollars were paid for lumber, which they were compelled to buy. They built a dam six feet high and three hundred feet in length, upon which thirty men labored nine days and a half. The cost of said dam was estimated at two thousand dollars. This Company left off working on the twenty-fourth day of September, having taken out in *all*, gold dust to the amount of forty-one dollars and seventy cents! Their lumber and tools, sold at auction, brought two hundred dollars."

A very small amount of arithmetical knowledge, will enable one to figure up what the "American Fluming Company" made, by *their* Summer's work. This result was, by no means, a singular one; nearly every person on the river received the same step-mother's treatment from Dame Nature, in this her mountain workshop.

Of course the whole world (*our* world,) was, to use a phrase much in vogue here, "dead broke." The shop-keepers, restaurants, and gambling-houses, with an amiable confidingness peculiar to such people, had trusted the miners to that degree, that they themselves were in the same moneyless condition. Such a batch of woful faces was never seen before, not the least elongated of which, was F.'s — to whom nearly all the companies owed large sums.

Of course, with the failure of the golden harvest, "Othello's occupation was gone." The mass of the unfortunates laid down the "shovel and the hoe," and left the river in crowds. It is said, that there are not twenty men remaining on Indian Bar, although two months ago, you could count them up by hundreds. . . .

My heart is heavy at the thought of IV,349 departing forever from this place. I *like* this wild and barbarous life; I leave it with regret. The solemn fir trees, "whose slender tops *are* close against the sky" here, the watching hills, and the calmly beautiful river, seem to gaze sorrowfully at me, as I stand in the moon-lighted midnight, to bid them farewell. Beloved, unconventional wood-life; divine Nature, into whose benign eyes I never looked, whose many voices, gay and glad, I never heard, in the artificial heart of the busy world, — I quit your serene teachings for a restless and troubled future. Yes, Molly, smile if you will at my folly; but I go from the mountains with a deep heart sorrow. I look kindly to this existence, which to you seems so sordid and mean. Here, at least, I have been contented. The "thistle-seed," as you call me, sent abroad its roots right lovingly into this barren soil, and gained an unwonted strength in what seemed to you such unfavorable surroundings. You would hardly recognize the feeble and half-dying invalid, who drooped languidly out of sight, as night shut down between your straining gaze and the good ship Manilla, as she wafted her far away from her Atlantic home, in the person of your *now* perfectly healthy sister.

# SUGGESTIONS FOR LIBRARY WORK

With the exception of the material from *The Shirley Letters* and the Marryat material the selections in this book have necessarily been limited to relatively short excerpts. You will undoubtedly want to go to the library and read further in the writings of Colton, Buffum, Taylor, and Buck.

The writers included here represent only a sampling of the Argonauts who swarmed into the Mother Lode country after James Marshall's discovery early in 1848. The California gold rush is significant not only because it was the first and most spectacular mining rush of the trans-Mississippi West, but also because it was the training ground for an army of miners who, by the turn of the century, had spread the mining frontier north to the Klondike, east to the Black Hills and south to the Mexican border. There are excellent opportunities for comparing life in the California mines with conditions in other parts of the mineral frontier. For example, Mark Twain's *Roughing It* (1872) and Dan De Quille's (William Wright's) *The Big Bonanza* (1876) contain delightful and largely reliable accounts of the Comstock Lode in Nevada and there are similar source materials, if not so well known, dealing with the discovery and development of mines in British Columbia, Alaska, the Inland Empire of Washington, Idaho, and western Montana, the Dakotas, and the Southwest.

From the vast reservoir of firsthand accounts of the California gold fields only a few of the more lively and substantial ones can be mentioned here. Well written and gently ironical is Alonzo Delano's *Life on the Plains and Among the Diggings* (1854). A reprint edited by R. R. Wilson with the title slightly changed to *Across the Plains and Among the Diggings* (1936) is available. Richard B. Mason, *Report of the Gold Fields of California,* House Executive Document #17, 31st Cong., 1st sess. (1849) is restrained and reliable as an official report should be. Enos Christman left a balanced and sensible picture of nearly three years in the diggings in his letters and journal edited by Florence Morrow Christman in *One Man's Gold* (1930). Other worth-while narratives include: J. D. Borthwick, *Three Years in California* (1857); William Kelly, *An Excursion to California* (2 vols., 1851); Sarah Royce, *A Frontier Lady* (1932), edited by R. H. Gabriel; Daniel B. Woods, *Sixteen Months at the Gold Diggings* (1851); and Felix P. Wierzbicki, *California As It Is & As It May Be. Or a Guide to the Gold Region* (1933), edited by George D. Lyman. Collections of gold rush narratives include: Valeska Bari, *The Course of Empire* (1931), Stewart Edward White, *The Forty-niners* (1918), and Owen C. Coy, *Gold Days* (1929).

Among secondary accounts the best comprehensive treatment is John Caughey's *Gold Is the Cornerstone* (1948), which also has a carefully sifted bibliography. A useful study of the first twenty-five years of California mining with emphasis on the mining process is Rodman Paul's *California Gold* (1947). Sooner or later anyone interested in the history of the American West will come to Hubert Howe Bancroft. For purposes of this book, Volume VI in Bancroft's *History of California* (7 vols., 1884–1890) is the basic work. It may be supplemented with the same author's *California Inter Pocula* (1888).

The pioneer interpretation of the evolution of law and government in the diggings is Charles H. Shinn, *Mining Camps: A Study in American Frontier*

*Government* (1885). A broad literary and philosophical approach to the same period is Josiah Royce, *California, from the Conquest in 1846 to the Second Vigilance Committee in San Francisco: A Study in American Character* (1886).

Cultural by-products of the golden era may be studied in: Franklin Walker, *San Francisco's Literary Frontier* (1939), and his editing of Prentice Mulford, *California Sketches* (1935); G. R. MacMinn, *The Theater of the Golden Era in California* (1941); Constance Rourke, *Troupers of the Gold Coast* (1928); William Taylor, *Seven Years' Street Preaching in San Francisco* (1857); George R. Stewart Jr., *Bret Harte: Argonaut and Exile* (1931); and Ella Sterling Mighels, *The Story of the Files* (1893).

The historical quarterlies furnish excellent and convenient sources for both primary and secondary accounts and should be consulted in connection with your research papers. Here are several examples to point the way. Walker D. Wyman, ed., "California Emigrant Letters," California Historical Society *Quarterly*, XXIV (1945), 17–46, 117–138, 235–260, 343–364; Raymond A. Rydell, "The Cape Horn Route to California, 1849," *Pacific Historical Review*, XVII (1948), 149–163; Charles L. Camp, ed., "An Irishman in the Gold Rush, the Journal of Thomas Kerr," California Historical Society *Quarterly*, VIII (1928), 203–227, 395–404, IX (1929), 17–25, 167–182, 262–277; and John Caughey, "Shaping a Literary Tradition," *Pacific Historical Review*, VIII (1939), 201–214.

Possibilities for research range widely and can only be suggested.

How was news of the gold discovery received outside of California? In Hawaii, in the Pacific Northwest, in the East, in Latin America, in Europe?

What were the routes the various gold seekers took to the mines? Compare the overland route with the Cape Horn and Panama routes.

What were the chief characteristics of life in a representative mining camp? How did the miner dress and what were his principal tools and techniques? What did he do for recreation?

As northern California filled up what did the miners do about government and the problems of control of crime and the administration of justice?

How did minority groups fare in the California mines?

What literary endeavors emerged from the California mining frontier? Would a paper comparing San Francisco and Boston at mid-nineteenth century as cultural centers be feasible?

How does the miner compare with the fur trapper or cowboy as a frontier type? What are the gold lodes like today? Where are they?

No matter which topic you pursue, you should pay special heed to bibliographies. Carl I. Wheat, *Books of the California Gold Rush* (San Francisco, 1949) is a good bibliography of the rush itself. R. E. Cowan's *A Bibliography of the History of California, 1510–1930* (3 vols., 1933) is also useful. Many of the books listed above have bibliographies, sometimes at the end of chapters, sometimes in the back of the book. Often footnote references supply helpful leads for further reading and research. You will find that one source leads to another and that you will have no trouble in finding plenty of original material in your library for almost any topic you choose.